"*Adopting the Hurt Child* thoroughly and realistically examines many issues affecting adoptive families. Through readable prose interspersed with actual case histories, the authors clearly outline the challenges of special-needs children, but also suggest ways in which parents can work with children to help them make sense of their past and build a better future."

—JOE KROLL, Executive Director, The North American Council on Adoptable Children (NACAC)

Adopting the Hurt Child

Revised and Updated

Hope for Families with Special-Needs Kids

Gregory C. Keck, PhD

Regina M. Kupecky, LSW

Edited by L. G. Mansfield

NAVPRESS⬤.

NavPress is the publishing ministry of The Navigators, an international Christian organization and leader in personal spiritual development. NavPress is committed to helping people grow spiritually and enjoy lives of meaning and hope through personal and group resources that are biblically rooted, culturally relevant, and highly practical.

For a free catalog go to www.NavPress.com
or call 1.800.366.7788 in the United States or 1.800.839.4769 in Canada.

ISBN-13: 978-1-60006-289-6

Cover design by The DesignWorks Group
Cover images: Left image: Corbis
                       Middle image: Getty
                       Right image: Getty

Some of the anecdotal illustrations in this book are true to life and are included with the permission of the persons involved. All other illustrations are composites of real situations, and any resemblance to people living or dead is coincidental. In an effort to preserve anonymity, our case examples are sometimes compilations of actual cases and do not include racial or cultural identifiers. In the absence of a gender-less third-person pronoun, we use the masculine form throughout this book to avoid awkward constructions and to facilitate readability. In addition, we refer to parents in the plural form when discussing the families of adopted children. This has been done solely for consistency and is not meant to slight the many single parents who have adopted hurt children. We hope our readers will understand and accept our rationales.

This publication is designed to provide accurate and authoritative information in regard to the subject matter covered. It is sold with the understanding that the author and the publisher are not engaged in rendering legal, accounting, or other professional service. If legal advice or other expert assistance is required, the services of a competent professional person should be sought. From a Declaration of Principles jointly adopted by a Committee of the American Bar Association and a Committee of Publishers.

Library of Congress Cataloging-in-Publication Data

Keck, Gregory C.
  Adopting the hurt child : hope for families with special-needs kids :
a guide for parents and professionals / Gregory C. Keck, Regina M.
Kupecky. -- 3rd ed.
    p. cm.
  Includes bibliographical references.
  ISBN 978-1-60006-289-6
  1. Special needs adoption--United States. 2. Older child
adoption--United States. I. Kupecky, Regina M. II. Title.
  HV875.55.K43 2009
  362.7340973--dc22
                              2008034434

Printed in the United States of America

1 2 3 4 5 6 7 8 / 12 11 10 09

To Brian,

whose journey should encourage us all

CONTENTS

SOCIETY'S CHILDREN

There was a time, not terribly long ago, when adopting a healthy infant was a simple task. In those days, social services agencies employed slogans like *Do you have room for one more?*—so great was the availability of such children. Birth mothers, usually unmarried, placed children for adoption because they were unable to care for them. There were few support systems—professional, familial, or societal—for an unwed mother who wished to keep her child. The stigma of illegitimacy was strong enough to make it difficult to raise a child alone.

Older children—then defined as more than two years of age—or children who had been removed from their families as a result of abuse or neglect were labeled "unadoptable," destined to spend their childhoods in the foster-care system. They were often moved from home to home, and many of them ultimately landed in public children's homes.

Today, the availability of infants has decreased dramatically due to birth control, social acceptance of the single parent, and legalized pregnancy termination. Prospective adoptive parents have begun to consider noninfants, a category that has rapidly expanded to include considerably older children and those with special medical and psychological needs. An entirely new component of the adoption system has emerged, and it continues to drive many adoptions.

As of September 2006, the U.S. Department of Health and Human Services states that approximately 129,000 children in the United States are waiting for adoption.[1] In fact, many of them are older children who will carry complex baggage with them if they are adopted. If they are not adopted, their issues remain with them and the families they eventually form. In either case, they are hurt children who need help. It is important to remember that the only reason they are available for adoption in the first place is because they experienced serious trauma in the birth family and were most likely removed involuntarily.

These children affect greater society in many ways. They attend school with our children, live next door to us, work in the businesses we patronize, date our teenagers, and ultimately become our coworkers, neighbors, or perhaps our spouses. As taxpayers, we support these children to the tune of thousands of dollars—some even cost millions before their journey through the system ends. This journey may continue well into adulthood—into our prisons, shelters, and mental health facilities. They are truly "society's children" because they belong to no one.

Some people may not realize the gravity and magnitude of the number of children who fall into this category. The U.S. Department of Health and Human Services has estimated the following for the year 2006:

- 510,000 children in foster care
- 129,000 children for whom adoption is the goal

It is further estimated that 51,000 children were adopted from foster care in 2006. The number of international adoptions stays at about 20,000. Approximately the same number of infant adoptions—20,000—occur each year. These figures do not include stepparent adoptions and adoption by relatives. Since uniform reporting systems do not exist, these numbers may, in fact, be an underrepresentation of children who live in temporary, ever-changing situations.

Unfortunately, many families expect to lose their children to "the system." As her fifteen-year-old was being removed from her home by a social worker, the mother noticed that her two-year-old was hurriedly running around the house gathering up toys and clothes and stuffing them into a trash bag—the most common form of luggage of the frequently moved child. She looked down at the toddler and said, "Honey, you can't go this time. You'll have to wait until you're older."

While the human losses are difficult to measure, the actual hard costs are clearer. One family alone could add up to the following estimated costs:[2]

One child in residential care for three years	$295,650
One child in a group home for six months	$59,040
One child in therapeutic foster care for two years	$24,000
Two children in regular foster care for one year	$56,000
TOTAL	$434,690

These figures are staggering, and we know that those in the foster-care system often end up needing care throughout their lives.

Newspaper reports suggest that 60 percent of the homeless people in New York City are products of the foster-care system; 80 percent of those in the prison system in the United Kingdom are reported to have been in foster care.

These figures reflect the large number of hurt children and indicate just how long the hurt lasts. The multiplier effect is even more alarming.

Children face many birth-family issues that significantly affect an adoption. They bring into their new families the remnants of the problems that began in the birth home and have never been resolved. These unresolved issues are the very foundation of the difficulties faced by the children and adolescents we will discuss.

Throughout this book, we talk about children and adolescents who experienced multiple traumas prior to adoption. They were removed from their birth homes because of these traumas—not because a loving birth mother thoughtfully and carefully planned an infant adoption. We have truthfully examined the critical issues that precede these adoptions, and by doing so, we may have offended some people. It is not our intention to cast aspersions on those about whom we write. Our objective is to provide a clear picture that may help enlighten those who seek to heal the children who have been hurt by people they should have been able to trust. We also hope to provide a means to enable the hurt children to become good moms and dads to their own sons and daughters.

This book will help define the new face of adoptions. It will dispel numerous myths and bring to light certain grim truths that many will find difficult to accept. It is a frank and candid portrayal of a sad, sometimes brutal reality. But it is most importantly a source of valuable insight and hope for adoptive and foster parents, therapists, teachers, social workers, and all others whose lives interact with these children.

ACKNOWLEDGMENTS

So how long does it take to write a book? About fifty years. Fifty years of combined education and work with kids and families. To the families, the children, and our colleagues who have given us knowledge and inspiration for this book, we say thanks.

To the late Barbara Roberts, who in her role as director of Northeast Ohio Adoption Services blessed our endeavors, we say, "We miss you, Barb." To our early editors and critics — Sandra Prebil, Father John McCarthy, and Regina's brother, Jim Breig — we extend our deepest gratitude.

We owe a special thanks to Elle Mansfield, an adoptive mother and author whose editing minimized our struggles, and to Vicki Mongan, whose editing brought a fresh perspective that fine-tuned our work.

We are especially grateful to Marita Rose, who keeps everything together and running smoothly at the Attachment and Bonding Center of Ohio. Without her organizational skills, we would be lost.

Kris Wallen and the team at NavPress were open to our candid examination of this sensitive topic, and for this we are grateful. A special thanks to Kris for suggesting the updates for both of our books!

To our friends and coworkers who offered their skills, love, and patience — a big thanks. We appreciate and respect the triad members who shared their thoughts and feelings in chapter 15.

And lastly, to our families — Greg's sons, Brian and James; Regina's husband, Don; our parents, Joe and Mary Breig and Don and Jane Keck, who taught us the meaning of good parenting; and our grandparents, whose family values have enriched and inspired us — we say thank you.

Since the first edition of this book in 1995, tens of thousands of people have read *Adopting the Hurt Child*. Many of them have taken the time to call or write to us to share their stories and to thank us for giving them some insight into their lives and the lives of their hurt children. Both of us have been invited to speak about adoption, the impact of early childhood trauma, and issues of attachment to many people throughout the United States, the United Kingdom, New Zealand, and Australia. We thank all of you who have been in contact. We value your interest and input because it continues to validate the need for support for adoptive families. We are most grateful for all the feedback that thanks us for telling the *truth*. Families have told us that this truth, although sometimes unpleasant, has empowered them as they undertake the difficult journey of adopting and parenting children who have been hurt.

We give heartfelt thanks to the many children and adolescents who have chosen to trust their parents—and to trust us—as they embark on their path to healing.

NEVER TOO LATE
TO HOPE

Picture her — all glowing cheeks and bright eyes and a smile to melt your heart. She is the child who is about to become your daughter. The thought fills you with love and hope and pride. But beneath the shy grin, beneath the tousled curls lies a little girl whose world has been less than safe and loving. She reaches out to you, but with reservations you may struggle to understand. She is one of the hurt children.

Picture them — he with a crooked, mischievous smile and uncombed hair, she with long, dark braids and a chipped tooth. They are finally going to live again as brother and sister. They fidget in their seats — sometimes poking each other, sometimes holding hands. When you enter the room, they sit stone still. They are hurt children.

Picture him — all long legs and big hands as his body struggles into adolescence. In spite of his awkwardness, he has a smile that could light the darkest corners of a room. You have a glimpse of the heartbreaker he might become as a young man, and you smile at the thought. But he has AIDS and will need treatment for the remainder of his life. He is one of the hurt children.

Hundreds of thousands of such children live in this country. First, they were hurt by the birth families who abused, neglected, abandoned, or rejected them. Subsequently, they were hurt by multiple moves and repeated failed reunification efforts. In many cases, their uncertain futures led them to develop a temporary mind-set — a thinking process guaranteed to hamper them throughout their lives.

Although these children have been hurt—and have often hurt others—there is hope for the families who adopt them and for the professionals who work with them. Certainly, those who choose to adopt a child do so with a great deal of hope, but their expectations are usually internally driven and may not be based on the realities of the situation. Adoption professionals, too, tend to suffer from generalized hopes—to find the right family, to place a child, and to legalize the adoption.

It is our intent to provide all those involved in the adoption process with a sense of balance—to show that while adopting a hurt child is a voyage into a complicated, entangled life, it is also a journey of joy and discovery. By sharing some of the dynamics and behind-the-scene views of hurt children, we will attempt to define an encouraging path through the adoption process.

It is a difficult course, to be sure. It is difficult for the children, who often wish for the worst or create it on their own so they can be assured of facing what they know best: loss, pain, and anger. It is difficult for the adoptive parents, who are ill-prepared for the feelings they are experiencing. While pre-adoption classes may enlighten them about loss issues and adjusting to a new home, they cannot possibly prepare them for the child who may not respond to their love. It is difficult, too, for the professionals who are involved in the adoption process. Often, they are like bystanders at the scene of an accident—wanting to help make things better but not knowing what to do.

We hope that our insights, theories, and case examples provide you with a perspective that will better prepare you for the voyage you are facing. To be sure, the adoption venture can be more completely experienced, managed, and mastered when the travelers not only know where they want to go but also have an understanding of what to expect.

The lessons presented in this book stem from our professional experience and include the following premises:

- Healthy attachments between child and parent result from repetitive early nurturing, protection, care, and stimulation. A child should remain with the birth family if the parents can provide a safe and nurturing environment.
- Adoption always involves losses.

- Losses prior to adoption affect the quality of attachment in adoption.
- Early abuse and/or neglect interfere with healthy attachments.
- Repeated failed reunification trials complicate future attachments.
- Developmental delays occur as a result of interruptions in the normal developmental process.
- Successful adoption of an older child is viable.
- Multiple foster-home placements adversely affect subsequent attaching.
- Supportive relationships need to be preserved as a child moves from place to place.
- Completely truthful disclosures help the child heal and grow.
- Confronting the child's dysfunctional patterns is therapeutic.
- Nurturing after confronting encourages emotional growth.

It is our firm belief that children hurt by abuse and neglect can learn to love and trust adults in a family setting. Growth and development continue throughout the life span, and it is rarely too late for a child to change. The better we understand what motivates these children, the better equipped we are to help them.

We will be the guides to help achieve this understanding—indicating the path to follow and pointing out important features along the way. While not all the scenery will be rosy, it combines to form a picture of truth. Some of the thorns will be painful, but the parents and children whose lives are depicted here will find comfort and relief in being understood and validated. We hope they will find solace in knowing that many share their voyage— tumultuous, yet ultimately rewarding and worthwhile.

THE CHILD WHO WAITS

A Long Road to Love

Dear Ex-Mom,

I am writing this to tell you I hate you. You were mean to my brother and me. You didn't take care of us or feed us, and you let your boyfriend have sex with us. You left us outside when we were so little we got sunburned and had to go to the hospital. You said you'd be back for us, but you lied.

I have a new family now, and I have been mean to them because I am mad at you. No more. My scars from the sunburn are still there, but you are out of my life. Good-bye forever.

Your ex-sun,
Sam

"Your ex-sun"—this slip of the pen by young Sam emphasizes the pain he endured when his birth mother's neglect caused him to suffer a debilitating sunburn. While the scars from his burns have begun to heal, the emotional scars are still raw. Sam's memories of physical pain mingle with the rage he feels toward his birth mother, and his negative emotions have transferred to his adoptive family. They are a group steeped in frustration and chaos.

It is hard for us, as a society, to accept the fact that children can feel hatred toward their mothers. We like to think that the mother/child relationship is always sweet and supportive, but for many children this is not true. Sadly, the capacity to reproduce does not necessarily impart the ability to be a loving parent.

We would like to believe that Sam is the exception, but a simple perusal of newspapers reveals many stories of abused and neglected children. Some of them never leave the horrors of the birth home; others find their way into the adoption system. As the long list of parents who want to adopt increases, the number of children waiting for permanent homes continues to swell. Why can't the matches be made? Why must these children continue to wait? They wait not because of who they are, but because of who they aren't.

WAITING FOR LOVE

Timmy was an active, aggressive child. His male role models included many of his mother's boyfriends and periodically extended to the man who might have been his father. Timmy had three brothers and two sisters and was next to the youngest in age. He was four; his siblings were eleven, ten, eight, six, and one.

The atmosphere of the home was generally loud and angry. Often, the usual level of noise was heightened by the sound of breaking glass, intensified screaming, and ultimately full-blown violence directed toward the children or Timmy's mother. Timmy, despite his young age, was no longer fearful of being beaten or thrown across the room. Such activity had become normal to him. Mealtimes, too, had the same level of turbulence. Food that was placed on the table most often ended up on the floor or smeared across the faces of those who had somehow, although unknowingly, made Mom's current male friend mad.

Timmy did not defer to the violence or the threat of it, and so he became the target more than anyone else. He was the family punching bag and grew into his role rather well. When his bruises were noticed and reported by the school, child welfare professionals investigated. However, when questioned, all of the family members denied or minimized the abuse. Over time, there were twenty reports documented in Timmy's case record that were declared "unsubstantiated," meaning only that there was no proof.

Only after an unexpected visitor to the home found Timmy tied to his bed was the abuse substantiated. Subsequent medical examination revealed numerous old fractures in Timmy's arms and legs. Cigarette burns were found on his buttocks and genitals, and Timmy finally confirmed what the authorities already suspected: He had been abused for years and tied up routinely.

Timmy was removed from his home by the child welfare agency. He was placed in foster care while a family reunification plan was begun. After years of failed attempts to rectify the home situation, plans for his eventual adoption were made.

Parents wait for healthy infants. They dream of the perfect child, and Timmy does not fit into their fantasies. Timmy joined the ranks of hurt children. They are often school-age and may have medical problems. Almost all of them have histories of serious abuse or neglect. Some have special needs, some belong to a minority race, some are members of sibling groups, and many are from orphanages in other countries.

Angela, age five, was removed from her birth home after she was found foraging in a neighbor's trash at two in the morning. Her mother, a cocktail waitress, had stopped for a few drinks after work and never made it home. Angela, used to being on her own, had ventured out of the apartment in search of food.

Her mother tried to do better at parenting, and Angela was returned home. When her mother's efforts failed, the child was removed again. This pattern was repeated four times, and at each removal, Angela entered a different foster home. Her mother finally met a man and married him. Angela was sent to them and was sexually abused by her new stepfather. At the court hearing, her mother announced that she couldn't give up her husband for Angela, who was now ten.

Angela wanted to return home. She believed that the sexual abuse was a fair trade for the opportunity to be with her mother. She was falling behind in school, she was frightened and alone, and she was told that she would never see her birth mother again.

Mark and Sally are siblings. Three years older, Mark has always been responsible for his sister. Their mother, a prostitute, often disappeared from their lives for long periods of time, leaving her son in charge.

In eight years, they have lived in three foster homes. They are considered among the lucky ones because they have always been together and their moves have been relatively infrequent. Their present foster parents have cared for them for three years but have no desire to adopt. Although the children want to stay where they are, plans are in motion to move them to an adoptive home.

Ted is fourteen and has been living in a series of group homes since he was ten. He was abandoned by his birth parents, who decided to move out of state without him. After exhaustive attempts to locate relatives and terminate his parents' rights, he is finally free to be adopted.

Ted has never really had a chance to be a child. When he lived with his parents, their neglect forced him to take care of himself most of the time. When he lived in the group homes, he never attached to anyone. But in spite of his history, he is expected by the system to fit into an adoptive family.

Southern Ohio's rolling hills and valleys seem the paradise that embraces the old-fashioned virtues of home, hearth, and tranquility. The small towns look like warm places where Norman Rockwell might have set up his easel. No one would choose these peaceful scenes to be the backdrop for the adoption of a troubled child, but such children are everywhere. To Mike, as he entered his thirty-fifth foster home, it was just another stop on his erratic journey through childhood and adolescence.

Mike was first surrendered for adoption by his birth family when he was four years old. Conceived during a heated divorce and unwanted by either parent, he failed to attach to his mother in a meaningful way. She took fundamental care of him and his brother but was unable to deal with Mike's special needs — a speech problem and hearing loss.

Eventually adopted, Mike had problems in his new home. His distancing behavior, aggression, annoying ways, and lack of reciprocity drove a wedge between him and his adoptive parents. Compared to their loving, lively, intelligent birth child, Mike never measured up. He began to be the "best at being bad."

Unable to access any meaningful help, the family members became angrier with Mike and with each other. Finally, Mike's adoptive father walked calmly into the local sheriff's office one day armed with a gun and announced, "Remove my son, or I will kill him, my wife, my daughter, and myself."

A social worker met Mike in the principal's office and then took him to his first of thirty-five placements. Mike describes this scene as unbelievable and shocking. For years, he says, people talked to him about the incident, and it was as if they were speaking in a foreign language. His first adoptive family lost custody, and Mike was left with a closed birth record and little information about his early years. (Adoption records are closed in Ohio, and the judge refused to open Mike's even for general information.)

By the age of sixteen, Mike could look back on a history that was blank for the first four years and murky, at best, for the next six. His journey through group homes, foster homes, and four preadoptive homes had left him with little trust, distancing attitudes and behaviors, and unresolved feelings. The only certainty in his life was that time was running out. Within two years he would be put on the independent living track, which meant that the social services agency would pay his first month's rent after high school graduation. Period. All the caring, loving social workers who had been searching for a solution for Mike would say good-bye and turn their attention to other children. He would be alone—with nowhere to go for the holidays, no one to turn to in time of crisis, and no one to help him grow into a man.

These are just some examples of the children waiting for adoption. As a group, they have experienced multiple separations, losses, and traumas, which combine to create serious problems in adoptive placements.

It is clear that those who choose to parent an abused or neglected child require some basic elements to help them do the job well: an understanding of the issues faced by the child, support from professionals and the community in which they live, and an honest portrayal of the child's history. The truth about the child's background, although sometimes painful, is necessary if families are to succeed in helping the hurt child.

Two

THE CHILD WITH ATTACHMENT DIFFICULTIES

Common Behaviors of Kids with

Attachment Disorders

There is a common children's verse that says, "Sticks and stones may break my bones, but words will never hurt me." For the abused child, nothing could be further from the truth. While the effects of physical abuse usually heal over time, the psychological insults experienced by the child bring deep, long-lasting pain. These wounds fester within, creating ongoing difficulties for both the child and the adoptive family.

Many adoptive children did not experience early childhood trauma, neglect, or abuse. The issues these children face are common to all children and are usually compounded by issues related directly to adoption. But for adoptive children who lived through a difficult start, there is a range of developmental diversity tied to the abuse.

DEVELOPMENT DELAYS

According to developmental models, all of us grow along a time continuum, starting from a simple state and moving toward a more complex, more integrated personality as we mature. Along the path to adulthood, there are several tasks that we must master to move to higher stages of personality construction. Life events, especially traumatizing ones, may cause a child to get stuck at one level for an extended time.

Very often, an abused child may appear immature because his development was frozen at an earlier stage. For example, an eight-year-old who suffered abandonment as an infant may cry uncontrollably when left with an unfamiliar sitter. A child who was removed at age four may throw tantrums similar to a four-year-old's even at age twelve. A child removed from home at Christmas may be frightened by the sights and smells of the holidays. This behavioral regression is a return to the developmental state where the child is frozen, even though he has developed beyond that on many other levels. The child does not lose the complexity of being an eight-year-old; he simply regresses to an earlier state when faced with trauma.

Tammy, a nine-year-old who is developmentally delayed—socially, psychologically, and cognitively—was terrified of gray cars. When a driver from the social services agency arrived in a gray car, she refused to be driven to her doctor's appointment. *Refused* is a mild word for the extent of Tammy's rage. Three adults could not get her into the vehicle.

Later in therapy, Tammy revealed that her mom's boyfriend used to pick her up from school in a gray car. On almost every trip, he forced her to perform oral sex on him. Due to her intellectual and developmental limits, she could not separate the car from the event.

Parents of these children often face frustration when their child, who has made good progress over time, seems suddenly to regress. Panic sets in as they cry, "We're right back where we were a year ago!" While this may seem to be true, it is not. Real gains in growth and development by the child are permanent. In addition—and as a ray of sunshine—even those frozen stages in development can be reactivated. That reactivation can be compared to going back to fill in the blanks and is, in fact, the key to lasting change.

As stated, true gains in growth and development are never lost. Once a child has developed a conscience, for example, he cannot act against it without feeling distress. Though it often seems to parents that it is "one step forward and two steps back," every movement forward for the child is permanent. Regressive behavior is a temporary reaction to real or perceived trauma.

The difficulty for parents comes when children have experienced severe developmental delays affecting major behavior patterns. Many children have not, for example, developed a conscience—a process that generally occurs around ages six to eight. Others may not have mastered the concept of cause and effect, which is a precursor to conscience. Parents naturally expect a child to feel remorse for an action or to feel empathy for another, without realizing that these are complex skills requiring the development of a conscience.

A child may step on an animal or break a treasured heirloom and keep right on going, perhaps staring vacantly at the scolding parent or mouthing a superficial apology. The frustration a parent feels at this is understandable; we have learned to expect certain behavior at certain ages. But the early trauma this child experienced may have inhibited his capacity to develop. The child is not "bad" for not feeling what parents assume is "normal"; he simply has not reached that developmental stage—yet. For this child, conscience development will occur only after he has identified with a parent and has been able to internalize that identification.

If a child has never seen a baseball, never been told about one, never been taught how to catch one—even though every other child his age has—we would not consider getting upset with him for failing to catch the ball. This lack of behavioral skill development is much the same. If a child has never been able to identify with a safe, rational adult and internalize adult values, we cannot expect the conscience to be present. Worse, if a child has been shown that there is no justice or predictability in his life and that trusted adults do bad things to him for no reason, we begin to see how developing a conscience may not even have been in the child's best interests. A child who has managed to survive by lying, cheating, and stealing, by acting offensive to prevent sexual advances, or by remaining quiet when questioned will not release those survival mechanisms easily. He may not even be able to see how those behaviors are wrong, for without them he believes he would have died.

Because developmentally delayed children fall somewhere on the continuum between birth and their present age, we need to identify precisely where they fit in order to help move them along the way. We cannot assume that a ten-year-old is a ten-year-old. He may be more developmentally similar to a three-year-old or an even younger child. Locating and identifying that child's individual developmental pattern is the first, most critical step in helping him grow. By doing so, the parents and therapist can deal with a child in a way that is individually specific and developmentally appropriate.

To understand how to undo the effects of early developmental delays, it is not necessary to know what interrupted the child's development. That may, in fact, not be possible with an adopted child. But knowing the possible interrupters can help parents empathize with the child who can bring such frustration and despair. The interrupters most commonly identified include:

- Prenatal drug and/or alcohol exposure
- All forms of abuse (physical, verbal, emotional, sexual, psychological)
- Neglect
- Separation from the primary caregiver
- Foster care
- Adoption
- Pain that cannot be alleviated by the caregiver
- Institutional care

Many children experience a mixture of these factors on a constant, though random, basis. Like a bird caught in a windstorm, they are battered from first one direction, then another, beyond predictability.

Consider the plight of a child whose mother suffers from alcoholism. Born with Fetal Alcohol Spectrum Disorder, the child's development has been compromised in the womb. In addition, he may be emotionally abandoned from the first day of life. Left alone for hours at a time while his mother is out drinking, he may then be greeted by a mother whose behavior ranges from raging anger to drunken affection, from impatience to indifference, with no connection to his behavior. One day she may be arrested and suddenly disappear, while he is shuttled off to foster care. Upon his return to his mother's care, he may decide the foster parents abandoned him, further complicating the issue of trust. There may be a period of relative calm as the mom tries to stay straight.

The calm ends, and the maelstrom begins anew. Throughout all of this, there are other players entering and leaving the picture—some providing emotional support, but the majority supplying further abuse. A child with such a background may well be the developmental equivalent of an infant.

On the other end of the spectrum, there are children who have experienced relatively minor disruptions but still display emotional problems. One case that comes to mind is an adolescent who was described by his family as being aloof and not affectionate. By contrast, the other children in the family appeared able to give and receive affection appropriately. The parents indicated that this son had always been the "different one" of the family and that he had trouble developing or sustaining friendships. Though nothing came to mind at first, the mother finally recalled an early separation when she had returned to the hospital for medical complications resulting from his birth. She had been out of the home for twelve days while his father and relatives took care of her son. When she returned home, he was not as responsive as he had been and, in fact, did not want her to hold him. As a result, she followed what seemed to be his wishes and held him less, so as not to bother him. Unfortunately, exactly the opposite should have occurred. If she had held him more after their attachment was interrupted, the break most probably would have healed and the attachment strengthened. Out of this one separation, a lifelong pattern of distancing began. Each time the mother avoided her son's intense reaction to closeness, the pattern deepened.

REACTIVE ATTACHMENT DISORDER

The types of problems that adoptive parents see in their children are most likely the result of breaks in attachment that occur within the first three years. Such breaks impair, and even cripple, a child's ability to trust and bond to other human beings.

Issues with attachment cause the greatest problems when adopting a child with special needs. As adoptive parents attempt to connect with a child whose attachment ability is impaired by developmental delays, the attachment will either be insecure, distorted, or focused on negative behaviors.

Children who have suffered abuse or neglect severe enough to bring them into the foster care/adoption system may meet the diagnostic criteria for Reactive Attachment Disorder. This clinical diagnosis identifies children who have not been able to attach appropriately to a caregiver in a meaningful way. Although highly technical, an explanation of the diagnosis is given here to help parents better understand their child. The criteria is reprinted from the *Diagnostic and Statistical Manual of Mental Disorders*, also known as DSM-IV. This official document is published by the American Psychiatric Association for mental health professionals to use in diagnostic work with patients.

DIAGNOSTIC CRITERIA FOR 313.89 REACTIVE ATTACHMENT DISORDER OF INFANCY AND EARLY CHILDHOOD

A. Markedly disturbed and developmentally inappropriate social relatedness in most contexts, beginning before age five years, as evidenced by either (1) or (2):

(1) Persistent failure to initiate or respond in a developmentally appropriate fashion to most social interactions, as manifest by excessively inhibited, hypervigilant, or highly ambivalent and contradictory responses (e.g., the child may respond to caregivers with a mixture of approach, avoidance, and resistance to comforting, or may exhibit frozen watchfulness)

(2) Diffuse attachments as manifest by indiscriminate sociability with marked inability to exhibit appropriate selective attachments (e.g., excessive familiarity with relative strangers or lack of selectivity in choice of attachment figures)

B. The disturbance in Criterion A is not accounted for solely by developmental delay (as in Mental Retardation) and does not meet criteria for a Pervasive Developmental Disorder.

C. Pathogenic care as evidenced by at least one of the following:

(1) Persistent disregard for the child's basic emotional needs for comfort, stimulation, and affection

(2) Persistent disregard of the child's basic physical needs

(3) Repeated changes of primary caregiver that prevent formation of stable attachments (e.g., frequent changes in foster care)

D. There is a presumption that the care in Criterion C is responsible for the disturbed behavior in Criterion A (e.g., the disturbances in Criterion A began following the pathogenic care in Criterion C).

Specify type:

Inhibited Type: if Criterion A1 predominates in the clinical presentation

Disinhibited Type: if Criterion A2 predominates in the clinical presentation[1]

While parents and professionals living and working with children in the foster care/adoption system may feel that the disorder exists all too often and that most of the children they know qualify for this diagnosis, there is a danger in overdiagnosing or assuming that every child in the system develops the disorder. Placing labels on a child must always be done with great care. We have found, conversely, that children who have untreated Reactive Attachment Disorder will most certainly manifest other problems and develop other diagnoses. Frequently, parents hope the child will "grow out of" behaviors associated with attachment disorder. Unfortunately, since the child is stuck on his path of development, he will not grow out of anything emotionally without significant repair work.

Children whose developmental interruptions have resulted in an attachment disorder may exhibit many, or even all, of the following symptoms:[2]

- Superficially engaging and "charming" behavior
- Indiscriminate affection toward strangers
- Lack of affection with parents on their terms (not cuddly)
- Little eye contact on parental terms
- Persistent nonsense questions and incessant chatter
- Inappropriate demanding and clingy behavior

- Lying about the obvious (primary process lying)
- Stealing
- Destructive behavior to self, to others, and to material things (accident-prone)
- Abnormal eating patterns
- No impulse controls (frequently acts hyperactive)
- Lags in learning
- Abnormal speech patterns
- Poor peer relationships
- Lack of cause-and-effect thinking
- Lack of conscience
- Cruelty to animals
- Preoccupation with fire

For parents who lovingly and naively adopt a cherub-faced child, the personality traits described above can be shocking. Instead of fulfilling hopes and dreams, the child threatens to become the parents' worst nightmare. The parents often feel isolated, as if they are the only ones coping with such bizarre behavior. That isolation is compounded by the child's outward charm to the rest of the world. The pain and heartache the adoptive parents feel cannot be underestimated, nor can the hope that comes with identifying this disorder. From identification comes treatment that can fill in the child's developmental gaps and allow him to grow to maturity.

One of our hopes is that by identifying the disorder, we can help parents see that they are not alone in their pain. Beyond that, we want to stress that *something can be done.* Attachment disorders are treatable. With patience and understanding, parents can help their child form the bond of love needed to heal.

The only attachment disorder listed in the DSM-IV is that of Reactive Attachment Disorder. Academicians, however, have identified and researched various styles of attachment. While the numerous researchers do not classify the different styles in terms of psychopathology, each style has corresponding behavioral patterns that may be perceived by parents as troublesome to live with on a day-to-day basis.

Clearly, the diagnostic description of Reactive Attachment Disorder in the DSM-IV is inadequate, and its limitations are apparent to clinicians and researchers. While parents are probably not particularly concerned about specific attachment styles, research offers the opportunity for clinicians to refine and differentiate their therapeutic interventions. Families are most interested in what is going to help their children with attachment disturbance finally get the necessary help to be able to live comfortable, reciprocal, productive lives.

Without going into great detail, we will mention the primary attachment styles most often cited in research: secure and insecure.

The National Child Traumatic Stress Network (NCTSN)[3] states that a secure attachment pattern, present in approximately 55–65 percent of the normative population, is thought to be the result of receptive, sensitive caregiving. The parent who provides nurturing in an ongoing manner helps the child develop a foundation that reflects trust, reciprocity, emotional attunement, self-regulation, and empathy. This individual will most likely develop conscience and live life in a typical manner.

Insecure attachment patterns have been consistently documented in more than 80 percent of maltreated children. Children with insecure attachment patterns may be classified as avoidant, ambivalent, or disorganized. The avoidant attachment style has been associated with predictably rejecting caregiving. Many parents have described this kind of behavior as they attempt to provide nurturing to their child or adolescent.

Ainsworth, Blehar, and Waters state that when children experience parents alternating between validation and invalidation in a predictable manner, they may develop ambivalent attachment patterns.[4] NCTSN goes on to say that these children may attempt to disconnect themselves from others when they perceive that important adults are either rejecting or overly engaging. Adoptive parents may see this reaction as they begin their interactions with their new child. They should be aware that this response may be the child's attempt to protect himself from rejection or from being overwhelmed by the adults' affectionate gestures.

Children who have experienced severe, unpredictable violence and/or abandonment early in life may develop disorganized attachment. This attachment style is associated with erratic behavior in childhood. Disorganized attachment in adolescence seems to reflect primitive survival-based interactions, according to NCTSN. The behaviors seen in individuals with disorganized attachment are closely associated with what we see in people diagnosed with Reactive Attachment Disorder.

Given the complexity of what research is discovering about the developmental attachment process, it seems that further differential diagnosis will lead to improved approaches to differential treatment. While the term Attachment Spectrum Disorder is not being used, it seems to us that it probably should be utilized to heighten the complex nature of attachment and to reduce simplistic approaches to diagnosis and treatment.

Since most of the people reading this book are parents or professionals working with adoptive families, we assume they have an interest in gaining further understanding of the kinds of behaviors they may be seeing in their children or clients. Below, we have provided more detailed information about the behaviors mentioned earlier in this chapter.

COMMON BEHAVIORS OF KIDS WITH ATTACHMENT DISORDER

Superficially Engaging and "Charming" Behavior

Parents of a child with attachment problems know just how superficially charming their child can be with people who do not know him well. New, unsuspecting adults are of much interest to the child. By leading others to believe he's an easy kid to be around, the child's behavior causes others to assume that his parents are the problem. Parents of children with attachment disorder regularly report that therapists, teachers, and other authority figures assume that the charming qualities they initially observe in the child reflect his normal behavior. For the parents — struggling with behavior that more typically approaches the bizarre — the strain grows each time their credibility is directly or indirectly questioned. They also continue to question themselves, wondering why a child can be so well behaved around grandparents, for example, and so difficult at home. "Maybe it *is* us," they reason unfairly. "Maybe he would be better off in another home."

But children who have not bonded and attached solidly in their earliest days, months, and years are frequently more comfortable around strangers. Closeness and familiarity makes them uneasy. In contrast, a normally developing child will always be more comfortable with parents than he is with strangers. A child without difficulties uses parents as a home base as he enters into tentative interactions with unfamiliar people. The child may reach out shyly, then retreat to the security and safety of mom or dad. Children with faulty attachment do not treat anyone as a stranger and prefer the unknown to the familiar.

As these children grow older, this attraction to strangers grows. Because they have no baseline for judging people, they are poor judges of character and cannot predict the outcomes of their interactions. As a result, they may experience one precarious situation after another as they move through life.

Tasha was transferred to her new school so she could be placed in its self-contained classroom for children with severe behavioral problems. This school change was her third in almost as many months. She sat quietly waiting in the office, chatting amicably with staff who wondered why such a delightful little girl was being placed in a program designed for children who could not be schooled in any other setting. In fact, Tasha was to be the only girl in her class. How bad could she possibly be? Why was her mom so mad and so controlling?

After three days at their school, the office staff quit wondering. Tasha had stolen lunches from the other students, put cleanser in her teacher's half-full coffee cup, and wet and soiled her pants each day. When she was caught in a closet engaging in sexual activity with a classmate, the staff's questions were answered.

Indiscriminate Affection Toward Strangers and Lack of Affection with Parents on Their Terms (Not Cuddly)

Affection toward strangers is coupled with a distinct, pronounced lack of affection toward parents. The child does not trust anyone and so avoids any real, intimate contact — except on his terms. Instead of seeking a hug at an appropriate time, the child may use affection-seeking behavior when the parent cannot reciprocate. He may want a hug when mom is on the phone, when company arrives, while dad is driving the car, or in the middle of a family crisis. He usually flees from closeness when the timing is appropriate and is initiated by the parent. To reverse this counterproductive pattern, parents must set up situations in which the child can be exposed to affection, whether or not he desires it.

> Lisa knew no strangers. Early in her life, people were amused by how comfortable she was being passed around the room from relative to relative. She greeted each new person with a bright smile, a big hug, and an affectionate kiss. While her adoptive parents thought it was cute at eighteen months, they became alarmed as she grew older and began approaching complete strangers in the mall, in restaurants, and at church.
>
> Most unusual was the fact that Lisa's affection was given only to strangers. She avoided any form of affection or close contact with her parents. She violently recoiled whenever touched or hugged, so they felt as though they were hugging a board. Lisa stiffened and held her breath, without reciprocating in any way. She occasionally uttered groans and sighs, and everything she did sent loud messages to her parents to stay away.

Little Eye Contact on Parental Terms

One of the earliest connections between parent and child is eye contact. Since this did not happen so early for the child with attachment disorder, he will tend to avoid eye contact—especially with parents. In therapy, these children often tell us that making eye contact gives the other person power over them. They almost seem to fear giving too much of themselves away by allowing parents to see their eyes. At the same time, these children can skillfully use eye contact to charm strangers, and they often use direct eye contact when lying in an effort to disarm parents. Parent after parent states in surprise, "He never looks at me while I'm talking to him, but he stares me straight in the eye when he tells a lie." The child will also have eye contact when he wants something or is intimidating others.

> Anthony's eye contact was his tool. With his deep brown eyes, he could catch and hold the attention of strangers in the park as he asked them for money. His apparently genuine eye contact served him well, as person after person handed over their pocket change.

At home, Anthony's adoptive parents could seldom catch his eye in casual conversation. When angered, however, his eye contact was direct. He intimidated and threatened with his eyes, maintaining piercing contact that caused his mother to say often, "If looks could kill . . ."

Anthony's eye contact also improved when he was lying. As his mother pulled a twenty-dollar bill from his pants pocket, he looked her straight in the eyes, assuring her that he had not taken it from her desk and that it was not the same twenty she had asked him about earlier that morning.

Persistent Nonsense Questions and Incessant Chatter

Parents often feel uncomfortable about their child's ongoing chatter and nonsense questions. At first, they feel an obligation to respond—after all, they just adopted a child who experienced deprivation. They want to be available to enrich his life at every opportunity. After a while, they begin to feel manipulated and controlled by the incessant, unrelated, and unrelenting questions and jabbering.

While most young children do this frequently, they stop the toddler-like behavior at some point. But for children with attachment issues, control seems to be the motive for this type of chatter. They keep a parent engaged to ensure that the parent does not forget, ignore, neglect, or abandon them and to remind themselves that they can maintain control of a situation.

Mack, age thirteen, just loved to ask questions. In fact, he loved questions so much that he began asking them as soon as his mother pulled out of the driveway. "Why do we have to wear seat belts? Why do we need to be safe? Why will we get a ticket? How do the police know we're not wearing them? What happens if we get killed? Where do we go after we die? Have you ever died? I don't like this seat belt. Do you like it?" On and on he went. His mother began to turn up the volume on the radio and make repeated threats. Nothing seemed to work, especially since she was Mack's captive audience while in the car.

Inappropriate Demanding and Clingy Behavior

The children we are discussing feel entitled, expecting to get what they want. They think that what they want is what they need, because they cannot distinguish the difference. The parents, dealing with a constant barrage of demands from the child, find that they begin to resent yielding to the child's insistent wants. They may feel every interaction is akin to negotiating or bartering for peace.

Clingy behavior is often designed to interfere with the parents' other activities. The child has figured out that his adoptive parents value physical contact and have a hard time refusing it, so he uses it to interrupt them. At first, the behavior seems like affection, but that flavor soon fades to overt manipulation. When parents diligently initiate and maintain physical contact, clingy behavior may be reduced.

> Easter Sunday, after church, the entire congregation gathered for a buffet lunch. Generally, it was an easy, orderly, comfortable meal. But Jennifer's family dreaded the affair and felt guilty for their apprehension. Jennifer loved to be difficult at church functions. She loved to make demands and hang on to her mother's legs and dress. At seven years old, Jennifer could have been playing with other children, but she preferred — demanded — to sit on her mother's lap and eat from her mother's plate. This successfully prevented her mother from interacting with anyone else. If someone tried to initiate conversation with her parents, Jennifer would do something that required attention.
>
> The superficial impression was that Jennifer was an unusually loving child. Church members had difficulty understanding the tension on her parents' faces, which made her mom and dad feel even worse about their parenting.

Lying About the Obvious (Primary Process Lying)

Before the ages of three or four, a child does not know that other people have minds of their own. He does not realize that they can evaluate what he says, so he is free to tell the truth or lie without any fear of what others think. If the child says it, he automatically assumes that the other person believes it. Imaginary friends are common at this age, as a child assumes his parents believe they exist. In early childhood, this behavior is appropriate and expected. But when the child continues to do this well into his teens, he is clearly displaying a developmental delay. The types of lies that kids with attachment problems tell are so preposterous they are almost impossible to miss. The lying perplexes and angers people. Parents and other adults frequently reply to such lies with, "How dumb do I look?"

When confronted with the lie, the child is often amazed that people recognize it. It isn't that the child thinks the other person is stupid; he simply doesn't realize that the other person thinks at all. If not treated, he may continue such lying throughout his life. Self-protective lying might develop as the child grows, but the childish, age-inappropriate lying also continues.

Children and adolescents who have developed a pattern of lying often become automatic liars. In other words, the first lie they tell in an interaction may be completely unintentional. Their follow-up lies, however, are most often deliberate and are meant to support and defend the original, automatic lie.

> Scott was sixteen and in love. He was excited about his recent adoptive placement and seemed to be doing very well. One day, a bill from a local florist arrived at his home, indicating that Scott had sent a single red rose to his new girlfriend. His father was surprised, but pleasantly so, and attempted to compliment his son for being so thoughtful. Scott, however, adamantly denied that he sent anything. He insisted for two days that the florist must have sent the bill to the wrong people, at the wrong address, yet charging for a flower sent to the right girlfriend. Not until Scott and his father went to the florist to correct the "error" did Scott even partially admit any involvement. Six years after the event, Scott finally told his dad that he sent the rose. He was still surprised that his father was so smart to have known the truth long before.

Stealing

Much like lying, the specific stealing behavior of children with attachment problems is unusual. They steal from their homes, their parents, their siblings. The way they steal almost guarantees that they will get caught. Rather than taking a cookie and hiding it away to eat, the child may eat it where the crumbs surely will be noticed. The child may take a parent's wallet and put it under his pillow. Entire packages of food are often taken to the child's bedroom for later consumption.

In a more normal type of stealing, the child may take change from his mother's purse. Here, the child is more likely to take the last twenty-dollar bill and will be genuinely surprised and perplexed that his mom actually notices the money is missing. In any case, the evidence is always that: evident. While some of these children shoplift, the majority of them limit their stealing to home or school. When caught, they immediately display anger and project blame. They may react by blaming the victim for leaving the purse on the sofa or for leaving them alone in the room with the cookie. While the blame is inappropriate, and even foolish, they predictably attempt to distort and reframe the situation.

> John, age thirteen, stole shirts and underwear from his adoptive father. He wore the shirts around the house, to school, and outside to play. When confronted, he would deny that he took them or even that they were his father's. Although he could have asked for and received any of the things he stole, he continued to pilfer openly with no attempt to hide it. At school, John "found" more things each week than his parents had "found" in their entire lives. Like his lying, his stealing was obvious.

Destructive Behavior to Self, to Others, and to Material Things (Accident-Prone)

Children with attachment problems tend to hurt themselves, possessions, animals, and other people. Toys, even if they are supposedly unbreakable, break. New shoes look like candidates for the trash in two weeks. If something can be broken, destroyed, or rendered inoperable, the child will find the way. Because no one cared for or respected the child's most precious possessions, his body and soul, he does not understand the concept. He damages things the way he was damaged, because destruction is the metaphor of his life.

> Jacob, age twelve, could break anything, even items guaranteed against breakage by the manufacturer. Knobs were a special attraction. If they could be removed, Jacob did so, hiding them in his pockets and

drawers. Every toy he received each Christmas morning was inoperable by dinnertime.

At first, he seemed accident-prone. He fell down constantly, even out of his bedroom window and off the roof. Three screens later, Jacob's parents began to suspect that many of his accidents were at least partially intentional. They watched as he fell on his little brother, over and over again. He showed no regret about hurting his brother or about breaking his own things. To Jacob, nothing had any value.

Abnormal Eating Patterns

One common problem with a child who has suffered early neglect, abuse, and deprivation is his approach to food. Depending on his history, he may steal, hoard, gorge, purge, or even refuse to eat. Food-related problems can be minor or severe, but they are often present. Some children even eat non-nutritive things such as wallpaper, paneling, blankets, animal dung, and pet food. Food-related problems are connected to the child's uncertainty about being fed when he was very young and are a sad reminder of the effects of neglect and abuse.

As anyone who has ever tried to change eating habits and patterns can attest, handling issues related to food can be very difficult. Most often, the unique food problems for a hurt child are likely to be managed rather than eradicated. The key is to recognize that filling emotional emptiness with food is destined to fail.

Theresa had experienced a great deal of deprivation in her early years. Now, at age four, she arranged her entire life around food, much the way an infant's life is normally arranged around food.

Theresa hid food in pillowcases. She gorged whenever she could. Night after night, she roamed the house taking food, eating it, and hiding what she could not finish. It took awhile for Theresa's new parents to realize that she was eating the dog and cat food, as well. One day they caught her going through the garbage, eating anything she could find.

Many parents become so frustrated with food issues that they attempt to limit the amount of food the child has access to or to restrict certain foods. Either of these interventions will be perceived as deprivation by the child and are nearly guaranteed to fail to be corrective. Actually, providing the food that the child seeks is more likely to minimize food-related obsessions.

No Impulse Controls (Frequently Acts Hyperactive)

We often hear parents describe their adopted child as impulsive or hyperactive. Superficially, this may be true, but a diagnosis of Attention Deficit Hyperactivity Disorder (ADHD) must be made independently.

Reactive Attachment Disorder is actually very different. And while we continue to hear from parents and some professionals that there are many shared symptoms, we do not concur. On the contrary, the most troubled children we see are not impulsive; they often plan to do the things they do. While their activity levels may be high, they know exactly what they are doing. Many of them share with us the elaborate plans they make and carry out with successful — but negative — results. Children with attachment problems have *intentional* difficulties and may or may not have *attentional* issues.

Another behavior that needs to be considered is that of hypervigilance. Many, if not most, children who have experienced trauma are hypervigilant. They need to know what is going to happen, when it is going to happen, and how it will affect them.

Unexpected transitions may cause them great distress. While children with ADHD might be distracted by the arrival of a police officer at school, the child who has had multiple traumas may be triggered into thinking about *why* the police are there. Did something happen at home? Are the police coming to take him to another home? The hypervigilant child/adolescent may actually be overattending to something, as opposed to being inattentive.

Charles knew what to do when he wanted to get out of doing something: He would "take a fit," as he called it. He became very active — running, jumping, climbing all over things. His parents and teachers began to worry that these fits were involuntary, since they seemed to overtake his body without any control on his part. After some therapy, Charles gladly acknowledged creating his fits. Each time he came to the office, we asked him to show us one. Over time, they began to decrease in frequency as we increased our requests to see more.

Lags in Learning

In addition to being mislabeled hyperactive, many of these children are also classified as learning disabled. Again, this is an area that must be evaluated carefully and independently of other issues. In our experience, most of these children actually have normal intelligence or better, but their developmental issues prevent them from tapping into it or from letting it show. In many cases, acting stupid has served their survival to such a degree that they now appear to be stupid.

Dramatic differences in results are often apparent when we test a child before and after treatment. Most often, there is no evidence of a problem in brain chemistry or dysfunction. Sometimes, however, fetal drug and alcohol problems or physical abuse have created organic problems that interfere with learning and cannot be corrected. Parents should have their child carefully tested by qualified professionals before making any judgments about whether his problems are physiological or psychological in nature.

Michael was in classes for developmentally handicapped children. Still, he was getting all failing marks—an almost impossible feat in a class designed to prevent failure and bolster self-esteem. Michael's parents and teachers felt he was much brighter than tests reflected; ultimately, his therapists agreed.

Yet Michael acted as dumb as he could. He spoke strangely, slowly, incorrectly, and in a chronic whine. Strangers often thought something was wrong with him, and they were right. But what was wrong was not what they thought. After treatment, Michael was retested. His measured IQ jumped thirty points over earlier scores.

Michael had not gotten smarter—he had improved his mental outlook and emotional state enough that he no longer needed to act dumb.

Abnormal Speech Patterns

Abnormal speech is a symptom sometimes seen in children with attachment difficulties, though by itself it is not evidence of attachment disorder. While any child may develop unusual speech patterns, the child with attachment disorder will display them along with other, more serious, symptoms.

Robert, a ten-year-old, had a habit of mumbling. His speech was so unusual that it drew people to him to listen to his strange ways of saying things. People were forced to pay unusually close attention. Adults often said, "What did you say? I didn't understand you," as they leaned forward to hear him. While it seemed to be a serious developmental problem at first glance, Robert's adoptive parents soon began hearing Robert speak quite clearly and correctly when he thought he was out of earshot.

Poor Peer Relationships

A child who cannot get along with his family will surely have problems with friends. His unusually charming behavior may help him make friends quickly, but he will lose them just as quickly. Lying, cheating, stealing, and casting blame do not go over any better with children than they do with adults. A child or teenager with this problem will consistently alienate others. He will invent rules for games when the standard ones do not fit his needs, and his friends will tire of the manipulation of standards such as "three strikes and you're out." "Not at my house" may be the child's angry response. Adults reason from a more advanced level and will show greater tolerance of this behavior than children. Children may eventually brand the child a social misfit, making his life even more difficult.

Children with developmental delays often experience difficulties connecting with peers due to the fact that they may not have developmental equals. In other words, the child who is developmentally diverse—for example, a little bit six, a little bit twelve, and a little bit fifteen—may not seem like a good-friend candidate to other children.

Randy's parents, though struggling with him themselves, were increasingly concerned and saddened that he had no friends at school or in the neighborhood. They watched as neighbor children initially befriended, then avoided, their son. On several occasions, they heard the children making fun of Randy's quirks—his squinting, constant movement, odd noises, and acting dumb.

When Randy's birthday was two weeks away, his parents invited ten children to a party. At first, the children's parents accepted for them. Then, one by one, embarrassed mothers and fathers called, giving flimsy excuses for why their child would not be able to attend. Just one person showed up for the party, but Randy was thrilled. He believed the lame excuses offered and seemed not to care. Besides, he said, those other kids were weird.

Lack of Cause-and-Effect Thinking

People's reactions to his behavior will often mystify the child who has an attachment disorder. But think about it: When a child does not experience a predictable cycle of nurturing, he never develops the ability to discern cause and effect. In this child's world, action A does not bring result B. Sometimes action A brings result B, but it may as often bring results F, R, J, or X.

A baby's crying, for example, may bring a mother's comforting presence and food, or it may bring a shrieking attack from that same person, isolation for hours, or a stranger shaking him to be quiet. What happens one time will not happen the next, so how could a child comprehend the concept of action/reaction? Life has demonstrated, conclusively and convincingly, quite the opposite. And without the ability to grasp cause and effect, the child cannot develop a conscience.

Every day it was the same thing: Ten-year-old Damien would take food, money, and tissues. His parents would find them in the same places—under his mattress, in his drawers, and above the mirror in the bathroom. Each day his mom presented the items retrieved from those places, and each day Damien vigorously denied taking them. It was a mystery to Damien, the only child in the house, how his parents always knew he had done it. Though his parents thought they would go crazy with the repetition, Damien never varied his pattern.

Though this example may seem far-fetched, it is a real story of a child who has never grasped the idea that one action brings about an equal and opposite reaction. Damien did not understand the relationship between his actions and his parents' reactions because a crucial step was missed in his development.

Lack of Conscience

In a typical setting, a child learns to identify with a parent's values, behavior, and ideas of right and wrong. As the child observes, he takes those values into himself and establishes a set of criteria by which he can judge himself and others. This process is critical to establishing a conscience.

In the child with attachment disorder, this internalization does not happen, which prevents him from becoming a responsible, productive, and contributing member of a family or of society. When the child is adopted by new rational parents he must begin a process that normally takes place between ages six and eight. Although it is challenging and presents perhaps the greatest barrier to creating a peaceful family, this developmental step can take place at any age. First, however, the child must attach to and identify with the new parents.

> Tracy was adopted into a close-knit family. Her parents frequently socialized with her new aunts, uncles, grandparents, and other relatives. On each of these occasions, Tracy would return home with many "new" things, including jewelry and money. When Tracy's parents confronted her, against the wishes of the grandparents who thought they were too quick to judge, Tracy had no remorse, feelings of guilt, or embarrassment. She appeared to feel nothing.

Cruelty to Animals

Long considered a hallmark of the disturbed child, this behavior is often present in the child with attachment disorder. Cruelty to animals may include incessant teasing, physical assault, torture, or ritualistic killing.

A child's cruelty to animals is a serious concern because it often escalates to hurting people. Parents sometimes deny the intentional nature of their child's harmful treatment of animals, and the child will support the accident theory when confronted. This can be a perilous denial because of the danger to animals, other children, and adults as the child grows.

Carl, age eight, started being mean to pets at age two. He squeezed the gerbil, pulled the dog's tail, intentionally stepped on the cat. The extreme anger he felt inside flowed out in his cruelty toward animals because they were much easier to get to than people. Animals cannot tell on a child and seldom defend themselves against abuse. In therapy, Carl expressed much anger and described, in detail, how he felt as he strangled puppies and kittens.

Preoccupation with Fire

Some of the most disturbed children we counsel display an unusual fascination with fire. Given the number of homes with fireplaces, it is safe to say that many people are attracted to fire. This preoccupation we are describing, however, goes far beyond the typical to the bizarre. The child may be attracted to the power that fire holds and his ability to create such a large effect even though he is so small. Most of his life, he has felt powerless to control situations and to create any effect on others, and fire offers a way to change that. Parents may find burned matches around the house, charred papers under the child's bed, or a pile of burned items hidden behind the garage.

Because this behavior holds much potential danger to the adoptive family, we regard this symptom of attachment disorder as one of the most serious. Parents dealing with a child who shows a strong attraction to fire would be wise to seek counseling immediately.

Along the same lines, a child may display an equally strong pull toward blood and gore. The pictures he draws often contain depictions of blood and wounded people, and his talk is peppered with references to injury. If given the freedom, he will select movies that contain graphic violence, and he may play-act the violence with others. Again, this child is dealing with intense inner rage and a strong desire to hurt in the same way he has been hurt.

When the police brought twelve-year-old Jeffrey home after catching him trying to start a fire at his elementary school, his parents were upset, but not surprised. Since Jeffrey arrived five months earlier, it had been a constant worry. His parents had found clothing and other items burned and often discovered piles of burned matches in unusual locations. It became so bad that they had gone through every corner of the house confiscating any items that could be used to start a fire.

All of these symptoms must be evaluated as part of a comprehensive diagnostic process. Reactive Attachment Disorder may coexist with additional diagnoses, which could either cloud or aggravate the situation. Keep in mind that not all hurt children develop attachment disorder, so they need to be recognized as individuals—each with unique wounds that may or may not require professional treatment.

We can never know a child's complete history or trace all the positive influences that may have been present even in the most abusive environment. In addition, children have varying degrees of resiliency, and some may survive even severe trauma relatively unscathed.

Leticia's adoptive parents were prepared for the worst when they first took her into their home. Their first adoptive daughter had displayed classic signs of attachment disorder, requiring ongoing therapy. They knew that Leticia's history included severe neglect and abandonment typical of a child who develops attachment disorder. Leticia, however, was a delightful, cheerful child who never displayed any of the symptoms expected. Although it took a few months for her to feel completely safe, she formed a deep attachment to her new mother that grew over the years.

When exploring resources to evaluate a child, check to see if the professionals you're considering are familiar with Reactive Attachment Disorder diagnosis. When determining treatment, ensure that the therapist is familiar with the latest information. Misdiagnosis or mistreatment will only make matters worse for your child.

As any adoptive parent struggling with these issues will confirm, many of these symptoms are very, very serious. The severity varies from child to child, but in the more difficult cases, the symptoms completely disrupt life for all who live in intimate contact with the child. They may even threaten the health and well-being of other children in the family.

While the severity of attachment disorder should not be minimized, neither should the hope for change. A child placed in an environment where he can be helped to fill in the missing developmental pieces in his past can change dramatically for the better. Attachment to other people is the natural desire of the hurt child. As he moves through the treatment process, he can develop a strong bond to the adoptive parents that allows him to change his behavior. The key lies in treating the cause of his behavior, not fruitlessly attempting to stop him from manifesting the symptoms. In our clinical practice, we have seen many children with attachment problems emerge from treatment as loving, responsible, contributing family members in whom parents can place their complete trust.

THREE

THE CYCLE OF BONDING

Interruptions from Abuse and Neglect

Even before a child is born, the building blocks of development are being laid. During the critical nine months the child is within his mother's womb, he must receive sufficient nutrition and be free of harmful drugs if he is to develop into a healthy baby. Many hurt children were born to mothers addicted to drugs and/or alcohol. These children can be viewed as life's earliest abuse victims since their systems failed to develop properly. Many times, they are not primed to attach to a caregiver. With immature neurological systems, they are often hypersensitive to all stimulation. They do not like light and may perceive any touch as pain. A child in chronic pain, even with the most loving caregiver, may develop attachment disorder as the pain short-circuits his ability to bond.

Sadly, a baby born with Fetal Alcohol Spectrum Disorder or drug-induced problems is most often tended to by a substance-addicted mother, incapable of providing even basic care. His heightened sensitivity and irritability may set him up for further abuse or neglect from his mother as she attempts to parent a baby who is often fussy and upset.

To better understand how abuse and neglect affect a child's development, it is necessary to understand "normal" development in an infant. Abuse and neglect interrupt the first and most important developmental process for an infant—the cycle of bonding, as illustrated on the next page.[1]

THE EFFECTS OF ABUSE AND NEGLECT ON THE CRITICAL CYCLE OF BONDING

Most professionals who work with and study the process of bonding and attachment agree that a child's first eighteen to thirty-six months are critical. It is during this period that the infant is exposed—in a healthy situation—to love, nurturing, and life-sustaining care. The child learns that if he has a need, someone will gratify that need, and the gratification leads to the development of his trust in others.

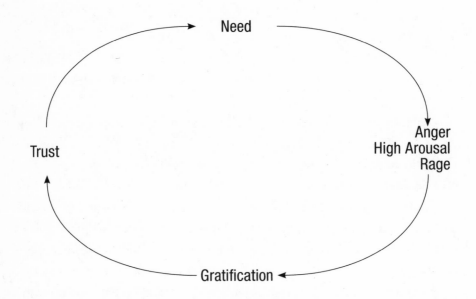

Prior to gratification, frustration is heightened. It is during this frustration that the foundation for delaying gratification is laid. This is critical learning with lifelong implications.

During the delay after his first cry, the infant may become increasingly angry or rageful, and his state of arousal is high. It is at this point that he is receptive to his parents' gratifying efforts, which include touching, smiling, rocking, feeding, changing, making eye contact, and vocal soothing. Presenting a valuable opportunity for attaching between parent and child, these acts allow the child to begin to trust that his parents can and will care for him and protect him. The cycle is repeated thousands of times in the first two years of an infant's life, forming the foundation of every other developmental task of human life.

This is not to suggest that later events will have no bearing on the course of a person's life. Instead, it is to say that without the successful completion of this cycle at some point, it is doubtful that an individual's growth will proceed normally without specific therapeutic intervention.

Failure to complete and repeat the bonding cycle leads to serious problems in the formation of the child's personality, which, in most cases, will have lifelong implications. When the bonding cycle is interrupted, problems arise in these areas:

- Social/behavioral development
- Cognitive development
- Emotional development
- Cause-and-effect thinking
- Conscience development
- Reciprocal relationships
- Parenting
- Accepting responsibility

A child born into a dysfunctional environment that features abuse and neglect as the overriding themes will not experience the bonding cycle with any predictability. In an abusive home, he may reach the point of high arousal and be physically silenced. Injury at the height of arousal is an effect — it's just the wrong effect. Abuse becomes gratification, and the child believes that he has the power to arouse others and cause them to act out anger and abuse. He begins to trust his power and control, and not that of others. Eventually he learns to lose his fear and may learn not to feel physical pain. The final outcome is that he learns he can trust no one except himself to gratify his needs. And that is a dangerous lesson. Because he trusts no one, he never learns to identify with other people and cannot develop compassion, empathy, love, or any of the other positive emotions that result from interaction. In fact, the only way he learns to interact with others is through aggression and violence.

An infant who is born into neglect or has lived in an orphanage learns slightly different lessons. For him, the bonding cycle is short-circuited. Instead of experiencing need, high arousal, gratification, and trust in others, he experiences need, high arousal to the point of exhaustion, self-gratification, and trust in self/self-reliance. Eventually this child develops less need, less arousal, more immediate self-gratification, and no involvement with others. He is likely to develop habits to gratify himself that may include rocking, head banging, sucking on his hands, and hair pulling. He may grow up detached from others, appearing vacant and empty. He has few emotions and desires no interaction from others, even acting as if no others are present in a room.

He has effectively learned that he can—and needs to—trust himself. We would all agree that no young child should have only himself to trust and that such self-reliance interferes with his desire and capacity to rely on others—his parents included. Often, parents report that their child never asks them for anything. He is frequently content with getting or taking what he wants—he does not think he needs anyone else to help him.

The neighbors noticed little activity in the trailer next door. Upon further exploration, they discovered that the three children who lived there—ages nine months, one and a half years, and two and a half years—were unattended. After reconstructing their memories about the last time they saw the family car, they concluded that the children had been alone for at least four days. The youngest child had not had his diaper changed throughout that period of time, and the two older children had been soiling and urinating all over the trailer. The dogs, as well, had been using the trailer as their yard.

The electricity was not in service, and the only food included moldy leftovers, soured milk, and plenty of beer and soft drinks. The rooms were strewn with opened, unfinished cans, which had been providing some liquid intake as the older child tried to care for her younger siblings.

When removed, the children were receptive and open to strangers—social workers and police officers—who were taking them away. The Humane Society was called to take the dogs, and the health department officially closed the trailer.

After two years of failed reunification plans and three foster placements, the children's permanent custody was given to the county. The parents' appeals lasted another two years before the children were finally available for a permanent family. They were nearly five, five and a half, and six and a half years old.

These children suffered from repetitive, extensive neglect—the factor most damaging to a child's emotional development. The bonding cycle is interrupted over and over. While there may be times when the child's needs are met, there is no predictability. He never knows what will happen when, and if, he lets out a cry.

The other type of abuse that disrupts the bonding cycle is sexual. Sadly prevalent in our society, this abuse creates a very distinct and unsettling pattern of behavior in a child. Sexual stimulation is pleasurable to the human body and may bring gratification to a child. But an adult sexualizing a child often may both hurt and please the child, creating pain, fear, and, ultimately, confusion. The child's cycle of bonding becomes very disordered as gratification becomes linked to sex. The cycle operates something like this: no need, high arousal, physical (sexual) gratification or pain, distrust. A child learns to both desire and fear sexual activity at a very primitive level. As he grows, he may attempt to meet his needs through sexualization with others. If violence has also been present, the child may be both sexual and aggressive—a frightening combination.

Dwayne, age eight, and Patty, age five, are siblings who were living with their mother. They frequently moved from place to place, most often living in shabby, by-the-week motels or their mother's car. Mom had many friends, all male, so the children had many "uncles." No system could keep track of them as they moved from town to town, county to county, state to state. Dwayne had never been in one school system for any length of time and had none of the academic skills of a normal eight-year-old. Days were for sleeping and nights were for partying with Mom and her friends.

Sometimes Mom would have a long-term relationship, and they would all move into that uncle's house. One time, they even stayed in the same place for six months. Despite all the moves, one thing was always predictable, always constant: Gross things were going on.

Dwayne and Patty were sexually abused by Mom, by her many friends, and finally by each other. They would watch Uncle Joe "do it" with Mom, and then Mom would watch Uncle Joe "do it" with Dwayne and Patty. Sometimes Mom even took pictures. Sometimes the things that were done to them felt good, sometimes they hurt, and sometimes they felt strange. But they always happened.

There was no escaping it. When Grandma and Grandpa babysat, they did the same things. They even told the children that they used to do those things to their mommy, too. Dwayne and Patty came to believe that their reality was everyone's. They believed that this sex stuff was what all families did as part of daily life.

One time, after the family stayed in one place for a while, the neighbors and teachers noticed that Dwayne's and Patty's behaviors were highly sexualized. In fact, the two of them were trying to engage in sexual activity most of the time. They approached both younger children and older children. They played games that turned sexual. They tried sticking things in their dog's private parts. They targeted adults as well — Patty grabbed the mailman's genitals one day.

Child welfare professionals were eventually notified. The children were removed from their home, and a sexual-abuse investigation was initiated. Abuse was substantiated, and Mom was incarcerated. From prison, she began a drawn-out appeal cycle to regain custody of her children. Dwayne and Patty are not yet legally adoptable, so they continue to move through the system.

While these case histories are graphic, they are certainly not unique or the worst that we have seen. Though they differ in method, both abuse and neglect systematically destroy a child.

To lose a child to foster care requires a serious offense. To lose a child to permanent custody requires proof that parents:

- Repeatedly harm the child
- Repeatedly neglect the child
- Repeatedly fail to protect the child

Talk shows sometimes feature birth parents whose children have been removed. In woeful voices, they tell of how the system swooped in to remove their children when the mother made an emergency run to the store for a quart of milk. What Mom fails to tell the audience is that on her way to the store, she picked up Dad, got drunk with him, and left town for several days. Their children, in the meantime, were found alone, filthy, cold, hungry, and scared. After several failed reunification attempts, when the same sort of thing happened repeatedly, the children were finally made available for permanent adoption. Although occasionally parents are unfairly targeted for child-abuse charges and their children are placed in temporary foster care, permanent placement requires far too many attempts at keeping the family together for an error to occur.

HOW A CHILD RESPONDS TO ABUSE AND NEGLECT

The child who has experienced abuse, neglect, sexualization, and chaos has a limited range of emotional responses. He frequently attempts to disconnect from his most uncomfortable feelings—specifically, sadness and fearfulness—because they make him feel vulnerable and weak. In trying to escape these feelings, he often heightens his arousal with anger.

Anger for him feels strong. It is familiar. Better still, it acts as an emotional anesthesia. Anger is a friend that can be called upon whenever the child is feeling weak, powerless, or sad. It is always available. It is always predictable. And people respond to it. They either disengage and flee or engage and fight. If the child has orchestrated the angry interaction, either response may be acceptable to him because he no longer feels vulnerable. On the contrary, he feels consumed with power. After all, if a four-year-old can get an adult to act like a four-year-old, that's quite an accomplishment.

In taking a child who has been neglected or abused into our homes, we must remember that behavior that may seem strange to us developed out of his attempts to:

- Gratify his own needs (food hoarding, head banging)
- Protect himself (lying, staying dirty to keep people away)

- Express his anger (destructiveness, cruelty to animals)
- Reenact early sexualization (inappropriate sexual activity)
- Emulate the behaviors he knows (swearing, violence, sexual activity, lying)
- Keep the fear away (keeping others at a distance)

None of the behaviors developed randomly or without a survival-based cause, so they will take much time and patience to undo. Is the effort worth it? Only if you want to save a child's life by providing him with a life worth living.

We have focused primarily on early neglect and abuse because that is the most damaging. A child who is abused after the age of three will be traumatized and may have problems as a result, but he will not be hurt in the same way as a younger child. Once developmental progress has been made, it cannot be undone. It is the abuse and neglect that occur during the early stages of personality formation that cause the deepest damage. Imagine the stability of a skyscraper built without a foundation, and you begin to see the fragility of a child denied the right to a healthy start.

With few exceptions, any child placed into adoption from the foster-care system is the victim of extreme abuse or neglect or both. While the child may not manifest attachment disorder as described in the previous chapter, he will almost certainly have unique problems, especially related to allowing others to get close. On top of the certain abuse and neglect in the birth home, the system adds the possibility of multiple moves through foster services and attempts to reunify the child with his birth family. The developmental interruptions that have occurred in the birth home are firmly cemented into place by the process of repeatedly moving him from home to home and back again.

Adoptive parents must understand that their child comes to them with a long unhappy history that all the love in the world cannot erase. But with that understanding, a good measure of patience, and a healthy dose of love, they can help their child face the truth about his past and move on to become part of a new loving family.

FOUR

THE TOLL OF IMPERMANENCE

A Child Welfare System in Crisis

Out of the problem of abuse, an entire social system has developed. It is made up of social workers, lawyers, judges, abusive and/or neglectful parents, foster parents, adoptive parents, and—finally—children. In an effort to put the child first, an elaborate bureaucracy has sprung up that often backfires, injuring its least powerful and most important participant, putting his welfare last on a list of less important considerations.

We strongly believe that it is in a child's best interest to remain in his family of birth—if it is a safe and nurturing home. Tragically, too many birth homes are dangerous and damaging. The child who is abused, neglected, and abandoned cannot be returned to a home that remains unsafe. In this case, that child should be swiftly moved into a permanent home where he can begin to heal. When this does not happen, the child becomes a victim of a revolving door that spins him through a series of temporary living arrangements. And everyone loses.

The lack of permanency, coupled with multiple moves and adjustments, is destructive to children, frustrating to foster parents and professionals, complicating for adoptive parents, and of no help to birth parents. Privately, most professionals agree that children benefit from moving to a permanent home as soon as it has become clear that the birth parent cannot, or will not, give appropriate care. Public policy, however, remains unchanged.

> Sue, a thirty-year-old mother, had eight of her ten children removed after they were repeatedly, and ritualistically, sexually tortured by several of her boyfriends. They were removed one or two at a time after lengthy legal deliberations about each one. They were returned as part of a reunification plan, only to be taken away again. No one has yet to document problems with the remaining two, so they continue to live in a home already determined unfit for eight others.

How do we justify this? How do we allow the parent's right to procreate to supersede the child's right to a safe, loving home? It seems reasonable to assume that the two remaining children will follow the same pattern — abuse, removal, return, abuse, removal, perhaps adoption, and ongoing conflict for the adoptive family. Into the mix, add the likelihood of multiple foster homes and the probability that no adoption will occur. What chance do these children have to grow up healthy?

Another case demonstrates how our system continues to put off the decision to terminate parental rights far longer than is healthy for the child.

> Jane, a single mother, suffered from both mental retardation and schizophrenia. During times when her schizophrenia was in remission or being treated with medication, she was able to provide limited, but basic, care for her child. However, she did not take her medication regularly or comply with her treatment plan. As a result, her mental problems flared and she repeatedly abused and neglected her child.
>
> The child was removed during these times and often stayed in foster care for a year or two before being reunited with his mother. From age two to thirteen, he was removed several times and placed in multiple foster homes before parental rights were finally terminated and he was placed for adoption.

We have to ask: whose interests were served here? Not the child's, not the foster parents', and not those of the mother, who was incapable of providing for her son.

The case of neglect is often considered more benign than blatant abuse, but it is not. Allowing an infant to lie alone for days without food or any human contact is devastating. Toddlers and children who wander their home and neighborhood seeking food and comfort are no less emotionally damaged than the abused child. A child who has been neglected or abandoned has missed even the most basic human contact. Like a wild animal, he learns to survive in ways that do not work within society. He may be terribly frightened by touch, have no manners or social skills, be unable to speak, and be emotionally shut down. And yet it may take years for him to be placed in a permanent home. By the time he is adopted, the damage is deeper still and compounded by the aftermath of constant moves.

We are not advocating capricious removal of children from their homes. Nor are we suggesting that a child be removed for any reason except abuse or neglect. We are suggesting that a permanency plan be developed — and implemented — as soon as it is determined that the birth parents cannot adequately care for the child.

Foster homes work to provide a safe temporary solution while a permanent placement is being arranged, but they were not intended for long-term stays. And, because of its temporary nature, foster care can create its own problem for the child. In healthy families, a child learns, "I mess up, I get a consequence, I remain in my family." In foster care, all too often, a child learns, "I mess up, I get in trouble, I leave." Leaving, rather than repairing, relationships is a difficult lesson to unlearn. It may easily turn into a permanent pattern that will follow the child long into adulthood and through multiple marriages. In addition, it makes a child leery of forming attachments and will certainly hinder his chances of forming a strong bond in an adoptive family.

KINSHIP ADOPTION

After appearing on a television talk show, we received hundreds of phone calls from people whose adopted children were demonstrating severe behavioral and emotional difficulties. Story after story echoed the familiar theme:

> Marcus is my daughter's son. She didn't take care of him and regularly left him with babysitters who abused him. Finally, social services

stepped in and took him away. I adopted him, but we're still having problems. My daughter keeps trying to interfere, and Marcus keeps acting up. He breaks things, lies, and steals all the time.

Today, we find more and more instances of people adopting or obtaining permanent custody of the children of family members. Grandparents, aunts, uncles, and cousins all seem to be getting involved in kinship adoption.

In most cases, children who move to the homes of other family members are among the hurt children. They have been neglected, abused, or born drug addicted — which is why they were removed from their birth homes in the first place.

Only a few of the calls after the talk show came from nonrelative parents, giving us some idea of the growing number of kinship adoptions. This scenario also reinforced the fact that when a child is neglected or abused prior to being adopted, there is a great likelihood that he will experience behavioral and/or emotional problems, regardless of his blood relationship to the new caregiver.

It is important to point out, however, that being adopted by relatives clearly minimizes a child's loss of family. He is still, in some way, connected to his birth family, and the identity issues that are so apparent with other adopted children are much less severe. Kinship adoption is definitely a viable option and should be examined whenever possible. Kinship adoptions should be eligible for the same supports—financial and service—as nonrelative adoptions.

It is important to look at the big picture when defining the word *kinship*. In many instances, the prospective parent is, in fact, genetically related to the child but is not known to the child. Aunt Sue, who lives 2,000 miles away and hasn't seen Aidan since he was three months old, will be a complete stranger to him. Therefore, the spirit of kinship adoption should take into consideration the degree of familiarity the relative shares with the child. Loving and caring foster parents with whom the child has lived for several years will likely have a much stronger emotional and psychological bond.

A SYSTEM IN CRISIS

The limitations of the foster-care system cannot be blamed on foster parents, who perform one of the most difficult, lowest paid, least understood, and most challenging jobs on earth. Many foster-care systems pay less for twenty-four-hour care of a child than people do to board a dog at a kennel.

Good foster parents are often treated with the same lack of respect the child received. They are abused, neglected, and abandoned by their agencies. Many times, after successfully parenting one or two difficult children, their homes are viewed as good resources. Soon, they become overloaded with special-needs children, resulting in chaos that can escalate to dysfunction and even abuse. Then the agencies — first adoring them, then ignoring them — swoop in to remove all the children.

While abusive birth parents can err and receive help, foster families are soundly condemned and ostracized for far lesser crimes. A birth parent may, in some areas, be assigned a case aide to help clean, a nutritionist to help plan meals, and a therapist to help resolve family issues and be given food stamps to help stretch dollars and parenting classes to help teach skills. The foster family seldom receives any of this, yet they are caring for children whose history almost surely guarantees a life of stress, punctuated by crises.

As with any bureaucracy, there seems to be plenty of money for some things and little for others. An agency may, for example, be able to find $100,000 a year to keep a child in a residential treatment program but not be able to find any money to cover the far lower cost of providing specialized therapy to help him adjust to a foster or adoptive home. Agencies may have the money to hire caseworkers for the children, but no money to hire adoption staff to help recruit permanent families. Great amounts of money are wasted on temporary or misguided solutions, while the best interests of the child fall through budgetary cracks. A case in point:

A grandmother wanted to provide a home for her grandson, Jerry, whom she had raised from birth to age five. The two were very close and had established a strong, attached relationship. The senior apartment complex where she lived did not allow children but had turned a benevolent blind eye to Jerry until he reached school age.

The school could not register the boy at her address, and the grandmother could not afford to move from her subsidized apartment. When the situation came to light, social workers made no attempt to find alternative housing. Instead, Jerry was returned to his drug-addicted, alcoholic mother's home, where he was abused sexually, emotionally, and physically. Starved and abandoned for weeks, he was removed again at age eight.

After five years in foster care, he was adopted by a family who simply endured his disinterest until he packed his bags at age eighteen and moved home to Grandma's.

For lack of housing, Jerry was abused, abandoned, removed, and adopted — costing society thousands of dollars for foster care, therapy, and adoption. It would have been far simpler, less costly, and, most important, significantly better for Jerry to remain with a grandmother he loved and trusted.

Penny-wise and child-foolish seems to be the fiscal theme of this country's child welfare system. The system has become so cumbersome and convoluted that it almost guarantees that once a child sets foot into it, he will find himself going in and out of home after home throughout his childhood years. And the chances are very good that he will suffer more of the kind of abuse the system was set up to guard against.

It all begins when child protection authorities are alerted to abuse or neglect and move in to rescue the children of a family. In some cases, the children are taken to an institutional receiving home established for emergency care. More often, the social worker reviews a list of "empty beds" and starts dialing numbers. The social worker then makes decisions based on the age and sex of the child, a convenient location, and who answers the phone and says yes. Because few foster-care homes have room for an entire sibling group, brothers and sisters generally separate at this first step, and many are never reunited.

This first foster placement is often the most difficult one for a child. Reeling from trauma and separation from his family, compounded by anxiety about the future and uncertainty about the present, he acts out. Finding himself in an enormous mental and emotional crisis that few adults could handle, his behavior may be understandably extreme and difficult. Because of the stress this creates, these first placements seldom last. And the moving begins.

Some systems design methods to prevent the stress of this first placement by establishing group receiving homes or designating special homes for emergency, temporary placements. While they do alleviate the original problem, they guarantee a new one by mandating moves for the child in turmoil.

Early in the process, a reunification attempt with the birth family is likely. When this fails, the child moves again, this time to a new foster home. It is highly unusual for a child to return to the first foster family for a second stay. Any sense of permanency the child develops is shattered as these moves continue.

Most often, the child is moved because of his unruly or destructive behavior. The same issues that plague adoptive parents assail the foster family as well, but it can be even more difficult for the child, since the foster family knows his placement is temporary and he can be asked to leave at any time. Often, there is no funding for therapy for foster families and children, and the family is hard-pressed to invest in a situation almost certain to be a transitory one. As a result, lacking other solutions, the foster family eventually requests that the child be removed. Children describe coming home from school to find garbage bags full of belongings and a social worker ready to move them again. It is ironic that a child's luggage is so often a garbage bag. Into the bag their few belongings are stuffed, usually quickly, for transportation to their next home.

Other moves are made by design. For example, certain foster families will parent only preschoolers or elementary-school children. As the child grows older, he is moved to a new home, treated more as a production-line item than a frightened child.

Each foster family situation that fails means another move for the child, and each move injures him further. Oftentimes, a move means more than losing the contact with a parent figure. It also means a setback in the child's education and the loss of friends, teachers, and siblings. Pictures of the child's birth family, awards, treasured toys, pets, gifts from family and friends, and other special possessions tend to be left behind with each successive move. Soon the child seems to have no history as he loses link after link of the chain.

REUNIFICATION PLANS — INJURY UPON INJURY

Within the cycle of foster-care moves, repeated attempts are often made to reunify the child with one or both birth parents. This compounds the issue of trust, since the child is very often returning to an environment that has changed little since he left.

Remember, he was removed because of abuse or gross neglect. Imagine that a woman who has been beaten repeatedly by her husband goes to a shelter for battered women. The shelter's first job is to provide security and safety. Let's assume that the shelter's second job is to develop a reunification plan to put the woman back into the home with her husband. After a few days or weeks in the shelter, the woman's husband comes forward and promises not to hurt her again, says he has stopped drinking or has completed a class on being a good husband—and besides, he is really sorry. At this point, attorneys, social workers, and judges all order the woman back home to live with a man she knows will abuse her again. We would not dream of being so casual with an adult woman, and we would not dream of forcing an adult to live in an environment proven to be violent, yet we do it to our children by the thousands every day.

In our society, it is the victim who is inconvenienced the most: Children who are hurt are removed, and women and children who are abused are sent to shelters. The bad guy stays at home and continues with his life—an arrangement that may last only awhile, or forever. He gets to sleep in his own bed. He gets to lounge in his own chair. He gets to do the things he wants. He doesn't move from place to place, from school to school. He doesn't lose his friends. It is no wonder the children who have been victimized come to feel that they are the ones at fault.

As a child is shuttled back and forth between foster care and his birth home, as he is repeatedly forced back into an environment of abuse, he begins to distrust all homes and all foster parents. He believes that since the foster parents were the adults in charge, they made a calculated decision to place him in jeopardy. He cannot comprehend the system machine that includes social workers, attorneys, judges, and case planners who do not always make his best interests their priority. After many reunification attempts, he may come to believe he will always return home—eventually. He stops making attempts to attach to a foster family because he knows he will always circle back around to the starting point—his birth family.

Because the legal system is so time-consuming and unpredictable, years may go by in a foster child's life before anyone can, with any degree of certainty, tell him whether or not he will return home. When legal delays are coupled with legal appeals, the child can remain in limbo for several years. He cannot make the emotional break from his birth parents since visits continue with promises of "I'll get you back." And since he's moved from foster home to foster home, he cannot rely on permanency there either. Reunification plans often drag on so long that the child is unable to work on any developmental tasks in a meaningful way. He spends his life on hold, waiting to see what and whom each day will bring.

Many of the factors that result in a child's removal from his birth home are difficult to remedy, such as addictions, family violence, and sexualization of children. Most professionals working with these problems agree on one thing: All three conditions are highly resistant to treatment. Yet reunification efforts often go on ad nauseum, usually ending only after repeated parental failures. Meanwhile, the days and years of a child's life tick by, unnoticed.

Although many people assume that once abuse is proved, the child is permanently removed from that home, his path may look more like this:

2/10/07	Patrick is removed to emergency foster home as a result of substantiated abuse.
2/12/07	Patrick is placed in Smith foster home.
2/16/07	Patrick is moved to Jones home.
3/26/07	Patrick has supervised visit with his mother.
4/10/07	Patrick has unsupervised visit with his mother.
4/11/07	Patrick reports abuse that occurred during previous day's visit.
4/12/07	Visits with mother are terminated.
6/10/07	Patrick is placed in Kosloff home for long-term foster care.
5/01/08	Reunification plan is initiated.
5/10/08	Patrick has supervised visit with both parents.
5/20/08	Patrick has supervised visit with both parents.

6/10/08	Patrick has unsupervised visit with both parents.
6/25/08	Patrick has unsupervised visit with both parents.
6/26/08	Visits are going well, and parents are cooperating.
8/15/08	Patrick is returned to his parents.
9/18/08	School reports that Patrick has bruises on his face.
9/18/08	Patrick is placed in Rogani foster home on an emergency basis.

Rather than burden you with additional pages of documentation, suffice it to say that this is truly an underrepresentation of the process. Children are traditionally moved so repeatedly that moving is more familiar than staying. Through all the moves, the only constant is the birth home. What this reinforces for the child is the familiarity, predictability, and constancy of the abusive environment. Ultimately, he gets the message that the one place he truly belongs is with his birth family. Home is familiar. Whatever the environment—and no matter how repulsive to others—home is normal and comfortable. Even though he knows something bad will happen and he will have to leave again, he is used to coming home.

Again, we are not advocating permanent removal of children from their birth homes without good reason. However, we must point out that even one year represents a large portion of a young person's childhood. And since children view time differently than adults do, a year may seem like an eternity.

Think about how long a year seemed to you when you were in elementary school . . . how summers never seemed to end . . . how the weeks before a birthday or holiday dragged on forever. Now think about how quickly a year passes as an adult . . . how there's never enough time to prepare for a special occasion . . . how birthdays loom menacingly near.

A family reunification plan—and the accompanying three-year stay in foster care—may seem like progress to the adults in the picture. To the six-year-old child, however, it means that half of his life is spent in uncertainty.

THE EFFECTS OF IMPERMANENCE ON THE HURT CHILD

Children who have moved frequently have their own subculture, complete with customs and language idiosyncrasies. For one thing, they think only in terms of past and present. After all, when you move from home to home so often, there is no tomorrow on which to depend. Why get excited about the Valentine's Day party at school when you probably won't be there anyway? Why participate? Why care? More important, why control your behavior, worry about consequences, or care what anyone thinks about you? For the hurt child, it is worse to care about people and lose them than not to care about anyone at all. And so his thinking becomes fixated on the present moment.

Because a child's crimes and history are not likely to follow him, he also develops a narrow scope on what "now" encompasses. For example, he may say, "I used to steal, but I stopped." Asked when he last stole, he will comfortably report, "I haven't stolen for two days." By using the past this way, he feels he is able to get himself out of trouble and avoid consequences for actions. He sets the stage for others to let him off the hook and give him a fresh start. After all, if anyone knows about fresh starts, he does.

While this one-day-at-a-time approach works well for children and adults who have developed clear cause-and-effect thinking, it does not work well for the child who has not. For him, it is destructive because it prevents him from grasping the idea of sequence. He cannot make a connection between his thoughts, feelings, actions, and choices and the outcome that results. The child who lives only for the moment will have trouble developing:

- Cause-and-effect thinking
- The capacity to delay gratification
- The ability to plan and set goals
- A conscience

The lack of ability to project into the future also makes it difficult for parents because the child never seems to learn from experience. "She does the same thing time after time" is a comment we often hear. "She never learns." "I've told her a hundred times that stealing is not allowed." "It seems like I have to remind him of certain things every single day." And it's true—the child does not learn. There has been no reason to learn something for tomorrow, and the rules will probably be different in a new family.

Other personality traits often develop in a child who has moved repeatedly:

He loses things. He has been left or lost and feels adrift. He has the attitude that things always disappear anyway when he moves, so there is no reason to hold on or be concerned. In fact, it's dangerous to become attached to something.

He breaks things. Again, he has little attachment to material things. But on a deeper level, he is also reacting to being broken physically, sexually, and/or emotionally.

He steals things. He feels that he has been stolen from home after home. His childhood — his very life — has been stolen by adults. If he obtains enough things, maybe the empty hole in his heart will be filled.

He lies. Because there is no development of conscience, he doesn't see lying as wrong. In fact, lying may well have served and protected him. The better he lied, the safer he could be. In addition, he has been lied to by almost every adult in his life, even the well-meaning ones who promised, "Your mommy is better; she won't hurt you again. We will keep you safe when you go back home." For this child, lying is the norm.

He wants to move. It's what he's used to, and he knows it will happen sooner or later. Sooner is better, he reasons.

He hoards and hides food. If he has gone hungry often, he lives with a primal fear that he will not get enough food. He stashes it away . . . just in case.

He gorges himself. Again, from past hunger, the child has learned to eat whatever he can, while he can.

He eliminates (urinates/defecates) in all the wrong places. Many children who were abused and neglected were never taught proper bathroom etiquette. Others came to believe, falsely, that smelling bad and doing disgusting things kept adults from having sex with them. Moreover, all the anger, pain, and fear inside must be eliminated, and this is one way to get rid of it. And boy, does this push adults' buttons!

He spends (wastes) money as soon as he gets it. Why not? If there is no future, and the money may disappear with the next move or be stolen by another child in the foster family, why hold on to it? Get what you can with it now.

He offends. He has been so offended so often that the concept of causing hurt feelings makes no sense. This is also a good way to get out some of that seething anger and to recreate a familiar situation where everyone yells and screams.

He controls. He has never been able to control anything in his life—the behavior of his birth parents, being "tooken" away, moving again and again—so he is driven to control anything he can. Even if he produces a negative result, at least he produced it. He has also been victimized repeatedly by others who control him, so he sees this as the winning position.

He distorts reality. Living with lies and being expected to believe them creates a situation in which there is no reality. "You're daddy's good little girl," she is told while being sexually abused. "You're mommy's good little helper," he is told while stealing from stores. "I love you and I'll never leave you again," she is told by her mother between drug-induced abandonments.

For a child to change his beliefs and behaviors, he must see and experience another way of life that features qualities such as permanence, honesty, respect, and plenty to eat. In addition, his adoptive parents must understand his culture and how he has lived. A child coming into an adoptive home is somewhat like a foreign exchange student moving to a new country. The major difference is that while the student is eager to assimilate a new culture, the adopted child does not care about it at all. Yet the parents are often insistent that they will not tolerate any culture other than their own. They may even find aspects of the child's past disgusting, alienating him from both his birth and adoptive families.

Like all foreign cultures, the language of children on the move has its own distinctive features. With no ability to think sequentially, the child may be empty, vague, disconnected, repetitive, nonsensical. He may appear stupid or out of focus, as if "nobody's home" . . . a telling phrase.

He may have a habit of leaving himself out of language connections, just as he has been left out of life connections. Frequently, sentences begin with his favorite friend: "it." It broke. It got lost. It didn't get turned in (homework). It just came out (urine or feces). It ran away (the puppy). It hurt itself (the baby). Having no connection also means having no responsibility when things mysteriously go wrong. These mysteries are often explained with a comment like, "I did it on accident!" What an interesting slip—most of us say "by accident" and "on purpose."

Some would argue that the language peculiarities of frequently moved children are a result of educational deficits from abusive homes and multiple moves. However, after years of hearing the same linguistic idiosyncrasies from so many different children and adolescents, we have come to believe that the language patterns are related. It appears the language not only communicates but also describes and reflects the child's inner workings. Because of this, it would be wise for parents, teachers, therapists, and social workers to pay close attention to what the child means, beyond what he says. It is an excellent way to learn about a child who is dedicated to letting no one learn about him.

For example, the child's use of disgusting, sexually explicit, profane language that most families would find intolerable tells volumes about his history. He may use it to point out how different and unappealing he is. The familiarity with sexual talk can offer glimpses into the possibility of sexual abuse. The extent and volume of profanity from a child shows us the depth of his anger.

Another common habit is to answer questions that were not asked. In responding to "Good morning, Jeff," one adolescent said, "My hair is a mess because I was sleeping." He was already anticipating a critical comment about his hair. In fact, his hair looked fine. His automatic anticipation of rejection led him to defend himself unnecessarily. When a child is used to being rejected, he will offer reasons in anticipation and explanation.

A child may also answer unasked questions to avoid answering other questions. This is a very common avoidance strategy that can be interrupted with direct confrontation or a bit of game playing. One method is simply to respond to the "wrong" answer with the question that would have accompanied it. For example:

ADULT: Good morning, Jeff.

CHILD: My hair is a mess because I was sleeping.

ADULT: What happened to your hair? (Or) Oh, I didn't mean to ask you about your hair—I was just saying good morning.

Another one:

ADULT: How did you do on your science project?

CHILD: I just fed the cat.

ADULT: What did you just do? (Or) Oh, I'm sorry, I didn't mean to ask you about feeding the cat.

If the child does not respond to these gentle strategies, a simple, direct question such as, "What did you hear me ask you?" may work. The child has defended himself with this mechanism for so many years that it is now a habit. He may need frequent, mild reminders to bring about a lasting change.

The culture of impermanence leaves a child disengaged from himself and everyone around him. But that's not a natural state for human beings. Most hurt children still have the desire to connect with others, though it is likely to manifest itself destructively.

Arguing is a favorite. After all, it demands complete engagement and complete attention. Parents and therapists must remember that the argument is the point—the goal for which the child has worked. How the argument turns out, who is right or wrong, what punishment will follow—none of that matters. Once the argument starts, the child has succeeded in activating the adult. In the child's mind, the formula works something like this:

Activation = Power

Power = Control

Control = Safety/Fear

While the first two equations are easy enough to see, the last one can mystify parents and professionals. The child expresses a desire for control through all of his actions. He seeks, demands, and forces it, but he also fears having it. Instinctively, the child knows he needs containment because he wants someone to stop him from hurting himself or others. The paradox is that if he succeeds in gaining control, he gets angry; if he is stopped from getting control, he gets angry. No wonder parents so often feel they can't win!

Kevin is protesting that he wants to attend a party and stay out later than his adoptive parents allow. Eager to avoid another prolonged battle, his parents begin to concede. However, they don't realize that Kevin's protests are for protest's sake rather than from a real desire to go to the party. What he really wants is a good hard battle that will allow him to tell his friends just how awful his new parents are. The truth is that he has no interest in going to the party and is hoping his parents will say no and offer him an excuse. In the process of trying to please their son, the parents lose both the battle and Kevin's confidence in their ability to set and maintain boundaries. Kevin is left feeling both powerful and vulnerable at the same time.

The key is for the parents to resist allowing the child to activate them. Although this is very tough to do, it is the family's only chance at succeeding. If the child discovers he cannot activate his parents, his behavior will eventually begin to shift. More important, when parents do not emotionally overreact, the child is assured that they will be able to handle anything and keep him safe.

A child on the move remains ready to leave in an instant. He may sleep in his clothes or dress in two or more layers—just in case. A common phrase parents hear is "Well, just kick me out." It is natural for parents to feel distress and rejection when their adoptive child seems ever ready to leave. What they fail to realize is that leaving is all the child knows. No one has ever wanted him for long, so he spends his life waiting for the other shoe to drop, signaling the time to move again.

While most children are moved only from birth homes and foster homes, there are many who have experienced failed adoptions, as well. The words "permanent" and "final" have no meaning to a child who reenters the system after an adoption has been legally dissolved. The family into which this child is ultimately placed faces increased challenges since the child now has even greater issues with trust and security.

It should be noted that prior failed adoptions are not necessarily a mark of doom. The reality that his behavior can lead to repeated rejection just may have sunk in enough to motivate the child to try harder next time.

Constant moving creates deep and lasting effects on the child, possibly no less traumatic than the abuse and neglect in his birth family. The more times a child is moved, the less likely it is that he will want to form meaningful relationships. Even if he is capable, he is fearful of getting close because he may be moved again. He adopts the adage, "Better never to love than to love and lose it."

STOPPING THE CYCLE

The children we see in our practice have typically been moved from seven to nine times in the course of a few years. Many have moved even more often. By the time they are adopted (if this ever happens), they are like bombed-out shells of children. Their behavior may be both difficult and dangerous. Needing—and deserving—more help than any other living thing, they often receive the least. At age eighteen, the system gladly wipes its hands and releases them on society as a whole. Soon they have children of their own who often enter the system. And the carousel begins again.

How do we stop the destructive cycle from repeating itself again and again? There *are* solutions. In talking to professionals within the system, a number of fairly simple ideas have come forth:

- Shift the focus from parental rights to the right of the child to grow up safe, happy, and healthy—in a loving home environment. Although we mouth that sentiment now, policy must be recast to support the ideal.
- Attempts at reunification should be made only when there are positive indications of success.
- Remember that foster care is a temporary solution. If the birth family can be helped, the child needs to go home. If not, he needs to be made available for adoption quickly. The determination should not take years, multiple failed reunification attempts, and countless moves that only further damage the child's psyche.
- Value must be given to the foster family. This includes paying people fairly for their skill and training. Typically, a foster parent with ten years' experience is paid the same as a brand-new foster parent. We must recognize the importance of the foster parents' services and offer them adequate compensation, training, and support. To prevent overcrowding and burnout, there must also be enough funding to

recruit the number of homes needed to serve the number of children entering the system.

- If a child returns to foster care multiple times, every possible attempt should be made to return him to the same foster home each time. Although this is not the ideal way to grow up, it at least gives the child some sense of history.

- We should recruit and support foster families who want to become adoptive parents if the child (or children) cannot be returned to the birth home.

- Foster families should be considered an important part of the child's life. When the child leaves foster care to move back with parents or on to an adoptive family, every attempt to maintain a positive tie should be made. The foster family often understands the child in ways no one else can and can serve as a source of respite care and support for new adoptive parents.

- Links with the child's extended birth family should be encouraged. Obviously, disruptive contact with abusive or neglectful relatives would not help the child move forward, but an aunt or grandparent who may not have been able to provide a home may offer a bond of love. Children moving into adoptive families must often look into the past to resolve issues in the present. Allowing connections to former foster families and birth family members provides the child with a history that can help him explore the mystery of how and why his life evolved the way it did.

Last, and very important, the system needs to speed up. While adults meet, plan, discuss, study, recommend, and so on, a child's life is ticking away. His growth and development won't wait until Mom or Dad completes his or her treatment program.

Childhood is short. We cannot afford to waste it.

PUTTING TOGETHER A FAMILY

Issues That Affect Placement

Once a child has been legally freed for adoption, it may take just a few weeks for him to find a permanent home—or it may take years. The time depends on the number of adoptive parents waiting and on issues such as race, age, gender, and sibling relationships. Agencies that deal with adoption vary on the criteria chosen to match children with prospective parents.

When there were many infants available, adoption matches were based on such tangibles as the child's hair and eye colors. Blond-haired, blue-eyed children went to blond-haired, blue-eyed parents. The children were typically infants, and there were enough children and families available to allow such frivolous bias. In those days, a red-haired infant may well have been difficult to place, unless there was a red-haired family waiting.

Placement jobs were viewed as the easy work. Most of the social workers placing children reached these comfortable positions after many years in the organization. In most cases, the workers were retired before the children they placed reached adolescence, so they saw few of the problems that may have developed as the children grew.

We live today with some remnants of the old system. The term *matching* came from the idea of using tangible markers to select parents. The other idea that remains within the system is the notion that adoptive placement is easy. Nothing could be further from the truth.

It is no secret that legalized abortion has greatly reduced the number of children in need of adoption, narrowing the availability of healthy infants to a trickle. As a result, parents are turning to other options, including children removed from their homes because of neglect and abuse, and international adoptions. While there are fewer infants to adopt, there are a growing number of children available at older ages and from sad circumstances. We applaud the loving spirit of parents willing to bring a hurt child into their homes, and we see these families as a very positive force in today's society.

But how are matches made now that both the child population and the criteria have changed? The answer varies from agency to agency. Knowing some of the basic guidelines can help parents as they wade through the piles of paperwork that are part of the selection process.

ISSUES THAT AFFECT PLACEMENT

Agencies that utilize parent-recruitment efforts often air television spots, run newspaper ads and articles, and send out flyers. Potential adoptive parents, seeing these materials, contact the agency and start the ball rolling toward adopting a particular child. Sometimes there are several families interested in the same child; other times there is only one. Agencies seldom reveal how many other parents are interested in adopting a particular child. Even if there is only one interested family, the agencies like to maintain the aura of a family being "chosen" to provide a home for a child.

When there are several families waiting, the standards for selection tend to be tougher. Such issues as employment history, income, education, number of children already in the family, parenting styles, and personal habits can come under close scrutiny.

Any specific needs of the child are also examined carefully. If he has a history of creating problems with other children, for example, a home where he can be the only child may be selected. Very often, the reasons a family is not chosen have little to do with the family but have a great deal to do with the child's special needs.

Recruitment efforts by adoption agencies always put a child's best foot forward. Public service announcements and flyers tend to be necessarily vague and positive to protect the child's self-esteem and to preserve confidentiality. As a result, it's wise to ask plenty of questions about statements made in the promotions. A phrase "should be the youngest child" could mean he needs nurturing and the security of the baby role in the family, but it could also mean that he has a history of sexually molesting younger children. Find out before proceeding very far with the adoption process.

Race

Many children available for adoption in this country are from racial minorities, and many of those adopted internationally are of a different race than their adoptive parents.

> Adopted from China by Sally, a single Caucasian mom, Susie was obviously not a birth child. One day, a Chinese woman approached mother and child in the grocery store and enthusiastically invited them to her home for a Chinese New Year celebration.
>
> Sally said, "It was odd — a stranger asking us to a party — but we went. While we were there, I felt what my daughter must feel every day: the isolation of being surrounded by people of a different race."
>
> Over time, Sally and her daughter have become close friends with the Chinese family, who have shared much information about their culture for Susie's benefit.

Despite noble claims of color blindness, most societies are not. Parents who choose to adopt across racial lines must be aware of the child's comfort level regarding the community, school, and family in general. They would be wise to incorporate cross-cultural art, books, and toys into their child's life.

Policies and practices regarding transracial adoption are affected by federal legislation, societal attitudes, and the availability of children. But however policies may officially change, individuals will still retain their own values and beliefs regarding interracial adoptions. So even when legal roadblocks are broken down, personal prejudices may still prevail.

Families who wish to adopt transracially will find many support groups, books, and research to help them (see "Resources" and "Related Readings" at the end of this book), but it is vital for them to understand that race is an issue that exacerbates other issues. For example, the greater the difference in appearance between parents and child, the more apparent the adoption. As a result, parents are often confronted by curious strangers who ask a host of personal questions. While this is awkward and painful for the parents, the effect on the child is even greater. He already feels different and doesn't need to have it pointed out on a regular basis.

In a society where blatant racism exists, same-race placements of children would appear to be the most convenient, desirable, and culturally congruent. However, the Interethnic Placement Act (IEPA 1996) changed the Multiethnic Placement Act (MEPA 1994) rule. While MEPA indicated that race could be one factor in making placement decisions, IEPA states that race, color, and national origin cannot be used as factors in placement except in very specific cases.

This federal legislation has increased the number of Caucasian children adopted by African American families, as well as African American children adopted by Caucasian families. In spite of these changes, interracial adoptions within the United States are still rare. It is estimated that 86 percent of noninternational adoptions are same race.[1]

Dan, a nineteen-year-old Korean, was constantly reminded of being an adoptee throughout his childhood. In checkout lines and restaurants, people frequently asked him and his parents, "Are you together?" Such questions drew attention both to the fact that he looked different from his family and that he was adopted.

We cannot offer an opinion on transracial placements by examining race alone. Other questions should be asked, and it is up to the adoptive parents to broach the subject. It is unlikely that agencies will bring up the issue because their priority will be to follow the IEPA law.

Some factors to consider include:

- Is the child already attached to a family of a different race?
- Is race more critical than the quality of the child's attachment to the family with whom he has bonded?
- Will the adoptive family help the child with racial issues? If necessary, are they willing to move to a more integrated neighborhood?

Bias

Potential adopters who are single, obese, physically challenged, interracially married, poor, or older; who are smokers, recovering alcoholics, and of certain religious beliefs may find doors closed to them without explanation. Foster parents, too, are sometimes told they cannot adopt a child because they are "not good enough to adopt." More agencies are coming to view foster families as the first in line for a child already settled into and attached to the family, but this is a recent and incomplete change.

Many biases against potential adopters are changing as society changes. Why, for example, should a single parent be prevented from adopting, when many available children come from single-parent families? Furthermore, an estimated 50 to 60 percent of all children in the United States live with single parents. The tendency remains to give single parents only the most difficult children, as agencies hold on to the bias that children with fewer behavior problems "deserve better."

Yet a single parent can often be the best placement for a child in need of undiluted attention. Couple and sibling issues are eliminated for the child, allowing him the complete focus of a parent for the first time in his life. Many success stories come from the homes of single adoptive parents.

Parents attempting to adopt sometimes run up against policies that serve more as a brick wall than a guideline. In making their way through the system, a family should be aware that the roadblocks may have nothing to do with their suitability as people and more to do with absurdities of the system.

THE "UNADOPTABLE" CHILDREN

Just as some potential parents face discrimination, some children face deep prejudice that undermines their chances for placement. Many agencies have a list of children they used to call "unadoptable" because they are too old, too damaged, or otherwise undesirable. Instead of being given a chance in a family or placed in homes of single parents, older parents, physically challenged parents, or poor parents, these children often grow up in institutions with no permanency plan.

Adolescents

While age may be a consideration, there is no magic point at which a child becomes "too old for adoption." Adolescent adoptions can be some of the most rewarding to those who rise to the challenge. Childhood is a relatively short time in the span of a person's connection to family. Most people spend many more years involved with their family as adults than they did as children. Adolescent adoptions offer children the opportunity to form positive bonds that will last for the rest of their lives.

An adolescent child in the adoption system may have a great deal of savvy when it comes to being adopted. Chances are good that he has been in and out of his birth home, foster homes, or orphanages, and may even have an earlier failed adoption before being placed. He is likely to have some very definite ideas about being adopted and is certain to make those known. An adolescent who wants to be adopted often tries extra hard to make a placement work because he knows it may be his last chance to have a family.

Ironically, an adolescent who has been in and out of the system for a long time may have developmental delays that will help the adoption process. He may want desperately to identify and connect with parents and may have far greater needs for affection than most kids his age. He may need to be cuddled, held, and even babied to make up for some of what he missed. Parents may feel awkward with this need but should understand that he is struggling to compact years of growth into the short time left before adulthood. A simple acknowledgment like, "Yeah, this is a little unusual at your age, but since it hasn't happened before, it's good to do it now," generally alleviates the discomfort.

Adolescents also come armed with the knowledge that "forever" is only a few short years. The option of soon moving out on his own may be comforting to a teenager struggling to adjust. Knowing he can leave in a few years may help the adolescent relax into becoming part of the family, a place he may actually choose to remain long after the magical eighteen has come and gone. Many children adopted during adolescence, in fact, remain at home far longer than their peers to make up for lost time.

Parenting any adolescent has its challenges, but a hurt child requires even greater tolerance. He comes into the family with already established tastes and styles and must be accepted for who he is. While his choices of clothing, music, friends, and jargon may make the adoptive parents uncomfortable, they would do best to practice tolerance. At this age, rebellion is the norm, so parents must carefully choose battles centered on issues that are truly important. Parenting in a spirit of relaxed fun with a desire to join with the child's efforts to learn and grow is far more successful than the authoritarian stance that encourages a teenager's active resistance.

Adopting an adolescent is sometimes like adopting a child, sometimes like adopting an adult. Walking the line between the two can present interesting challenges for parents. The rewards of being available to give a child that last chance for family, however, can more than compensate for the difficulties.

Kids with Medical Problems

The increasing number of children who are HIV-positive or have AIDS also have difficulty finding adoptive homes. Some of them are born with the disease, others contract it from childhood sexual abuse and still others contract it as teenagers. All are in need of a loving home, but few are given that opportunity. Many are abandoned by birth parents and end up in foster care. But there are parents trained in universal precautions who are willing to reach out to these children.

"The way I see it," explained one mom of an AIDS-infected child, "is that I didn't cause it, but he has it and he needs to live somewhere. It might as well be here with us. The joy and love he has brought us will have to be enough to help us heal when he is gone. Besides, I am forever the optimist. Maybe they'll find a cure soon enough for him."

Other children with fragile medical conditions or physical challenges sometimes find their way to the unadoptable list as well. But many parents exist who are willing to take on the challenges with an eye toward improving the quality of a child's life.

There are no magic formulas. And there are few ways to predict who will do the best job as adoptive parents or which children will bring the greatest joy.

At a recent adoption party, new parents proudly presented their three-year-old son. Recently placed, he is confined to a wheelchair because of severe cerebral palsy. Another single mother proudly introduced her fifteen-year-old, obviously pregnant daughter.

Both families felt immensely blessed with their new children and were in awe of each other. "We never could have adopted a teenager," the couple said. "She sure is special." "Wow," said the single mom, "I really admire people who can cope with a child in a wheelchair."

The issue of who will make the best parent for a child needs to be examined in light of reality. It may be that a child could benefit most from a "perfect" family situation. But if such a family is not available, we believe the child would fare better in what agencies might consider a less-than-ideal family than in a continuing series of foster homes or institutions. Besides, what may seem less than perfect to us may be heaven to the child. We spend hundreds of hours in parenting classes teaching people that there are no such things as perfect parents. Perhaps we need to deliver that lesson to social workers, judges, placement workers, children, and therapists. There are no perfect families, but there are families waiting to be joined.

EXAMINING YOUR MOTIVES TO ADOPT

In the early stages of deciding to adopt, parents must closely examine their own motives to determine what expectations they hope to fulfill. If their decision to adopt stems from personal loss — infertility or loss of a birth child — they must assess where they are in their own grief cycle to maximize their ability to help their new child. After all, adoption is about loss, and facing that loss is one of the first steps in the child's healing process.

It is, therefore, critical for parents to take stock of how bereavement is handled in the family so the child's loss can be addressed appropriately. Those who rely on silence or denial to get through the grieving process will have a difficult time helping a child who may need to talk about losing his birth family. Recognizing the child's emotional needs and adapting to meet them better will ultimately help all family members.

When infertility is the reason for adoption, it is vital to understand the dynamics of the problem. Adoption does not cure infertility. While it provides an end to a couple's childlessness, it does not alter the fact that they are unable to have birth children. Dealing honestly and openly with their feelings about infertility is necessary if they are to rise effectively to the challenges of adopting a child with special needs. Just as adoption is a lifetime event—viewed differently at different stages in an individual's life—so, too, is infertility. A couple's response to the problem will vary throughout their life cycle, affecting them differently at thirty than at forty-five.

Loss issues may also affect single people who make the decision to adopt. While for some it is a lifestyle choice, for others it is the loss of a dream—the dream of marrying, raising a birth family, and living happily ever after. Although they are not faced with medical infertility, many prospective single parents feel the same emotional loss as infertile couples because they are not going to reproduce.

Some families make the decision to adopt as a reaction to the empty-nest syndrome. As their children grow and move on and their roles as parents change, they realize that they miss having little ones around. They decide to do it all over again—to relive the good times of parenting. This may provide a resource for children who have some good times to give. For these experienced parents, the scars they have earned and the rocky roads they have traveled equip them well for some of the tasks they will face.

But these parents need to realize that it takes more than experience to ensure success. Even parenting their birth children was not all good times. And a special-needs child poses challenges different from those of the children they raised in the past. Since the child comes to them with his own painful issues, he will test the competency of their parenting in a completely different manner than their birth children did.

We might add insult to injury by pointing out that the parents are now older and are faced with new issues of their own. If they're used to feeling valued and accomplished for their parenting skills, dealing with a hurt child can gnaw at their self-esteem. They are suddenly faced with the reality that their tried-and-true techniques simply aren't working, and their reactions can range from disappointment to devastation. To compound the problem, their grown birth children may resent the adopted child, especially if he hurts a beloved grandchild. Once again, the more realistic parents' expectations are, the more equipped they are to handle the task of parenting a hurt child.

Adoptive families come in all shapes, sizes, religions, colors, sexes, and circumstances. They are single parents, remarried couples, traditional couples, and interracial couples. They are young, old, and in the middle. Some are childless, some have step, adopted, or birth children. They are white-collar, blue-collar, and pink-collar. They are farmer and CEO, workaholic and unemployed. They are wealthy, middle-class, and poor. They face challenges that may unite them or separate them from other adoptive families. But as they move through the adoption process, they all share some beliefs, characteristics, and hopes—some common issues and dreams. They view parenting a child as an important lifetime goal and as a fulfilling, fun, and meaningful experience.

All families, regardless of their composition, share hopes and expectations for the child they will adopt. They are an optimistic group—resistant to the realities addressed in training sessions, horror stories in the press, and their own uncertainties—bent on adopting a waiting child. They believe that any child will thrive in a sound family environment, nurtured by love, commitment, and guidance.

They frequently envision the adopted child as a "warm fuzzy"—someone to cuddle, to snuggle, to be close to. They want a child with whom they can build a snowman, go on an Easter egg hunt, explore the zoo, romp through fallen leaves, and tromp through mud puddles. While they know the child has experienced loss, they expect to be able to fill him with enough love to overcome that loss.

They anticipate a reciprocity of caring, sharing, and growing that will eventually lead to the closeness of a family. Sometimes, they see themselves as the child's rescuer. They believe that any child—particularly an abused and neglected one—would be grateful to have wholesome meals, a warm bed, a clean home, and the security of a loving, nurturing, and respectful family. They hope that the rescued child will show his appreciation by rejecting his own family and embracing the new one. After all, if someone rescued us from a horrifying situation, we would be extremely grateful. Or so we think.

It is important to recognize that the child's loyalty, love, and attachment are usually connected to his birth family. He may feel as if he's been snatched from them and live in hope of being returned. Seldom does he feel gratitude for being rescued; instead, he feels angry for being taken away from his home. Adoptive parents can weave a fantasy about how thankful a child will be for "all we can give him," but it is a fantasy that is seldom realized. A clean room filled with toys and video games, a vacation at the lake, and a birthday party in the park cannot heal the wounds inflicted in a child's early years.

If adoptive parents could view the situation from a child's perspective, the adjustment to a new family would be easier for all participants. To better understand what we mean, try this exercise:

Imagine that you're sitting in your living room on a warm summer evening. Your spouse is dozing peacefully on the sofa, having consumed one too many beers at dinner. Your two children, who have spent all day bickering, are quietly playing with their favorite toys. You're curled up with a good book, and your feeling is one of contentment. Perhaps this isn't the perfect family, but they're yours, and you love them.

Suddenly there's a knock at the door. You rise to open it. Standing there is a tall man you've never seen before. He gently takes you by the arm and ushers you into his car. Before you can comprehend what has happened, he's driving you away from your home.

Soon you stop in front of a beautiful house with a broad, manicured lawn. The man leads you inside, where he introduces you to the people there. They are warm and pleasant, and they smile sweetly at you. The tall man tells you that this is your new family.

Your new spouse doesn't have a problem with alcohol. Your new children never argue and are well behaved. They show you to your new room, point out all your new belongings, and tell you to make yourself at home. All the while they're smiling.

You look over your shoulder at the tall man, who's smiling too. He assures you that this new family will love you forever. And all they expect in return is for you to love them back.

You slowly look at your new surroundings. Your emotions are swirling out of control. You feel as if you are moving through a dream. This new family may be wonderful — they may be superior to your old family in every way — but they're not your family. You don't even know them so how can you be expected to love them?[2]

Once adoptive parents realize that this is usually how the adopted child feels, they are better equipped to help him adjust to his new situation. They can deal first with his issues of confusion and fear and focus less on assuming that he should demonstrate love and appreciation from the start.

While it is natural to wish for the best and envision wonderful times with an adopted child, it is important to establish realistic expectations to help ensure the success of the adoption. It is noteworthy that the adoptions of children with physical disabilities often work well for all parties. Parents who adopt a child who is missing a leg, for example, don't expect love, stability, and permanency to recreate a limb. They simply expect to help the child secure the best prosthesis and cope well. Since their hopes and expectations can be met, they can be satisfied.

However, a vast majority of children with special needs have emotional, not physical, problems that are manifested through behavior. It is much harder for parents to accept a child's stealing money or hoarding food than it is for them to accept the inability to walk.

One day, perhaps years from that initial arrival, the child may indeed become the one first envisioned in those dreams. Far more often, parents make the inner changes and adjustments needed to create new, more realistic dreams.

DREAMS AND REALITIES

Phases of the Adoption Process

Waiting to adopt a child can be a frustrating time for prospective parents. Control of their lives has been turned over to a stranger—more than a stranger, an entire agency! They may have their hearts set on a specific child, only to be told he will be placed elsewhere. Such a development poses a loss to the waiting family even if they have never met the child.

It is difficult for them to wait for contact from an agency and never hear a word. It is difficult for them to know that thousands of children need homes, while their spare bedroom with the dinosaur wallpaper remains empty. It is difficult for them to have their lives, finances, and homes scrutinized by professionals whose job it is to decide if they are suitable to parent. In the bureaucratic Bermuda Triangle of law, social worker, and paperwork, they are often lost.

In addition, the waiting game seems to make little sense. Since each adoption is unique—involving a diversity of players that includes adoption and foster-care workers, therapists, the child, his siblings, foster parents, perhaps birth parents, and occasionally more than one county, state, or country—it is impossible for parents to prepare for every eventuality. So, while a child waits, one player checks to see if the parents have toilets that flush. While brother is being separated from sister, another player reviews the monthly budget. While a child suffers alone from AIDS, still another player investigates the marriage of the couple who want to adopt him. Children wait, families wait, and no progress seems to be made.

On the other side of the equation is the placement worker, who is likely to be overworked and harried with demands. In smaller agencies, adoption is just one part of a mixed caseload that also includes training and evaluating parents, preparing children, placement, post-placement, and pre- and post-legalization work. The worker may be expected to have basic knowledge of sexual abuse, neglect, attachment issues, legal issues, and adoption issues, as well as normal childhood development. He is also expected to know about any special conditions of the children on his list, such as spina bifida, blindness, and Tourette's Syndrome. In addition, he may be expected to organize parent support groups and to attend to the financial and legal issues that arise from each case. And he must respond to every crisis, working to prevent any disruptions of adoptions that are not going smoothly.

Many adoption workers become so overwhelmed that they "manage by crisis," giving each squeaky wheel a quick dab of grease as they fly through. Stack all of this against the fact that many of these agencies are losing personnel, and it becomes a wonder that any children are adopted. Parents who hear nothing for weeks or months may have to become the next squeaky wheel in line for attention.

PHASE ONE: THE EMOTIONAL ROLLER COASTER

Most parents adopt out of the purest motives. They want to love a child who has been abandoned. They want to help a child who needs them. They want to parent a child who has no family. Their greatest wish is to fulfill their own needs to parent and to save a child from a life alone. They carry with them an optimism that angers many professionals. "Listen to the problems," these professionals say. "Acknowledge the issues. Face the challenges."

But as with any new experience, people retain hope. Before cancer surgery, the elderly man holds on to the belief that he will survive. Before her first baby is born, the mother believes he will be fine and robust. Before the young bride walks down the aisle, she believes that her marriage will be fulfilling. Before a couple signs papers to buy their dream house, they believe the water heater will never break. Before the family takes off on vacation, they believe they'll experience seven days of sunshine.

But some people die in surgery. Some babies are stillborn. Some marriages fail. Some water heaters leak. And sometimes it rains in Puerto Rico.

It is a natural human response to filter the success stories from the tragedies and to hang on to the odds for success. Thank God. Otherwise, no one would ever have surgery or a baby, no one would ever get married or buy a home, and no one would ever go on vacation. No one would ever adopt a child, and then what would society do with the thousands of children who wait for new families?

But waiting families frequently minimize or tune out relevant information that is passed on to them by the agencies. Because they are so eager to be selected as ideal parents, they often indicate that they can handle anything. Since they haven't experienced some of the behaviors that abused and neglected children can dish out, it's easy for them to feel "it's no big deal."

To avoid getting in over their heads, to keep themselves from plunging into disillusionment when faced with the reality of a special-needs child, waiting parents could best educate themselves by becoming respite providers and/or foster parents. To further this education, they should read books, view videos, participate in parent support groups, and attend presentations that address adoption issues. Most agencies now sponsor informative sessions and discussions for prospective adoptive parents. These events should be viewed as an opportunity to learn, not as an evening to be endured.

Families who adopt are planning to love, nurture, parent, and help their child. They are fiercely optimistic and ready to tackle the multiarmed monsters that might plague the most troubled youngster. They want to enjoy the good times and play down the bad times. They want picnics not panics, boat rides not beatings, communicating not counseling.

They must be strong, maintain a sense of humor, and, most of all, acknowledge that their hopes and expectations may be fantasies that will need to be adjusted to realities when the time comes. They must also recognize that these same hopes and expectations serve to sustain them during their anticipation and waiting.

As the wait continues, prospective parents usually experience a cycle that consists of hope, excitement, and expectation, followed by fear, uncertainty, and insecurity. Their fantasies range from adopting the perfect child to adopting the child from hell. One minute they are thinking, "Everything will be fine; we can do this. It will be fun." The next minute, they are wondering, "Can we handle this? Should we do this? Will it turn out okay?"

Then the call comes. There's a real child out there—one for them. The adoption moves forward, and parents and child begin their journey toward family.

PHASE TWO: GATHERING INFORMATION

Between that initial phone call and legalization is an important process for both parents and the child. Simply because the agency says there is a match, it does not mean that the parties involved will agree. Instead of running off in excitement to bring the long wait to an end, parents must ensure that this is the right child for them.

It is remarkable that normally sane people, who would never dream of making a major life decision without plenty of fact-finding and discussion, can get so caught up in the emotion of the moment. In their excitement, they trivialize or negate the need to learn about their prospective child. To do so is a little like agreeing to a marriage without the bride and groom ever having met. Information gathering is the most important step prospective parents must make. Chances are they will still agree to adopt the child, but the information they glean now can prove critically important as they parent the child.

The term "full disclosure" is often heard among families, social workers, therapists, judges, and talk-show hosts. Agency policies vary on the subject—from complete, open sharing of information and court records to a flat refusal to disclose anything. In the interests of making successful adoptions, we urge agencies to be forthright in disclosing anything they know that will help parents make the right decision.

Mr. and Mrs. Collins had adopted from a private special-needs agency the first time. They felt satisfied with the open honesty of the agency and had gone on to successfully parent their daughter. The experience had been so satisfying, in fact, that they decided to adopt two sisters through another agency.

"We asked the adoption worker how many placements the girls had been through, why they were moved, and when they came into care. She told us that the information was confidential and that we could either choose to adopt the girls with no information or leave. We left."

Though they always wondered if the girls were okay, they knew better than to agree to a blind adoption. After all, something had gone very wrong in the ten- and twelve-year-old girls' lives. As parents, they felt entitled to any information that could help them do a better job.

When full disclosure is not the policy, parents often later blame the agency for not telling the truth when their adopted child's problems become evident. Adoption workers are often equally frustrated at parents for failing to listen to the truth when offered. Lawyers and administrators are caught in the middle between what is known, what is suspected, and who has a right to the information.

For example, if the birth parents' psychological reports are stamped "May Not Be Released—Confidential," is it all right to give a copy to the adoptive parents? If a man with alcoholism or another genetically predisposed condition is named as the birth father but denies paternity, should that information be shared? These are the kinds of questions that various parties face daily.

Some information cannot be shared because it is simply not available. A child who was sexually abused may not reveal this information until he has been in an adoptive home for years. A child may be suspected of starting a fire in the foster home that went unreported. A child's sibling may have been given to a relative and never reported to the agency, remaining alive only in the child's memory.

There is often little information available to families who are participating in an intercountry adoption. Many of the children available from orphanages have been abandoned and found in the countryside or on the streets. Birthdates and names are made up by orphanage personnel. It would be helpful for the prospective parents to have a lot of knowledge about the country from which they are adopting.

Our recommendation is that any relevant facts, even suspected facts, should be shared with prospective parents. If, for example, no evidence has ever been uncovered to support a suspicion of sexual abuse, yet the child's behavior indicates it as a real possibility, the parents have a right to hear those suspicions. Agencies have an ethical responsibility to be forthright for the good of the child. Withholding information they think may jeopardize the child's chance for adoption does everyone a disservice. It is better for the parents to make an informed decision against adopting a child before meeting the child than to proceed with the adoption and feel betrayed and regretful. And it is essential that the adoption social worker translate professional jargon so the family can comprehend and digest the information.

Parents can get the facts they need from willing agencies in several forms. They can:

- Pay close attention to everything said about the child.
- Ask questions of the adoption worker.
- Read the child's file.
- Talk to the child's therapist.
- Talk to the child's current and former foster parents.
- Talk to any social workers who have been involved in the case.
- Talk to any available birth family relatives.

At the very least, adoptive parents should be able to answer these questions:

- Why was the child originally removed from the birth home?
- When did initial removal occur, and how old was the child?
- How many reunification attempts have there been, and why did they fail?
- How many placements has the child been through, and why did they end?
- How does the child do in school?
- How well does the child get along with others?
- Does the child have any dangerous behaviors—such as a history of fire setting, animal abuse, sexual abuse of other children, or injuring others?

- Does the child have any diagnosed conditions—such as dyslexia, Attention Deficit Disorder, or Reactive Attachment Disorder? Is there reason to suspect that any such conditions exist that have not been diagnosed?
- Do the child's birth parents have addictions to drugs or alcohol?
- Is it likely that the child's mother used drugs or alcohol while pregnant?
- Has the child been tested for communicable or hereditary diseases?
- Does the child have any other health issues that should be of concern?
- Are there any genetic issues that may affect the child later on in life?
- Does the child have brothers or sisters? How many? How old? Where are they? Why aren't they being placed together? Will they visit?
- Are there any birth relatives, foster parents, or others who have had a significant positive impact on the child? Are they willing to remain in touch with the child after adoption?
- What does the child like to do?
- Does the child have any particular hobbies?
- Does the child have any favorite toys, foods, television shows?
- Does the child attend religious services, and if so, what kind?
- Does the child participate in any sports or scouting activities?
- Are there any photos available of the child in his birth or foster homes that he can bring to his new home?
- Does the child have any treasured possessions that should come with him?
- Does the child have a pet that he would like to bring along?
- How do his current caretakers discipline him? Is this method effective?
- Is there anything else about the child we should know to ease his adjustment to his new home?
- Does the child take medication? For what condition(s)?

As we discussed in chapters 2 and 3, many behavioral problems stem from early attachment issues. When possible, it is important to find out everything available about the child's first three years of life. Questions that might be asked include:

- Is there any reason to suspect the child was abused, neglected, or abandoned?
- Was there anyone who provided consistent loving care?
- Were his needs met satisfactorily and regularly?
- Was he seriously ill or in pain?

In addition, parents need to ascertain exactly what services and supports will be available to them once the adoption is complete. It may be that the state will continue to pay medical bills, that therapy will be provided for a certain time period, or that the family will receive a small amount each month to help raise the child. Or it could mean that all services and supports will end when legalization is complete. Subsidies, assistance, Social Security benefits, and medical coverage vary from agency to agency and from child to child. Parents should not be embarrassed to ask about exactly what help they can expect.

Some benefits stay with a child until he is eighteen, some depend on family income, and some end at legalization. If the parents are adopting a child with a known history of severe abuse, for example, they need to find out what kinds of therapy will be available to the child or if they will need to include that bill in their monthly budget.

The availability of money can also be tied to politics since some administrations support services more than others. Previously promised services can be lost as new politicians are elected, new budgets are voted on, and counties or states suffer economic reversals.

Some agencies understand the children's special needs and the financial cost to parents and consider it the agency's responsibility to help. Other agencies feel they should not provide money to help a family adopt. "After all," said a board member from one such agency, "I adopted an infant in 1970, and no one helped me." He simply did not understand that the needs of a newborn infant and the needs of an abused, neglected, repeatedly moved older child might be different. The issues of finance and support may seem mundane, but they should be firmly established before the adoption agreement is signed.

While it may not be possible to get all the answers to each of the questions listed earlier, enough information should emerge to give a reasonably accurate picture of the child. Then it is up to the parents to determine whether they feel comfortable with what they have learned. It is important that couples honestly discuss the information and all possible ramifications since the child is sure to affect their marriage in both positive and negative ways. Being upfront about fears and concerns in the beginning lays the groundwork for honest communication when problems arise.

It would also be wise to talk over the information with other professionals, such as child psychiatrists, medical doctors, and geneticists. Finding out what the information may mean over the child's lifetime can help parents make a completely informed decision. They must realize, however, that all the information and all the experts in the world still cannot predict how the child will grow or if he will fit into the family. No one has a crystal ball. Even if given the same parents, background, and upbringing, each human being grows to become a distinct, unique individual.

PHASE THREE: GETTING TO KNOW EACH OTHER

Once the information is gathered, examined, and evaluated, the prospective parents must make an honest decision about whether or not to proceed with adopting the child. Different families can tolerate different behaviors. A child with high energy may drive a laid-back family crazy, while the same child may fit perfectly into a family focused on sports and other outdoor activities. If one family decides not to adopt a child, he may find another that will be a better match.

Although many people feel guilty when deciding against adopting a particular child, they are almost always pursuing the right course. Hurt children are difficult to parent when all parties are 100 percent behind the adoption. As with marriage or any other life-changing decision, parents must enter the adoption fully willing and prepared to handle whatever comes along. It is far better for the child not to enter the family at all than to experience the failure of an adoption later.

Parents must make careful decisions about how much of the child's information to share with others. Grandparents, teachers, friends, and casual acquaintances all need varying degrees of knowledge, depending on how involved they will be in the child's life.

The best guide is to share only what is absolutely necessary while protect-ing the child's dignity and privacy. When different needs arise later on, more information can be disclosed on an as-needed basis.

After the prospective parents decide in favor of pursuing adoption, pic-torial and written introductions are often made through photos of the new family, home, school, neighborhood, and activities, aimed at lessening the child's anxieties. This process then moves forward to actual visits.

Parents-to-be have often become so entrenched in information about the child that they have made a superficial connection before ever having him in their home. Visiting solidifies those feelings by adding the real, living, breath-ing human being to the piles of paperwork. Their every hope is that the child will fit in and soon become part of the family. While most parents view visit-ing as a time to begin bringing a child into the family, it is meant to be a way for the parents to decide if the child should move into the family.

If things do not go well at this stage, it is not too late for both parents and child to think things over. Parents should pay close attention to their own feelings when they meet the child for the first time. Of course, it is an awkward time for everyone, but honestly assessing your emotional reaction to a child is an important piece of the puzzle. Sometimes visiting activates feelings and realities that may cause adoptive parents, agencies, or children to want to change their decision. This should always be respected. Although visiting is a step on the road to adoption, it is only a single step.

Still, visiting is the fun part—the waiting is over, the information is in, the decision is fairly certain, and the honeymoon is just beginning. There are exceptions, but most often, this is one of the most enjoyable steps of the pro-cess. Most families plan relaxed activities that include introductions to impor-tant people, such as the extended family, friends, and church members.

Families are often spurred on by excitement. They are so delighted to be connecting to the real child that they often go overboard, plunging the child into the family's life. Before he has had the opportunity to accept Mom and Dad, he is meeting grandparents, aunts, uncles, cousins, neighbors—a dizzying array of new friends and relatives.

The child may feel very uncomfortable but is usually quite docile, dis-playing his best, most friendly face to all. Behavior difficulties mentioned by the social worker are seldom seen as he feeds into the family's fantasy that their loving home has already made a difference. Inside, something very different may be happening. None of this fuss was ever made during his multiple moves in and out of his birth home and various foster homes and institutions, so it may be confusing to him. He may resent being introduced as the new son. He doesn't feel like a son yet, so he may internally reject the family by feeling, "I'm not your son," while smiling at strangers and pretending to play his part. Instead of genuinely joining the family, the child may be watching the connections and interactions, learning the buttons he can push when the time is right.

The child will usually take advantage of the situation. He will encourage the parents to spend money on him and will gladly accept all gifts. His philosophy is often jaded by earlier rejections and may go something like, "Well, if it doesn't work out, at least I'll get something from these people." In restaurants, the child may automatically choose the most expensive thing on the menu, the largest soft drink, and the biggest dessert—even if he doesn't like the food or can't possibly eat that much.

The child may also be preparing to leave his current home by making negative comments about it, while flattering his new parents. His new mom's cooking may be much better than that of his foster mom. The adoptive dad may be told he is much nicer and smarter than the foster dad. The child may dredge up past arguments with his foster parents that illustrate how this will be a much better place. Because the child has left other placements in chaos and anger, he knows only how to leave in turmoil. If anger and rejection—his familiar friends—are present, he feels comfortable leaving.

The child is also gaining points with the new family. He hopes that if he downgrades the old home, his new parents will feel good about themselves, what they are doing, and him. Along this line, he may begin to call the parents Mom and Dad, which thrills the adoptive family. It would be wise, however, for new parents to realize that this may be the tenth woman he has called Mom and the seventh man he's called Dad, so the words may have little meaning to him beyond their use as effective tools.

Children adopted from orphanages may use the terms *Mom* and *Dad* long before those words are connected to an emotional tie. People working in the orphanages may have begun to teach the child the English words for parents, but the adopting family should remember that the child may not have even know these words in his own language.

Foster parents who have decided not to adopt their foster child can help prepare him for adoption—and make visiting time more special—by working with him. They need to be honest with him and with his new parents about why they have elected not to adopt. They need to be open about his strengths and weaknesses with both the adoption worker and the adoptive parents.

Foster parents can also supply the adoptive family with pictures of their family and any other people who have been significant in the child's life. Having a good-bye party provides the child with an opportunity to see everyone before he moves and allows him to have a happy closure on the time he spent in the foster home. It may help the child immensely if the foster parents can stay in touch with him and even provide respite care for the new parents as they need it.

As visiting continues, loss issues for the parents and child may begin to surface. The child may begin to experience grief over losing his current foster parents. Especially if he has established a connection to them, this move will be seen as yet another loss in a long line of losses. He is also certain to be moving through the final realization that he will never go home to his birth family—it really is over.

A child has no comprehension of the big picture as an adult might; he sees only this moment as another in a string of painful "this moments." But because he has been expected to deal with and suppress his grief so many times, the painful feelings may come out in distancing or angry behaviors. It helps if the prospective parents understand that their thrill may not be shared by the child for some time.

Parents may also experience their own loss issues during the visits. It is highly unlikely that this child is exactly what the parents had in mind—no child could meet the fantasies we create. And it is possible that the realization that this may be the end of the dream for a birth child could renew a grief cycle regarding infertility or singleness. Acknowledging that these feelings are normal and valid helps the parent stay on top of the situation.

PHASE FOUR: TO BE OR NOT TO BE A FAMILY

Visiting ends either in permanent placement or in the decision not to adopt the child. If the decision is made not to adopt, the parents must go through a grieving process and work through painful emotions stirred by the high hopes they brought into the adoption process. It may take months before they are ready to think about adoption again, or they may decide that it is simply not something they can do. It takes courage and wisdom for parents to tune into their inner knowledge and to let go of the dream, if necessary.

Parents who decide in favor of adoption are ecstatic at this point—the moment has finally arrived. What may surprise them is the amount and depth of grief the child may show. Tears, sadness, long hugs from foster parents, foster brothers and sisters, and other important people may be followed by a silent car ride punctuated only by quiet sobs. The happiness of the parents clashes quietly against the grief of the child as all struggle to move forward to create a family.

Though it is hard on new parents to stand by helplessly while the child they want to love grieves, either audibly or silently, they must keep in mind that grieving is a healthy, normal step in the child's process toward joining with his new family. He has to be allowed time to make the transition to his new home, and he must be given the opportunity to integrate the positive features of his old home into his new living arrangement. Letting him know that his feelings are normal and a part of the process is the best thing his new parents can do.

Parents have more cause for concern if their child displays no sadness, only a detached or glib amusement. If the child acts unusually excited about moving, he may be displaying evidence of attachment difficulties or he may just need permission to express his grief. Parents need to pay close attention to the transition period to see how real his emotional responses are. By noticing when his emotions do not seem to fit the situation, a parent can gain valuable insights into future issues that may need attention in therapy.

Happy, sad, or indifferent, the child is making the biggest and most important step in his life. Together, he and his new parents embark on a journey that may be exceedingly difficult—and enormously rewarding.

SEVEN

INTERCOUNTRY ADOPTIONS

The Unique Challenges

Advances in modern communications and the growth of instant media have given us more access than ever before to the realities unfolding in other countries. Some of the more sobering of these realities are the poverty, war, and domestic unrest in some nations, which always injure the weakest in a society. Because children often suffer the most in this social turmoil, their plights grab the heartstrings of many prospective adoptive parents in more stable countries.

Intercountry adoptions have been occurring for many years, but as the number of children available for adoption decreases at home, more and more people in the United States, Europe, Australia, Canada, New Zealand, and other countries experiencing peace and domestic prosperity have turned to adopting from abroad.

According to statistics compiled in 2006 by the Child Welfare Information Gateway, 20,679 children were adopted internationally that year.[1] Asia was the number one provider of these children, Guatemala ranked second, and Russia was third.

After World War II, children came to the United States from Germany and Italy. They arrived from Korea and Vietnam when the wars in those countries ended and from India, South America, Ireland, El Salvador, and Haiti during periods of crisis.

The current spotlight, because of media exposure, is on China, Russia, and Eastern Europe. China has a policy of allowing each family to have only one or two children in certain provinces. The culture places more value on boys than girls, so female children are often abandoned.

The breakup of the Soviet Union has created an economic and political atmosphere that allows for international adoption. Guatemala is now placing many children in U.S. homes. However, the adoption climate throughout the world ebbs and flows, so prospective parents must always check for a particular country's current status.

Today, there are approximately fifty countries that allow their young citizens to be adopted by parents from other countries. These children generally live in orphanages and institutions, facing a grim future if they remain in the land of their birth. Most developing countries have inadequate or nonexistent child welfare systems and do not have the ability to meet the needs of children whose birth families cannot take care of them. Native families who might want to adopt these children often do not have adequate funds to provide for them.[2] Some children with correctable medical problems, such as a cleft palate, may never receive adequate medical treatment. Education, job opportunities, and even marriage can be denied to children with no families.

While many similarities exist between domestic and intercountry adoption, some issues are unique to the international scene. When the harsh realities of Romanian orphanages hit the news, many adoptive parents rushed overseas to rescue children, thinking it was the best, fastest way to obtain a young child. But many adoption professionals shuddered at the prospect, knowing that very little information about the child's history would be available. They also knew that the kind of inhumane treatment experienced by many of the children was almost certain to create serious attachment issues down the road. Concerned but uninformed about such issues, parents hoped that providing a loving home with good food and a clean room would be enough to compensate for the early neglect and trauma.

What these parents usually failed to consider was the fact that children from overseas lose contact with everything familiar — their language, people, food, housing, and culture — thereby exacerbating an already difficult adjustment. To compound this problem, children from orphanages may have different issues than those raised in foster care. Prenatal exposure to drugs and alcohol, genetics, number of placements, and quality of care are more critical matters than a child's country of origin.

We urge anyone who plans to adopt—or has adopted—from another country to read this entire book since most adoption issues transcend borders. In this chapter, however, we will explore some of the unique issues and myths surrounding intercountry adoption.

SOCIAL AND MEDICAL HISTORY

People often choose to adopt from other countries because they believe that children available in the United States are too damaged by social and/or medical issues. While this is sometimes the case, American children at least have *known* social and medical histories, while children adopted internationally usually have little or no documentation of their backgrounds. They could have a family history of disease, such as mental illness, cancer, or alcoholism. They might have been exposed to alcohol or drugs while in the womb. They could suffer from any of a host of maladies that plague populations all over the world. A smoking and drinking birth mom with no prenatal care in Cleveland does the same damage to her developing fetus as a birth mom with the same habits in Moscow.

While an unknown or incomplete history is a factor in most adoptions—and a risk adoptive parents must take—it is important to learn as much as possible about a child's social and medical history. Gathering such information helps prepare for the future and enables the child to deal with issues surrounding his identity. Sometimes information that seems mildly interesting at first can turn out to be the key—perhaps a life-saving one—to aiding a child if physical or emotional troubles emerge at a later date.

In some instances, the medical records of children adopted from overseas are purposely vague or exaggerated to facilitate placement approval by the local government. Some countries will not allow healthy children to leave, so a false diagnosis may be made to help expedite adoption. An experienced adoption agency can help parents sort this out.

It is important to get the child's history—whether it is officially recorded or presented orally by foster parents, caretakers, or orphanage staff—into the hands of professionals who can answer questions that are unique to that child. An excellent American pediatrician, for example, may not be familiar with parasites that have invaded a child's digestive system in another country, so it is best to consult experts in the birth country before the child leaves for the United States. Calls to local hospitals, universities, the American Medical Association, and support groups can help locate these experts. Companies that do business overseas, veteran groups, and travel agents may also be able to help. (See the "Resources" section of this book.)

BIRTH-FAMILY AND IDENTITY ISSUES

A myth exists that most domestic adoptions are tenuous and in constant danger of disruption or catastrophe. This is simply not true. The parents of children who wait for adoption in the United States have already had their parental rights terminated. The instances of courts reversing adoptions are extremely rare, which is why they are so newsworthy. These stories, however, can feed the insecurity and distrust that some prospective parents have of governmental agencies. The child welfare system in the United States can often seem chaotic, and it is sometimes difficult for parents to access services or to trust that their needs will be adequately met.

The real issue that adoptive parents must face is that birth-family issues exist in an adopted child's heart and therefore move into a new home with him. No matter what the child's age, sex, race, or country of origin, no matter how far away the biological parents may be, all adoptees share the painful knowledge that out there somewhere, someone other than their adoptive parents gave them life. Children who come into care as infants have particularly poignant questions: Who am I? Why was I taken away, given up, abandoned? What is my birth family like? Do I look like them? These questions about identity and deep feelings of loss are shared by all adoptees, no matter how they come into the family.

George, abandoned at age two, was adopted from a South American orphanage when he was four. Now ten years old, he has a habit of stealing, lying, and defiance—behaviors that brought his parents to family counseling. In one session, George's beautiful brown eyes overflowed with tears.

"I miss my birth mom so much," he sobbed. "And even if I go back to find her, I can't talk to her. They took me from my country. I lost my mom, and I lost my language."

His adoptive parents were astounded. They never suspected that their son harbored such a deep sense of loss. With this new recognition, they were able to understand that his behaviors had roots that were previously unknown to them. Comprehending, sharing, and helping to resolve George's pain and loss became the goals of the family's therapeutic work.

Parents who adopt from other countries must be realistic—not only about their children's probable feelings of loss but also about their possible need to reconnect with their culture, country, or even their birth families at some point during their lives. The umbilical cord is strong and is capable of stretching around the world. As we will discuss further in chapter 11, a child's need to search for and/or reunite with his family of origin is normal. The tug is often very strong and is sometimes necessary to complete the emotional healing from loss. In many cases, people who were adopted internationally have completed successful searches and have found their birth parents.

A child's need to reconnect can be strong—even if removal from the family was because of abuse or neglect. In intercountry adoptions, where many children are taken away from their countries because of intentional or unavoidable parental abandonment, the adopted child's need to discover his roots can be especially intense. Children receive great gifts from their birth parents—their appearance, intelligence, health, some personality traits, prenatal care—and they will always be attached to these parents to some degree.

It is imperative that adoptive parents support their child's interest in resolving personal and cultural identity issues. The age at which an adopted child begins to question varies, and sometimes the questions remain hidden and never materialize in a search-and-reunion process. But adoptive parents must be willing to accept that, for most children, birth-family issues are a reality.

One way that parents of overseas adoptees might help with identity issues is by planning a homeland tour. Certainly, not everyone adopted from another country will want to participate in such an activity, but if the child expresses an interest, parents can help facilitate the process. Their openness and receptivity to exploring the child's country of origin will, at least, allow the child to know that he has parental support if he should choose to consider a trip or a search for birth relatives in the future.

A variety of agencies plan and coordinate homeland tours. Interested families should contact either the adoption agency with which they worked or another agency that organizes such tours. Within the adoption community, it should be relatively easy for families to access information about these trips.

Adoptees who make homeland tours have a variety of goals and expectations. Some want to see the country from which they came. Others want to visit the foster home or orphanage where they lived prior to arriving in the United States. Some want to search actively for birth parents, siblings, or other relatives. If and when a trip is considered, the child's interest and opinion should be primary. A trip should not be planned simply to satisfy the parents' desires to expose the child to his culture. This meeting of the parents' needs would not necessarily be in the child's best interest.

It is difficult to establish an age at which a homeland tour is appropriate. It seems, however, that the timing should coincide with the child's expressed interest in his identity and culture. The trip should not be undertaken by families in distress or for the purpose of "finally resolving" identity and transcultural conflicts. A vacation with a purpose, as opposed to a therapeutic venture, might be a better motivation.

Keep in mind that a homeland tour will not resolve or cure an adoptee's complications regarding loss, separation, and adoption. It should be seen as only one piece of the overall process of coming to terms with being born in one country and raised in another by adoptive parents.

With that said, the majority of intercountry adoptees do not make homeland tours, and adoptive families should not be pressured into believing that it is a necessity. The United States is home to many culture camps — both day and overnight — that are sponsored by adoption agencies or support groups. These camps, most often held in the summer, offer a variety of ways for children to learn about their cultures. To find out more about their availability, check with local adoption agencies.

One of our adolescent clients recently returned from a Korean culture camp. He was exhilarated by the experience and expressed renewed personal confidence. He enjoyed being around so many Koreans, eating Korean food, and playing Korean games and was delighted to share details with his parents and his therapist. Each year he looks forward to camp, and it seems to address adequately his interests in his origin.

Many adoptees do not explore these issues until adulthood, or they may never feel the need to do so. There is no right answer to whether or not a child needs such experiences. "It depends" is probably the best answer — hinging on whatever serves the child's best interests and wishes.

One twenty-two-year-old Korean adoptee said, "I have as much interest in Korea as my American-born Korean friends do — very little. We're Americans. My friends' parents push Korea, Korean activities, and Korean friends, but my friends all want the opposite: America, American activities, and (Caucasian) American friends."

Clearly, everyone has his own perspective, and that may or may not be in sync with what others think might be best.

RACIAL AND CULTURAL DISPARITIES

As we pointed out in chapter 5, adopted children whose race differs from that of their parents face special challenges. Not only is their adoptive status clear to all, but they encounter a society where some people make insensitive or racist remarks or expect certain behaviors based on racial stereotypes.

Parents who adopted transracially in the United States before the Interethnic Placement Act of 1996 were often required to make a cultural plan. Although this is no longer a requirement, it's a good idea to think about the issues that will inevitably be raised. Questions for you and your family to consider should include:

- How racially varied are your everyday interactions? Are your librarians, teachers, grocery clerks, church members, dentists, doctors, coworkers, neighbors, and friends of various races and cultures? How much are you willing to change your routine or lifestyle to accommodate your child's need to interact with people whose race or culture is different from your own?

- How accepting is your family of different races and cultures? Are you ready for in-laws of a different race or culture? Your extended family may be racially different forever. How will your biological family react at weddings, funerals, or holiday celebrations?

- Many children adopted transracially tend to identify with their own racial or cultural group more as they grow older. Is that all right with you? Is it acceptable to you and your family if most of your child's peers and dates are racially or culturally different from you? Are you ready for grandchildren of a different race?

- How far will you go to make your child's world more culturally and racially diverse? Will you move? Change churches? Hire babysitters who share your child's heritage? Refuse a promotion to an area that is not culturally diverse?

- How inclusive of your child's native culture can you be? Does he need to forget his native language and use only yours, or do you need to help him become bilingual? Are you prepared to learn about his country's history, literature, and culture so you can teach him about his roots?

These can be touchy issues, but they certainly deserve some honest pondering before you make a decision to proceed with adopting a child from another country. Adoption is a lifelong reality, and adopting across racial and cultural lines changes your family forever.

NEGLECT

Much of this book is devoted to discussing the effects of neglect and abuse on a child as he develops, and this problem is not limited to the United States. Children from all over the world can become victims of neglect and abuse, and the effect is the same whether the damage is done purposefully by a birth parent or inadvertently because of circumstances (such as too few caretakers in an orphanage setting).

The adoptive mom of a ten-year-old adopted in the United States as a toddler was watching a show about the effects of neglect on Romanian orphans. "I just began to weep," she said. "The looks on their faces, the emptiness in their eyes were just the same as my little girl's." Her daughter had come into care as a result of neglect and abandonment by a cocaine-addicted mother. While the Romanian neglect had its roots in government policy, poverty, and too few caretakers, the result in the children was the same. Lack of nurturing for any reason does the same damage.

Institutional living also leaves its mark on children. Adoption researchers have learned much about children raised in institutions. In institutions, children learn tolerance, distance, and routine. The focus is on the group rather than on individuals, so children learn the values of belonging to a group and receive stimulation through programs rather than people. They seldom learn age-appropriate language and play. Their development is delayed.

These issues can complicate a child's integration into a family. A child who is cared for in an orphanage by multiple caretakers can have a difficult time establishing trust since the bonding cycle discussed in chapter 3 is not completed by a primary caregiver. Because the feeding of infants in institutions is likely to be on a prescribed schedule rather than on demand and therefore his cries do not lead to comfort, the child may have a hard time with cause-and-effect thinking.

Instead of asking to have a need filled, a child may wait passively for someone to gratify him. This passivity may seem, at first, like a gift to a parent who also has a more aggressive child, but the passive child's detachment can make him difficult to connect with on a deep level.

Control issues are often prominent with such children, who believe that remaining in control is linked to their survival. Ironically, they have trouble connecting with a parent who cannot control them and therefore keep them safe. Conversely, because no primary link was made to a specific individual early in life, these children may not view anyone as a stranger—charming everyone they meet and being willingly led astray by adults or others in authority.

Because of staff shortages in most orphanages, some children may have been understimulated, which can cause them to be unresponsive or hyperresponsive to pain, sound, or touch. As an example, stiff materials or tags in clothes can seem like torture to children who are hypersensitive, and they will need to be avoided.

Simple games such as peekaboo (which helps develop object permanency) or rolling a ball back and forth (which helps build reciprocity) are often overlooked by burdened staff. Playing these games with children — even when their chronological age makes the games seem inappropriate — may facilitate emotional development.

Food is an issue with many children who have spent their early years in institutions. Bottle-feeding may have continued too long, delaying the chewing reflex. Choking, gulping food, and discomfort with textures of food are common to children raised in this way. They may also gorge on or hoard food in an attempt to make sure their basic needs are met. After all, their adoptive parents are untrustworthy strangers at this point.

Sleep disturbances can also occur once an institutionalized child is adopted. Unused to sleeping alone, in the dark, or in a large bed may cause restlessness, nightmares, or night terrors. Other problems common to institutionalized children are delayed language, poor fine and gross motor skills, attention problems, self-stimulation such as head banging and rocking, and intense clinginess.

Medical problems can result from limited prenatal care, poor nutrition, or lack of adequate medical care in early infancy. Specific problems can include, but are not limited to, an increased risk of tuberculosis, hepatitis, HIV, opportunistic infections, and parasites.

For some children who have spent time in institutions, these special issues will be quickly remediated. Others, because of variables such as personality, genetics, length of stay in an institutional setting, age at adoption, and perhaps a special connection to one caretaker, will exhibit several of the characteristics discussed. For some, these dynamics will create serious barriers to both development and bonding with a permanent family.

If your adopted child experiences any of these problems, the earlier you get help, the better. Trained therapists, occupational therapists, speech therapists, and medical doctors can assist. Support groups can be an excellent source for referrals to appropriate professionals and can also provide help by listening and offering suggestions on how to successfully integrate a child into the family.

Some of the best ways to connect with support groups are by contacting your area's adoption agencies, becoming active in the adoption community, attending workshops, asking to be included in mailing lists for newsletters, and contacting your local or state Department of Human Services. Even if these resources specialize in domestic adoptions, they can direct you to the proper support groups for families adopting internationally. The agency that helped you adopt your child should also know about local support groups.

Your child may also need help in some very basic areas. Following are some factors to keep in mind:[3]

- He may be used to a strict routine. Food, bedtimes, even going to the bathroom may have been regimented. The rhythm of a normal family may need to be more structured until he gets in sync with it. Establish rituals to take the place of the routines your child has left behind.

- Everyday objects (televisions, freezers, electrical outlets, toys, stairs, cars) may be new, frightening, or enticing to your child. Be sure that his environment is safe.

- Your child may never have seen a pet, so don't leave him alone with your family dog or cat too soon. Help him get to know and enjoy the animal first.

- Toys may not be familiar to your child. You may need to teach him to play.

- Your child may be terrified to sleep alone. Nightlights and a radio may help alleviate this fear.

- Because your child may have been understimulated and neglected, you may need to exaggerate your facial and vocal inflections to show emotions. The child can then learn what word (sad, mad, glad, or scared) goes with what facial expression. This will help him learn these subjective concepts in a new language and effectively communicate his feelings to his new family.

- Even if your child is preverbal, your language will sound foreign to him, so lots of vocal interaction is important. Talk to your child as much as possible. Name activities and objects, talk with expression, and use short sentences to help stimulate language development.

- Be your child's primary caregiver for as long as possible so he can clearly identify you as the reliable provider of his essential needs.
- Keep in mind that some of your child's behaviors — such as stealing or lying — may have been learned in the institution in order to survive. They were useful and powerful tools that may have served him well at the time, so they won't be given up easily.

ABUSE

A child can be physically or sexually abused anywhere — in a family, foster home, institution, orphanage, or on the street. Most often, such abuse is not documented in other countries, but it can nevertheless severely affect the child.

Gabriel, now three, was eighteen months old when he came to the United States from an orphanage. One of his many issues was choking on food. There were no medical reasons for this behavior. After role-playing his many moves — from birth mom to orphanage to foster care to adoption — he told his adoptive mom of the oral sexual abuse he had experienced at the hands of the "monsters in the orphanage." Although there is no way to validate his memory, it is probably true since most three-year-olds cannot describe this specific behavior. Gabriel's mom, as shocked and horrified as she was, responded well by reassuring him that she loved him and that she would protect him always.

Daniel, a handsome twelve-year-old, joined his adoptive family at age six. He had lived in "one of the best orphanages" in his native land, yet his behaviors were becoming more complex and dangerous. By getting more information from the orphanage, the family was able to find out that for the first eighteen months of his life, Daniel was tied down in his bed while his bottle was propped in his mouth. This was not done with malice but simply to keep him still so the bottle would stay in place.

Besides being routinely restrained, he was seldom held. Although the caretakers were doing the best they could under the circumstances, the child perceived their actions as abusive. Daniel's family is working hard in therapy and at home to help resolve these early hurts, and he still has many issues to resolve.

TRAUMA

Many foreign children available for adoption are orphaned from war, disease, epidemics, famine, or natural disasters, and the effects of the trauma may not become clear for some time. Children raised in war-torn countries have often witnessed murders, bombings, and other atrocities. They may have been burned, hit, had bones broken, or been injured in local battle zones. The unimaginable trauma some children experience before coming to the United States is an issue that adoptive parents need to be aware of and address.

Sofia was about two when the enemy came in and gunned down her family as she watched from under the bed. A missionary found her after several days, swatting flies from her mother's rotting body. She was taken from her home, placed in an orphanage, and later adopted by an American couple when she was five. Although her history was clearly tragic, her new parents initially had no idea what impact it had had on their daughter.

She was terrified to love anyone ever again. She had night terrors and would awaken the family with her screams. She felt survivors' guilt — surely, she thought, she could have done something to help her birth parents. Why, she wondered, was she left alive?

Said her adoptive mom, "People told us how good we were to adopt her, but we did it for ourselves because we wanted a younger child. If she had stayed in her homeland, she might be dead by now, but sometimes I wonder if we did her any favors."

It is important to remember that many neglect and abuse issues that manifest in a child being released for adoption are based on human responses and development. They are the same regardless of the child's country of origin, and the same—or a greater—level of commitment and resourcefulness on the part of the adoptive parents is required to heal the hurt child.

LACK OF SUPPORT

An adoptive mother of three Eastern European siblings—adopted at ages six, three, and one—admitted, "I knew there were many children in the United States who needed homes, but I also knew they had abuse issues. I truly thought that if I went far away and spent enough money ($30,000), I would get 'easier kids.' I didn't. If I had adopted in the United States, I would at least have the support of the agency and financial assistance."

Tension sometimes arises between adoption professionals who work on domestic adoptions and parents who adopt children from other countries, especially when the children need services once they're in the United States. With shrinking available resources, it seems that some professionals think they should be preserved for children born in this country. Agencies responsible for placing thousands of American children do not always understand the motivation of a family who goes far away to adopt a child with similar needs and issues. Adoptive families of a child from overseas, faced with that child's special needs, cannot always understand why services such as medical cards and subsidies are denied to them.

Parents who have adopted internationally and seek local services must be educators and advocates for their children. They must help service providers understand that no matter where the child comes from, he is now a resident of the United States and requires assistance. They need to give schools, therapists, and other service providers information regarding the child's past and adoption issues. Meeting with the providers, giving them adoption-sensitive information, and being resolute in pursuing help for the child are all advocate tasks that parents must take on. They may also have to become advocates in their state to educate politicians on the need for postadoption services.

HOW TO MAKE INTERCOUNTRY ADOPTIONS SUCCESSFUL

People who choose to expand their families through intercountry adoption can best prepare by reading, joining support groups, and doing Internet research.

The purpose is to connect with other families in the process—families who have already adopted internationally and can give advice—and professionals who can help with adoption issues that span cultural lines.

The "Related Readings" section of this book lists many helpful publications. Tapestry Press (www.tapestrybooks.com), among others, has lists of adoption resources. Many useful Internet sites can be accessed through a word search. These sites and chat rooms can also help you locate support groups, books, and other resources. In addition, several national support groups are listed in the "Resources" section of this book.

Before choosing an international adoption agency, conduct interviews so you're sure to find one that does more than just paperwork. You'll want to be able to rely on them for education, support, and postadoption services. If education is not offered, contact local adoption agencies—domestic or international—to see if you can sit in on education meetings. Topics should include discussions of loss, attachment, adjustment, and potential problems, as well as the positives of adoption.

Check on the agency's reputation and contacts in the child's country of origin. This can best be accomplished by talking to others in the adoption community who have used the services. It is a good idea to ask historical questions, such as how many placements have been made and how long the organization has been in practice. Also inquire about the training and qualifications of the staff.

Carefully preparing for an international adoption is key—both when you're in the child's native land and after you return to the United States. Most, but not all, countries require adoptive parents to travel to that country to pick up the child, but if you do not personally make the trip, ask your adoption agency to take on some of these tasks for you:

- Arrange for a review of materials on the child (videotape, written documents, pictures) by professionals (doctors, occupational therapists, developmental specialists) before you agree to placement. Most agencies supply this to you, and it should be reviewed by objective experts.
- Get as much information about the child as possible. The agency may have specifics on birth-family history, number of placements,

developmental issues, feeding problems, and medical records. In cases of abandonment, this historical data might not be available, but any current data will be useful.

- Review the list of questions on pages 94–95 in chapter 6. They are the same ones you need to gather information for an intercountry adoption.
- Do as much as possible to prepare your home for your child before his arrival. You will be far too exhausted and busy to do this once he joins your family.
- Identify potential service providers and explore medical insurance coverage.
- Take pictures of the orphanage, caretakers, foster parents, peers, city that your child is from, vegetation, and anything else that seems appropriate. This may provide your child's only validation of his early memories and culture.
- Tape-record the caretaker talking or singing in whatever language the child has been exposed to or learned.
- Bring home everything you can. If possible, trade new sheets, bottles, clothes, and toys for the ones the child is used to. What looks faded, old, or beat up to you may feel just right to your child. Do not throw away any of the child's possessions, but cherish them instead. The smells, sights, and feel of familiar possessions are comforting.
- Find out what nipple, formulas, food, routine, music, and smells the child is used to so you can replicate as much as possible when you get home.
- Purchase books, music, and artifacts you can use later to help your child understand his native culture.
- Pay attention. Even though you are stressed, tired, highly emotional, and in the throes of jet lag and culture shock, you need to remember everything you can for the sake of your child. Take notes or make an audio recording so you will have a record of important facts and feelings to share with him as he gets older.
- Bring home all the documents and information you can. Don't worry if they're in a foreign language — you'll find someone to translate them eventually. Remember — this may be your only chance to get

information that could be critical to your child at some later point in his life.

- Talk to everyone connected with your child. The judges, lawyers, and officials probably don't know your child as well as the orphanage staff, nurse, cook, janitor, and/or foster family.

- Accept that you are the foreigner in this culture and you are taking a child away from his home. Cooperate with the nationals involved.

When Your Child Comes Home

- If you traveled to get your child in his homeland, you likely experienced an abundance of stress and culture shock. When your child arrives home with you, he'll go through the same emotions. Slow your pace and be patient.

- Have your child evaluated by professionals as soon as possible. Most medical and developmental problems respond best when addressed early. Have your child's emotional needs — and your own — checked out by a qualified mental health therapist. Your child may need occupational therapy, physical therapy, developmental therapy, attachment-based therapy, or sensory integration work. Now is not too soon to start.

- Take care of yourself, your spouse, and your other children. Don't try to be Superperson. Some things will just have to wait. Take time to pamper yourself and your significant relationships.

- One parent should remain at home as the child's primary caretaker as long as possible. Several years is not too long for a child to learn about his new parents. Rushing into day care can be difficult for a child who just joined a family.

- Hold, cuddle, tickle, and play! Don't push developmental tasks such as giving up bottles or thumb sucking and potty training. If your child reverts to less mature behaviors, parent this "younger" child.

- Remember that your child may be scared. Give him time to get used to new smells, foods, languages, pets, and people. Don't force anything.

- Review Regina's Bag of Tricks in chapter 10. Make a life book or timeline for, or with, your child. Depending on the child's age, engage in activities together to build your relationship. If he is old enough to remember holidays in his homeland, you might want to incorporate some into your family life.

- Let your friends and relatives know exactly what you need. Don't assume that they know. If doing your laundry or cooking dinner would be a better gift than another outfit for your new little one, speak up.
- Avoid stereotypes about adoption or your child. Every situation is different, and you are the expert on your family life.

Choosing to adopt a child from another country is an exciting, challenging, and unique experience. It is one that can open a family to new cultures and abundant rewards. Most intercountry adoptive families find satisfaction in the experience and, like the majority of families who adopt domestically, would repeat the experience.

Education and preparation are important prior to placement, but it is never too late to learn. Open-mindedness, reaching out to others, and accepting appropriate help are vital in this process. Remember, you are not alone. Others have walked this path before you, will walk it with you, and will walk it after you have completed your journey. Use every available resource to prepare yourself, your family, and ultimately your child for a lifelong journey from his place of birth to his future and forever home.

We share with you now the best summary on intercountry adoption we have heard, presented by Susan Soon-Keum Cox, adopted from Korea, when she spoke to a United States Congressional Hearing on Adoption:

> The mandate for those agencies or individuals involved in international adoption should be, indeed must be, to find families for children rather than children for families. This is a very real and significant distinction.
>
> Without question, every child should grow up with his birth family — and every effort should be extended to make that possible. When that is not a child's reality, the next choice should be a family in the child's country. But if that cannot happen, then it is wrong for a child to grow old waiting in an institution if there is a family in another

country who will love and care for him as their own.

To make that possible, we who are committed to that goal must understand that inter-country adoption is a matter of privilege, not a matter of right. Nations are responsible for the care and protection of their citizens. This includes homeless children who may be potentially adoptable.

It must be a priority to respect both the dignity of the child's birth country as well as the dignity of the child. Whenever a country supports inter-country adoption as a way for a child to have a family, they are giving a great deal. A nation's decision, as a matter of policy, to permit inter-country adoption of its homeless children is not an easy one for any country. They do have the right to define the system as they feel it should be.

Sometimes, especially in the beginning, the system is cumbersome and slow. However, care should be taken not to circumvent the system put in place by sending countries. Adoption agencies, facilitators, adoptive parents, and adoption advocates must look at the bigger picture and be aware that how they facilitate the process could jeopardize the future of children who would be served later.

It is important to be honorable and aware of cultural sensitivities in approaching the possibilities of inter-country adoption. Assumptions that it is preferable for a poor child in a developing country to be part of a family in the U.S. is arrogant and foolish. Rather, it is the birthright of every child to have a family.

Adopting families need to acknowledge, accept, and care a great deal about the cultural heritage of the child they are adopting. Inter-country adoption can be complicated and complex, and sometimes difficult and frustrating. But it works. It is a wonderful way for a child who would never have a family to be loved, nurtured, and cherished.[4]

EIGHT

GETTING USED TO EACH OTHER

Early Issues in the Adoptive Family

The prospect of adding a new family member can be scary. Talking about it and actually doing it are two very different issues. Acknowledging the awesome responsibility of adoption may raise many anxieties for the new family. After all, the forever aspect of the adopted child not only alters the nuclear family but also changes kinship ties for every generation to come.

For previously childless couples and new single parents, the thought of school registration, after-school care, scheduled mealtimes, household rules, and pediatricians may seem overwhelming. Furthermore, these housekeeping challenges are usually compounded by the need to reconcile the reality of the adopted child with the fantasy of parenthood. First-time parents may also discover that they have made assumptions about their own roles and those of their spouse, and one may be unaware of them or unable or unwilling to meet the other's expectations. Once again reality sets in, and many new parents toss and turn at night agonizing over the fear of having made the biggest mistake of their lives.

For more experienced parents, the day-to-day issues may be less stressful but will still consume great amounts of time and energy. More complex problems occur when trying to assimilate the adopted child into the existing

family as birth orders shift, sleeping arrangements change, and roles are rede-
fined to accommodate his arrival. Siblings may feel resentment toward the
new child as he assumes the family spotlight, forgetting that they, too, were
once the center of attention.

Adoptive parents frequently try to help the new child adjust by making
few demands on him. Expectations, rules, and chores are put on hold "until
we get used to each other." In fact, this posture should be avoided because
it makes it even more difficult for the child to accept a role of responsibility
further down the line. Wise parents give their adopted child a realistic view
of family life from the very start.

Just as everything is new to the adoptive family, so is it new to the child.
School and siblings, food and clothing, family rituals and religious preferenc-
es—all present new experiences and challenges. Different socioeconomic circumstances, cultural issues, and neighborhoods all contribute to the newness
of the situation. A child from a rural area who is used to participating in 4-H
will have a difficult time adjusting to life in suburbia, where skateboarding
is an expected social skill. An African American child raised in white foster
homes may struggle with cultural issues if moved to a family of his own race.
Similarly, a child who is used to being one of many siblings in a foster family
will face major challenges if he suddenly becomes an only child in an adoptive home.

In addition to adjusting to the new aspects of his life, the adopted child
must address the concept of the adoption itself—a permanent plan that can
be terrifying. Most children view adoption as the final step in the lengthy process of letting go of their fantasies of being reunified with their birth parents.
And if the birth family is slated to lose all contact once the adoption takes
place, the child may feel especially lost. While this permanent separation may
spell safety for some, it sparks a painful resurgence of grief for others.

When the fantasy of reunification ends, a child often builds a new fantasy about adoption. Since the new parents tend to talk about how wonderful the adoption will be—usually touting the benefits of security for the
child and the chance to form long-lasting, positive attachments—the child
may begin to fashion a dream world using the adults' fantasies as a reference point. He begins to see the adoptive home as a place where problems
cease to exist. Adolescents, in particular, may talk about the freedom that

adoption will bring. While the new parents may see this attitude in a positive light, that is not necessarily the case. The adolescent often defines freedom in terms of increased autonomy, and the desire for autonomy is related to the psychological events of separation and individuation that are a normal part of adolescent development. However, when the adolescent has not yet formed an attachment to his new family, two developmentally incongruent psychological processes occur simultaneously: attachment to new parents and the need for separation from them. This poses difficulty for both the teen and the parents.

Younger children, too, often build fantasies of adoptive homes that fulfill their every wish, desire, and demand. Here, there is no homework. Here, there are no chores. Here, there are no consequences. When this dream world does not materialize, they respond with wails of "You're not my real parents!" They refuse to comply with any adult expectations because their own expectations were not met.

Clearly, adoptive families face many challenges. Parents often experience feelings of anger, terror, anxiety, and inadequacy. When they share their feelings with professionals or support groups, they learn that such feelings are normal and should be expected. Similarly, the child's feelings of loss and confusion, as well as his inability to bond, are also normal. Let's face it: It takes time to become a comfortable member of a new family.

Some families feel a connection from the start. "It's hard to believe he's been here just for a few weeks," they say. For others, their child continues to be a stranger for what seems like forever. "I keep thinking he'll be leaving any day now," they confess sadly. Both sets of feelings are valid and should not be denied. One attitude is not superior to another. Just as some couples fall in love at first sight while others date for years before committing, so children integrate into families at different paces.

THE PROCESS OF INTEGRATION

Testing the Rules

As the child begins his life in the new family, he starts to explore the behaviors and personalities of the family members. He learns how far he can go before consequences occur. He learns how much he can push before someone becomes angry. Rules can be exciting opportunities to test and manipulate parents. This is especially true if the parents do not always give the same message or enforce rules in the same way. The child may use such inconsistency to come between his new mother and father, causing them to question each other's parenting style and methods.

If the family has many rules, the child can manipulate by breaking a few and bending them all. Every time he succeeds in doing so, he sees himself in control of the family because the chaos he creates gives him a sense of power. Even minor violations, which the parents may choose to ignore, are perceived as major victories to the child. He truly believes, *The adults around here can't control me. I'm on my own.*

> Vance, age fourteen, found himself in an adoptive home where there were no rules regarding food. The refrigerator and cupboards were always open to him, and he could eat whenever he pleased. One of his earliest complaints to his social worker was, "Things are going pretty well, but I break the food rules." Vance needed so badly to be out of compliance that he made up rules and violated them. Whenever he had a snack, he then felt as if he'd gotten away with something.

> Joella, age eleven, would take a bath every time her adoptive mom told her to shower and would shower every time she was told to take a bath. Her mother truly didn't care which method Joella used as long as she was clean, but the child felt autonomous each time she went against her mother's instruction.

As time goes by and the child begins to trust his new environment—often after much testing of behavioral alternatives—he usually starts to comply with the adoptive family's expectations. This period frequently develops with a pattern of approach-avoidance: While the child will play by the rules in some instances, he continues to test the family's boundaries and limits. Families with whom we work often report that their child was a joy to be with for a few days, only to revert to his old, familiar behaviors.

During these times, the child's behaviors may be even more intense and negative than they were at the very beginning. His efforts to recreate the negativity that is so familiar to him are his way of feeling secure and safe — *I was born into chaos. I'm comfortable with chaos.* As he begins the transition into a more compliant mode, two things may occur simultaneously. The fear of losing his old life emerges — or, more accurately, erupts. This eruption interferes with his attraction to the new life, and so he retreats to the old, where he finds a sense of comfort.

In many cases, periods of compliance seem to occur without the child's conscious awareness. When he finally becomes aware, the cycle activates. The dynamics are similar to a child learning to ride a bike. He wobbles down the sidewalk on his new two-wheeler, a look of concentration mingled with triumph on his face. Suddenly, his excited dad declares, "Yeah! You're doing it!" The child's awareness is suddenly heightened, he gets frightened, his new-found skills evaporate, and he topples into the nearest rosebush.

The adoptive parents' line that parallels the excited dad's cheer is, "Honey, you've been a great kid to be around for the past two days!" The same cycle begins: Awareness is heightened, fear sets in, and the child retreats to his old behaviors.

Because of this pattern, we encourage parents to avoid global praise, which usually just scares their child. A scared child who is a survivor will not stay frightened for long since he will mask his emotion with anger. Ultimately, the gushing parents will have nothing to praise for a very long time.

Specific task-oriented praise is much more helpful and is generally received without the panic that accompanies global praise. A statement like, "Good job cleaning your room today," is focused and direct. Under most cir-cumstances, the child will respond appropriately to specific praise and receive it as it was intended.

Many adoptive parents find it difficult to hold back on the generous praise. After all, they want to help the child heal, boost his self-esteem, and encourage his efforts to behave and do well. Don't get us wrong — if lavishing your child with accolades does not cause his behavior to decline, then there is no immediate problem. Just keep in mind that most hurt children will view constant praise with suspicion and distrust. They will begin to wonder, *Why do I get fussed over for doing what is expected of everyone? Am I supposed to be doing the wrong things?*

Trading the Old for the New

New patterns are just that—new. Given the fact that habits of interacting take a long time to develop, it is perfectly normal for a child to practice them a little at a time. The exception is the overly compliant child, who readily accepts every new situation. While many parents would be thrilled to adopt such a child, parenting him is not necessarily easier and the child is not necessarily healthier. He is simply continuing to survive life in a passive, shutdown manner.

As a child continues to add new responses to old stimuli, changing patterns emerge. When these patterns start to work for the child, they become a part of his new life. None of us develops new behaviors without relying on past experience. Looking back provides us with a frame of reference and allows us to measure our change. If we view the change as desirable, we welcome it. If, on the other hand, the change is perceived as something scary or threatening, we resist it. As one adolescent told us, "I don't want to give up my anger. It's been with me longer than anything else." His identity had formed around this anger, and to let go of it felt as if he were giving up a part of himself.

It is critical for parents and professionals to understand this dynamic if they truly want to be a part of the child's change. The adults involved can achieve the necessary level of understanding by asking themselves a few questions:

- Could I give up what I learned in the first several years of life?
- Would I give up the very things that I now believe kept me alive and reasonably safe?
- How would I know when it was safe to do so?
- How could I be sure that the new way would work for me?
- If I let go of the old way, how would I get it back if I needed it again?

One of the hardest things for many hurt children to let go of is the dynamic of anger they often experienced and participated in while in their birth family. They have an amazing ability to recreate this dynamic with their new parents, who once considered themselves patient and loving.

When adoptive parents respond to situations with intense anger, they are replicating something their child has most likely seen before. While this anger may be unusual for the parents, it is very familiar to the child and helps him keep the old ways alive. He learns to trust that his new home will yield to these old ways when subjected to sufficient pressure. If this is the case, why should he bother to accept the new? It is fragile. It is fleeting. If he can suceed in getting his new, loving parents to respond to him in the rage-filled ways his birth family did, why shouldn't he? That's what he knows best, and that's what's comfortable to him. When his parents comply, the message he receives is, *Keep the old! It works better. You can get your new family to act just like your old one. What a powerful child you are!*

The less successful a child is at getting people to act the way he wants them to, the more likely it is that he will begin to be drawn to the new family's ways. When he fails to recreate old patterns, he can begin to trust new ones. When he relinquishes control, he gets the message that he does not have to take care of himself. He is not responsible for the adults in his life, and he does not have to worry about his safety.

Once these facts become evident, trust gradually emerges. As he experiences the role of a child — perhaps for the first time in his life — he learns that to accept his parents' direction does not mean that he will lose something. On the contrary, it is actually helpful to him. He can begin to make choices that are consistent with his new family's values. More important, he can feel comfortable with those choices. The result of his new decision making isn't merely his parents' happiness but his own sense of well-being, too.

This outcome is not only unexpected but also surprising to the child. In the past, he was not accustomed to family contentment — when one person was feeling good, others were often sad or angry. As the child becomes used to the notion that all members of the family can actually be happy at the same time, his comfort level increases. Retreats to the old ways decrease, and a new kind of familiarity develops. And repeating the familiar is exactly what parents expect in the course of a child's normal growth and development.

Consider, for example, how often a child returns to crawling while learning to walk. It is only through many falls that he learns to balance trust and confidence and step into a new experience. It is only with time and practice that this relatively simple developmental task is learned.

The adoptive parents of a hurt child can feel encouraged when they see him doing things a new way more than just once in a while. Repetition of acceptable behaviors will increase, and the parents will begin to say things like, "We had a bad day or two in the past week," instead of, "We had two good hours over the weekend." They begin to define the bad times as rare and unusual—a clear indication that their child is getting it together and keeping it that way.

These are positive indicators of lasting changes in the child:

- Abbreviated, although perhaps intense, retreats to old behaviors
- Faster recovery time after the retreat
- Decreased frequency of retreats
- Child's acknowledgment of his responsibility for the retreat without blaming others

Frequently, families—stressed, feeling guilty, and knowing that the child has conned them before—have great difficulty acknowledging or appreciating change. It often appears phony—which can be true, since a child may have to pretend to be a normal, loving, attached kid for some time before he really is. His parents may get stuck noticing the relapses and not the progress.

Once the features listed above are witnessed over a period of time, we can assume that the child's growth and development have been activated from an earlier, dormant state. Subsequently, all other change is made with less resistance, reduced turmoil, and little complication. Getting unstuck is the key to adjusting to a new life, and once this happens, the child will most likely continue to grow into a more integrated individual.

Of course, this does not mean that the future will be problem-free, but it does mean that the most difficult times are over. Adolescence, if yet to come, will bring with it a new set of variables, as it does with all individuals. However, if a solid connection has developed between child and parents, the family can expect to survive this stage with less serious wounds than if the bond had not been forged.

The parents' processes of adjusting parallel the child's. No one in a family can change without creating a corresponding response in another. Let's take a look at how the adoptive family moves through this process.

Staying in Charge

Anyone who has visited a friend or family member for a week is familiar with the stress and strain experienced by both guest and host. Daily routines, meals, bedtime, and leisure activities change as the visitor is incorporated into the family. As exciting as it is to see guests arrive, there is always some relief mixed with sadness as they depart.

Imagine, then, how much more complex it is to integrate a permanent new member into a family. The adopted child is not even remotely familiar with the dozens of unwritten rules that the family employs to ease tensions, cope with difficulties, or promote a good laugh. He knows nothing about customs such as, *Don't talk to Mom until she's had her second cup of coffee. Don't look at family bills. Don't go into Dad's study without knocking. Never try to get through to your sister when she's reading. Don't mention the fact that your brother wets the bed.* Consequently, he unknowingly breaks these rules repeatedly as he learns the expectations of his new family.

Besides being a source of aggravation for everyone, this rule bashing serves to further alienate the stranger. Often, the child will continue his unfavorable behavior to distance himself from the family.

It is therefore important for the family to exercise control by establishing a few clear-cut rules and following through on them, while at the same time realizing that no one can abide by unwritten rules until they are deciphered. As order and control are being established, patience and tolerance are required by everyone in the family.

However, being too easygoing in the beginning is a major mistake. While parents often think that bending the rules and overlooking infractions will help a child ease into his new home, the results can be disastrous. A child who has experienced chaos and abuse needs to know that the adults in his life are in control. If he fears that his new parents are uncertain regarding their lives, panic may follow and soon anger will rule. It was the uncertainty in his previous life that led to abuse and neglect, so a hurt child is extremely ill at ease with unknowns.

Families must establish control very early and as simply as possible. Despite the fact that modern society has come to equate control with harshness, discipline with cruelty, and order with militarism, the child needs control, discipline, and order to help him learn the family's expectations from the very start.

During the early—or honeymoon—stage, it is likely that he will comply with basic family guidelines. Ideally, there should be a few rules that can be enforced, rather than several rules that cannot be enforced. They should reflect the values of both the family in particular and society in general. A family rule might be, *We don't watch television before school.* A more general rule would be, *We don't steal.* Families need to sort through their expectations and decide what is important in order to help a child learn and grow.

When the family focuses solely on the child's needs and allows him to gain control, chaos reigns. When parents don't take charge, the child is frightened most of the time because he knows he really can't do a good job of running things. Ultimately, his scared feelings transition to mad ones.

The greatest danger of family disruption occurs when the parents and child are struggling with issues of control. Parents soon run out of energy, and all the hopes, fantasies, and expectations that urged them on prior to adopting are shattered. Their outlook for a happy family appears bleak, and any positive interaction with the child seems hopeless.

It is important for parents to rethink and readjust their hopes and wishes for their child. As one parent said, "When I adopted my ten-year-old daughter, I worried that I wouldn't have money for her college education. Then I hoped she'd finish high school. Now, I'm just proud she's never been in jail and can hold down a job." Parents need to face their fantasies and realize that they cannot control the future. They can only do their best to provide the child with the skills he needs to create his own life.

Self-Care and Support

It is important for parents to be clear at the very outset of the relationship that they are the bosses of the home and that their happiness, marriage, personal time, and needs are important. It is a powerful message for a child to see his mother and father take good care of themselves.

Unfortunately, meeting their own needs can pose a challenge to parents. As their child's needs become all encompassing, it can seem overwhelming—even impossible—to find the time or space to care for themselves. But they must.

A few well-planned strategies can make all the difference. Make a fifteen-minute coffee stop on the way home from work, take turns having a night out during the week, even verbalize your fantasies about flying off to Bora Bora together (while the difficult child sleeps). Maintaining a sense of self, a sense of fun, and a sense of worth can feed a relationship and help couples cope with trying times.

Outside support can often seem elusive when the family is in crisis. Individuals who can usually be counted on for a kind word and a comforting shoulder frequently desert the family because of the abundance of pain and confusion. Sometimes they disappear simply because they don't know how to help. For everyone involved, this is a completely new experience.

People know how to help new birth parents who pace the floor with a screaming infant. While everyone might wish he were quieter, no one would dare suggest giving him back. Medical doctors would give advice but wouldn't blame the obstetrician. Grandma would try to soothe him but would never say, "If I knew you'd give birth to a colicky baby, I'd have told you not to get pregnant." Coworkers would sympathize with the dark circles under Mom's eyes but wouldn't remind her that she "brought this on herself."

On the other hand, new adoptive parents with a special-needs child often get little or no support from family, friends, and the community. Therapists are quick to blame the child's past or even the adoptive family for his problems. Remarks like, "What did you expect?" "Give him back," and "They gave you a bad kid," are common as adoptive parents cope with plummeting hopes and fading dreams.

Most families find their best support in other adoptive parents. Many agencies offer support groups or link families with others who are willing to discuss similar experiences. Respite is an extremely valuable service, providing parents with a break from their child that gives them a chance to rest, recuperate, and readjust.

Many adoption agencies and community service organizations offer respite programs. Former foster parents and other adoptive parents can take a problem child for a day or two to allow the parents time to replenish their resources. By taking care of themselves, the parents send a clear message to their child that they are the ones in control.

Therapy
Therapy is often required for adoptive families, and the role of a therapist can either help or hinder the family relationship. In many cases, parents resent

participating in therapy because they "were okay before the adoption." Although this may be true, a therapist cannot treat a child in isolation. The conflicts that arise from his adoption into the family call for family solutions.

It is imperative to find a therapist who can help both the family and the child. Many times, a child will continue to see the therapist he had prior to placement. While this may offer the advantage of continuity, it can also divide the family if the therapist has bought too heavily into the child's needs. It can also be a detriment if the therapist knows little about the dynamics of special-needs adoptions. Often, his training is such that he believes the child is behaving in a certain way because of the family, rather than in spite of the family.

The most reliable sources for knowledgeable and helpful therapists are other adoptive families and agencies. If therapy does not appear to be helpful, a new therapist should be considered. Searching for the right match is far more beneficial than continuing for years with no progress or terminating therapy completely. The issue of therapy is discussed more thoroughly in chapter 11.

TEACHING A HURT CHILD RESPONSIBILITY AND COOPERATION

Demonstrative Love and Fun Strategies

Unfortunately, it is often during difficult periods that the family must face the prospect of deciding to legalize the adoption. In some cases, in order to maintain financial support, parents must legalize within a time frame that is not compatible with the family's emotional situation. In other cases, legalization is an irrelevant factor: The parents are certain that they will not ask for the child's removal under any circumstances, and they proceed with the process. In still other cases, the parents perceive legalization as a magic cure. They hope that by legally adopting the child, he will feel secure and his negative behaviors will end. While this concept may seem valid, it is never the solution. After all, from the child's point of view, "My birth parents got rid of me, so why should these parents be any different?"

It is important that the child is not led to believe that he can behave in any way he chooses and never be sent away. He can still be your child, even if he's in a residential treatment center or a detention facility. Just as an abusive spouse cannot be allowed to behave in hurtful ways and physically remain in the marriage, children need to know that they cannot continue to abuse parents and siblings and have things remain status quo. This knowledge serves to ensure their own safety, as well, but should not be used as a threat for every transgression. The idea of leaving the family loses its effectiveness very quickly, and the child may simply up the ante to get the removal to happen sooner in the belief that it will hurt less.

While parents need to be in charge of the family so everyone feels that there is direction and safety, we are not suggesting that they run their households like military camps. Having fun as a family should still be a top priority. Movies, picnics, and other outings should sometimes occur spontaneously as part of the rhythm of family life. When good times must be earned through an elaborate reward system, the child will most likely sabotage earning the event rather than risk having it taken away. And let's face it, waiting for weeks of good behavior in order to have fun with the child dooms the family to weeks of unrelenting "un-fun." This simply creates resentment and makes memory building difficult.

Many of our family memories are based on humor or fun. We are more likely to recall the time that Dad dressed up as a ballerina for Halloween than the time we lost privileges for swearing. A great deal of attaching can take place when the family shares silly events from the past and present. The new child already missed years of family fun, so it is important for him to build new memories based on fun. It can also be helpful to ask the child to talk about any funny memories from his past.

Laughter can often shift tense situations. For example, if a child lies much of the time, his parents might spend a day acting just like him. Such behavior can provide a learning experience that is far more effective than lectures. When a child says, "What's for dinner?" answer "spaghetti" and then serve meatloaf. When he asks where his favorite jeans are, tell him they're clean and folded in the clothes basket when they're really still in the hamper. Although normally truthful parents will have trouble with this exercise, it's worth a try. When done with the right spirit and a casual "I lied" when confronted by your child, he will usually get your desired message in a fun way.

> Mr. and Mrs. Brown had an eleven-year-old birth son when they decided to adopt two boys, ages nine and ten, who were both physically and rather emotionally healthy. One day, all three boys refused to comply with anything Mrs. Brown asked.
>
> "Fine," she commented. She retired to the sofa with a novel and a glass of iced tea, and the boys were stunned. Where was the anger? Where was the fight? Where were the consequences? Confused, they began to test her.
>
> "We're not going to do our chores, you know," they began. "We're going outside to play."
>
> "That's okay. I'll guess I'll just do the chores myself."
>
> A few hours later, the boys returned and requested lunch.
>
> "Well, maybe you guys can make something on your own," responded their mom, "since I haven't finished all of the chores yet. Or if you want to wait until I'm through, I'll be able to get your lunch in an hour or so."
>
> The three boys exchanged startled looks, and the thought of no food crumbled their resistance. They readily gave up their stance.
>
> "Okay," they said. "If we do our chores, will you make our lunch?"
>
> "Sure," Mrs. Brown replied with a smile. "That would be great."

Letting the Chips Fall

One of the most important lessons any child must learn is that he has choices, and with those choices come consequences. Four books we recommend to help raise children who make good choices are *Parenting the Hurt Child*, which we have written, and *Parenting with Love and Logic* and *Parenting Teens with Love and Logic* by Foster Cline, MD, and Jim Fay and *Parenting Adapted Adolescents* by Gregory Keck. The tools presented in these books will be effective only if the parents are willing to allow natural consequences to happen. While the role of the family is to be loving and supportive, it is not necessary to protect the child constantly. Too often, parents rush to rescue him because of his past. Unfortunately, the rest of the world will not be as sympathetic. Adults in the judicial system are not as compassionate as adults in the family. Allowing the child to experience consequences—provided they do not endanger him—is the best way to teach him how to make choices. And if the lesson is learned in childhood, it may prevent an onslaught of negative consequences in adulthood.

Parents must be willing to let go of all kinds of rules if they are to be successful. The first point to remember is that any rule that cannot be enforced should be canceled. It is impossible to enforce a rule such as "You can't smoke" because every time a child lights up at school or in the neighborhood, he wins (and simultaneously loses). A far more realistic rule is "You can't smoke in my presence," which is completely under the parents' control.

If telephone privileges are taken away, the parents must either stay home twenty-four hours a day or take the phones with them when they go out. Some parents we know actually drive around with phones in the trunk of their car to enforce this rule. In spite of this, all it takes is a friend's cell to give the child all the phone access he wants.

Grounding a child should generally be avoided since it tends to punish the parents as well, forcing them to remain on guard to ensure that their child stays put. Also, a child stuck at home will often adopt an in-your-face attitude, causing further grief for the parents. A more effective solution is a quick consequence instead of a lengthy grounding. Children are often restricted for so long that they lose sight of any link between cause (behavior) and effect (consequence). For learning to be effective, the consequence must be related directly to the infraction.

> Brian, age twelve, spent a lot of time doing the dishes because it was his parents' favorite consequence. He did the dishes when he received a bad grade, he did the dishes when he talked back, he did the dishes when he used Dad's power tools without asking permission. Doing dishes never changed his behavior because the consequence didn't relate to his behavior at all. There was no cause and effect. So he did dishes, got angry at his parents, and learned nothing.
>
> When a visiting neighbor asked Brian why he was always at the kitchen sink, the boy replied, "I have no idea. I have to do the dishes for the next six months, and I figure I'll have to do them forever."

The fewer and simpler the rules in a family, the more likely it is that a child will comply with those expectations. Traditions, rituals, and family expectations will most likely click in as the child develops a need to become part of the group. All unnecessary rules should be abandoned. If a child's bedroom is always messy, a simple solution is to close his door rather than argue about it. If he goes to school in wrinkled, dirty clothes because he tosses them on the floor instead of in the hamper, so be it. If he forgets to take his lunch to school every day, let him miss a meal instead of rushing to deliver it to him. (Unless, of course, he needs the food because of a medical condition.) Odds are he'll get food from his classmates anyway.

It is only by letting go of many unnecessary rules that parents can help their child comply with the rules that are really important. These rules must be enforced at all costs so the child learns that his parents are serious. When he begins to comply, his cooperation should be noticed but not necessarily rewarded. After all, rules, compliance, and self-control are important to help him become a functioning adult.

We don't get applause when we arrive at work on time, do our job, and get home at a reasonable hour. By the same token, a child shouldn't be praised when he gets to school on time, participates in class, and returns home when he's supposed to. His reward is simply not having a hassle. Instead of making a big deal out of normal, expected behavior, it is better to respond with a simple tousle of the hair, a smile, or a comment like, "Good job getting home on time." Just as detention is the punishment for tardiness, getting to go home at the end of the school day is the reward, and both are natural consequences. Leave it at that.

One of the most difficult lessons for parents to learn is to stop lecturing their children. We need only to reflect on our own childhood to remember how our eyes glazed over and our ears blocked out all sound whenever an authority figure began to carry on and on. To supplement a comment like "Good job getting home on time" with add-ons like "See? I said you could do it," "Isn't it easier to obey?" "I knew you had it in you," or "Bet you feel better about yourself, don't you?" simply turns the child off. Just saying what you mean — simply and concisely — is the best formula for success.

NAME CHANGES AND IDENTITY

Whether or not name changes should be made as part of the adoption process is an issue that most adoptive parents and children face. A person's identity is linked, in great part, to his first name. It may have special significance to either the name holder or the name giver. It is one of the first sounds a child learns to recognize, and it helps to shape his concept of self. There is no hard and fast rule that applies to name changes; each case for each child warrants its own evaluation.

We generally suggest that the adoptive parents refrain from being the ones to initiate the name change. Even though they may wish to pass on a name they've always fantasized about, the psychosocial elements may be more complicated. In the case of an infant, of course, the name issue is less significant. But with an older child, the complications may be great.

Loss issues are directly related to abuse, neglect, multiple moves, and adoption, and to add the loss of one's name may be an unnecessary disruption. It is therefore critical that older children and adolescents make their own decision about whether or not to change their names. If a child chooses to do so, there is no reason for parents to deny the request. He may be attempting to fulfill a specific need, such as leaving a part of his past behind or shedding the connection to a birth parent whose name he shares.

Will had been known as Little Will in his birth family because he was named after his father. Once the child was permanently away from the man who both named him and abused him, he wanted to break the connection completely. To continue to be an extension of his birth father was not desirable in any way, and he wanted to make a clean transition into his new family. He made this wish clear to his adoptive parents, who allowed him to select another name. While it was awkward at first for him to suddenly become David, the entire family eventually adjusted to his new identity.

The change of a last name at the time of adoption is the rule rather than the exception. Some families choose to incorporate the last name as a new middle name for the child. In some cases, an adolescent may prefer to keep his birth surname for a variety of reasons: convenience, fear that people won't be able to find him, resistance to joining the new family, and maintenance of his identity. Under such circumstances, we encourage parents to respect the feelings of the child and to work out a decision that makes sense in their specific situation.

The issues that affect the family in the early phases of adoption can set the stage for the eventual outcome of the placement. Families who have shored up their support systems, maintained their sense of humor, and presented a united front invariably fare the best.

Wise parents keep sight of the fact that change is often a long, slow process. The results they seek may take years to be realized, but small victories can be celebrated along the way.

Keeping fun in the family is vital to the success of any adoption. In many cases, parents become so involved in managing their child's special needs that they forget to manage the child himself. Frequent breaks from worry and difficult issues can prove to be therapeutic for all. Forget the household chores for an afternoon and spend a few hours in the park playing ball with your child. Forget your commitment to healthy eating and teach him how to bake your grandmother's sugar cookies. Watch a movie together, play a game of cards, take turns reading aloud from a book you'll all enjoy. These family activities can help weave the first precious strands of attachment between you and your new child.

NINE

SIBLINGS

The Old, the New, the Feelings!

It is estimated that 65 to 85 percent of children entering the foster-care system have at least one sibling. Thirty percent of children in foster care have four siblings or more. It is estimated that 75 percent of siblings end up apart when they enter foster care.[1] This sometimes happens by design because the children cannot live together safely, but more often it occurs as the result of bureaucratic incompetence. Most children adopted internationally also lose siblings — either brothers and sisters or orphanage mates who have become as close as biological siblings.

During a discussion about sibling placement, a worker commented to an associate that her entire caseload of children waiting for adoption was comprised of only children. Since a majority of the children in foster care have siblings, her coworker pointed out that it was statistically improbable for her caseload of thirty to be made up exclusively of only children. After doing some further investigating, she called her associate to apologize.

"You were right," she said. "One hundred percent of the kids on my caseload have brothers or sisters — I just didn't know it."

How could this be? It's easy. Siblings often have different last names. Some are still living with the birth mother; some are in custody in another county or state; some are half siblings living with relatives on the other side of the family; some come into care at a later date and aren't on each other's fact sheets; some are even in the same large agency and assigned to a different worker. Anyone who is working with or adopting a child in the system should investigate sibling ties. Even if it is unrealistic to place siblings together, their importance to one another should not be underestimated.

Sisters and brothers are an important part of any family. Who better to share with, fight with, tattle on, confide in, torment, and protect? Our siblings share our experiences—both the good times and the bad. Bonds between siblings can be incredibly strong and resilient since they are the longest relationships we experience. Even if parents or caretakers are neglectful or abusive, siblings often learn to lean on one another for support. In the traumatic life of a child removed from his birth family, brothers and sisters can validate both the horrors and the good times for each other. Older siblings, in particular, can help younger ones better understand past abuse and losses.

> Luke, a teenager with a reputation for being emotionally unstable, rocked his younger sister and comforted her as she cried for her deceased birth mom. As he assured her that "Mom would want us to love our adoptive family," his physical and verbal caresses soothed her in a way that hundreds of hours of therapy never could.

The words, touches, glances, jokes, and laughter that only family members understand should not be stolen from these children who have already lost so much. They can often rely on one another as important anchors in a sea of losses, and their ties should be preserved whenever possible. Adoption, foster care, and the child welfare system are built upon the belief that children belong in families. While money, time, and energy are rightly spent on the ideals of family reunification, more time and energy should be exerted to maintain sibling ties in foster and adoptive homes. Agencies need to affirm that siblings are best served by being placed together in foster care and adoptive homes. Only in rare situations does it benefit a child to be separated from siblings as well as from parents.

Even though placement together is not always possible, it should always be considered. Despite all the roadblocks faced when trying to keep these children together — despite the complicated issues faced by each child in the sibling group — it must be recognized that they have a fundamental need for a stable, loving, and permanent home together, if possible. They have survived the multiple losses of birth mom, birth dad, home, pets, school, innocence, safety, relatives, and friends. The loss of their brothers and sisters need not be added to the list.

In spite of this fact, siblings are often separated when they are adopted. Separation frequently occurs because of the children's sexual or aggressive involvement with one another. While separation initially appears to be a sensible solution, it does nothing to address the heart of the problem. Siblings engage in abusive or sexual behavior not because they are siblings but because they themselves have experienced such abuse by others. Separating them will end their destructive behaviors with each other but will not prevent them from seeking substitute victims. A prospective adoptive family should first determine if an effective course of treatment has been provided for the children. With appropriate treatment, there is great likelihood that an abusive child can be placed successfully with his siblings.

This is not intended to make light of a very serious dynamic. No one wants children to be hurt. If the abusive child has not received treatment for his behaviors, placing him anywhere will be risky, whether he is separated from siblings or not.

Another issue often cited as grounds for separating siblings is the case of the "parenting child." In many cases, the eldest child has assumed responsibilities in the birth family that far exceed what would be considered age appropriate. While some professionals may think that it is best to relieve the parenting child of such extreme responsibility by separating him from his brothers and sisters, it seldom works. It does, however, succeed in driving the parenting needs of the child underground. Deprived of the task of actively parenting his younger siblings, the child may become worried, anxious, and often angry.

We believe that the parenting child can be placed with his siblings if the issue of trust is addressed from the start. Trust of the new adoptive parents is essential if such a child is to express a willingness to turn over the reins of parenting. Since his instinct is to undermine parental authority and demand loyalty from younger siblings, it is critical for new parents to respect his past and assure him that it's okay to be a kid.

> Allison, age sixteen, was the eldest in a family of four children adopted by first-time parents. She constantly directed and corrected her younger siblings, daring her new mom with dagger-like glares to intervene. Her mom simply smiled and said, "I'm so glad you like to be Mom, because I'm new at this. But whenever you want to, feel free to be a kid yourself, and I'll take over as the mom." Within six weeks, Allison was through being a parent and settled comfortably into her new home.

Many families wonder if they will be viewed as suitable for, or capable of, adopting a sibling group. Although agencies and social workers frequently think that some sibling groups are too big for a single family, this is not necessarily true. While some families see themselves as complete with one or two children, others can parent a dozen at a time and still have room for more.

A family with six adopted children expanded to accommodate a sibling group of four. Now a family of ten children, they were advised by other parents who had adopted sibling groups to expect chaos at first. Armed with this information, they waited for mass confusion. But it never came. The couple, already used to parenting six children, discovered that routine chores—such as preparing school lunches, coordinating bath times, and scheduling appointments and activities—were not much different for ten. "You throw more potatoes in the pot and do a few extra loads of wash. No problem," was their assessment of the domestic front.

What constitutes a large family to one person seems average to another. Parents should have the opportunity to work with agencies to determine what size group is too large for their particular family to handle.

Providing a home for a sibling group can open up a family in new and exciting ways. By enabling the children to experience fewer losses and keep their family and memories more intact, the parents also help the siblings move into their adoptive family with greater ease. The message the parents send to each child is, *Your birth ties are important and should be preserved. Your birth family is as valuable to us as it is to you, and you deserve to have contact with them. You are loved by and precious to us, and so is your birth family.* In return, a sibling group often expresses a unique dimension of loyalty to the parents who adopted "all of us."[2]

CREATIVE COPING STRATEGIES

The first six months for a family with a new sibling group are usually exciting, exhausting, and confusing. Issues of logistics and finances tend to coexist with more mundane concerns such as "How many hot dogs do they eat?" "How often do I need to do laundry?" and "Who wets the bed?" Add to these questions the details of coordinating school registrations, scheduling dental appointments, and juggling visits with social workers and sessions with therapists, and you've got a lively household on your hands. Rather than struggle stoically to rise to every challenge, parents must understand that it is perfectly acceptable to reach out for support and help.

The children's former foster parents are an excellent resource since they usually know the siblings well and can offer safe respite for weary adoptive parents. Agencies need to recognize the importance of open relationships between foster and adoptive parents and support them so the children can prosper.

Establishing a relationship with a "buddy family" who has already adopted a sibling group is another good form of support. Having been through it themselves, they can share their firsthand knowledge with the new parents. Their tips and suggestions — even their recipes for casseroles that feed a small army — can be invaluable, particularly when the road seems so unendingly long and the rewards so painfully insignificant.

During the early adoption period, agencies should strive to be extra supportive of the parents who adopt sibling groups. A daily telephone call from the agency can alleviate much pressure and enable simple situations to be handled and resolved as soon as they arise. Since the social workers know the children better than the adoptive parents do at this point, they can easily answer questions such as, "Is Barry really allergic to green beans?" "Can Sally be allowed to climb a tree?" and "Did Joey really get kidnapped when he was three?" By being available to provide information to parents when they need it, the agencies can help facilitate the transition to a unified family.

Agency staff can also assist the family by visiting from time to time. A helpful attitude goes a long way in demonstrating concern for families, and frequent contacts enhance the sentiments. When a warm, positive relationship is established—enabling parents to feel comfortable sharing their concerns and difficulties—an agency staff person is ideally positioned to direct them to appropriate services.

Support from the community, relatives, and friends is critical for the new family. A kid shower or welcome party sponsored by any of these groups can significantly alleviate the financial stress of a houseful of new children. Ideally, gifts should be practical: clothes hangers, towels, sheets, and dishes. Jumbo-size packages of food, toilet paper, toothpaste, and detergent are extremely beneficial, and we can't imagine anyone not appreciating the thoughtfulness of a wholesale grocery membership, a family portrait, or a night at the movies for the entire group. Virtually any assistance during the early adjustment phase will help the family shift into their new roles far more easily.

The start-up costs of buying beds, a freezer, large cooking pots, and any other items needed to accommodate the sibling group can be extensive. Parents should look into the resources available from agencies to assist families who adopt several children. In addition, parents can approach community groups such as churches and fraternal organizations to help out with initial supplies.

When parents assume the responsibility of adopting several children, the integration of these new family members consumes a great deal of time and energy. Spouses frequently drift apart as their focus on the children reduces their time together. Several couples we know have managed to work around this problem by establishing some foolproof patterns guaranteed to give them time alone together:

- Get up a half hour earlier than the children and enjoy a leisurely cup of coffee or tea together. While it may seem difficult to reset your body clock at first, the quiet time alone will far outweigh the loss of a little sleep.

- Announce to the children that you're going to spend the day cleaning out the garage. We can just about promise that they'll disappear like snowflakes in July. Once they've fled the distasteful task, you'll find yourselves alone to enjoy each other's company. (And if this plan doesn't work, at least you'll gain a spotless place to park your car.)

- Add an hour or two to a planned event. For example, if you hire a babysitter so you can attend an adoptive parents' support group meeting, leave a bit early and go out for dinner. (We know one couple who did this and decided to get take-out food because it was so quiet and peaceful in the car. They fell asleep and missed the meeting, but the refreshing nap was worth it.)

Most parents report to us that the rewards of adopting a sibling group far outweigh the costs. While they never refer to the experience as easy, they use words like wonderful, exciting, miraculous, and—you guessed it—exhausting. But with their newfound weariness comes a newfound satisfaction as they look at their new family and can't imagine living without them.

Adopting a sibling group is an adventure. And like all adventures, there are peaceful times, dangerous times, exciting times, and times when you feel there will be no tomorrow. Most assuredly, this is not a journey for the faint of heart. But parents who respond favorably to variety, rewards, challenges, and accomplishments may find that this is the road for them.

WHEN SEPARATION IS UNAVOIDABLE

Sometimes two or three families will adopt members of a sibling group, pledging to preserve the birth family ties. While this type of arrangement is not uncommon, we rarely see it work on a long-term basis. In most cases, the families consider two or three visits a year to be adequate. Based on a child's thinking and development, however, it is clear that two or three visits a month is more appropriate if ties are to be preserved.

Children who meet infrequently with their siblings have little time to deal with the past issues they share, let alone the excitement that such visits cause. Contrary to the initial intention, the occasional visits usually leave the children with a deeper sense of loss. In addition, they may feel unresolved anger toward the adoptive parents, whom they perceive as destroyers of their family ties.

When siblings are placed in separate adoptive homes, it is imperative for the new parents to be sensitive to the loss that their child is experiencing. Just because he doesn't talk about his missing sister doesn't mean that he has forgotten her or no longer cares. His parents should gently encourage him to acknowledge her by calling, writing, or e-mailing, if possible, or simply by talking about her if contact is unrealistic. In this way, the parents can help the child face his feelings and begin to resolve the issue of separation. They will provide great help if they can express empathy, support, and understanding for his sense of loss, abandonment, and grief.

Sometimes these feelings are further complicated when prospective parents have two siblings placed in their home, only to return one child to the agency and adopt the other. The remaining child is likely to blame the adoptive parents for the sudden separation, regardless of the facts of the situation. He won't view the sibling as the one responsible because he perceives adults as the ones in control.

An adult adoptee who was adopted at the age of five while his eight-year-old brother was returned to the agency said, "The day my brother left was the day they stopped being my parents. I lived with them for thirteen more years, but as soon as I turned eighteen, I was out the door. If they couldn't love my brother, they couldn't really love me." Twenty years later, he still has had no contact with his adoptive parents. Sadder still, he has not managed to locate his brother.

Another situation that is difficult for a child to accept is to be adopted while his siblings remain with the birth parents or are adopted by relatives. As he deals with the hurt of family rejection and tries to comprehend it, his adoptive parents must strive to be empathetic. Statements like, "I don't understand why your grandmother took your sister and not you because I sure think you're a special kid," can help soothe his pain. Although facing the situation honestly will not always provide answers, it can help validate a child's feelings of confusion and provide a cushion of understanding and love.

When discussing the issue of siblings in adoption, it is also important to consider the effect that adoption has on the birth children of families who take in a troubled child. Just as the new child's special needs take their toll on the parents' energies, occupations, plans, and finances, so do they affect the emotional atmosphere of the entire household. Birth children often resent losing their parents' attention to an adopted child and feel cheated. Sadly, their feelings are frequently justified. They may have to lock their bedroom doors to prevent theft and/or destruction. They may fear physical or sexual victimization, and the parents must take preventive measures to ensure their safety.

If the child entering the home has a history of sexual abuse, it is imperative that parents help their other children understand the behaviors associated with such a problem. If the birth children are not old enough or capable enough to comprehend the situation, parents must take practical precautionary measures. Baby monitors, separate bedrooms, off-limit rules for bedrooms, and alarms on doors are solutions that should be considered to enable everyone in the household to sleep safely and soundly.

If the new child has special developmental or medical needs, parents should prepare the other children in the home by offering straightforward, age-appropriate information regarding his condition. The children need to know that they are not responsible for the well-being of their new sibling and that the parents will take care of everything. If the adopted child has a terminal illness, the prognosis should be presented openly and honestly. Some children fear they might catch the disease or disability, so the issue should be clarified to provide reassurance.

Adoption always changes the dynamics of the family. Children who are already part of the family must make room both emotionally and physically for the new child. There is great likelihood that their behaviors will change, and parents must remember to be patient and not to overreact when temporary shifts occur in grades and attitudes.

Oftentimes, the "old" siblings resent the time and money spent on the "new" sibling. And if the adopted child has behavioral problems, the negative feelings are intensified. Adolescents in the family may be embarrassed by the ongoing troubles created by the disturbed child. If they attend the same school, the discomfort will reach beyond the home and further complicate the relationship.

While the birth children may need supportive therapy, they often resent having to participate because of someone else's problems.

A recent letter written by a birth child, who is now the sibling of a difficult adopted child, reads:

Dear Betsy,

    I can't believe Mom and Dad ever adopted you.
They already had five of us and did not need you. Why
couldn't they be happy with us? What did we do to
deserve you? You've made my life a living hell. My friends
won't come over because of you.

    I have to lock up my room because you steal. Mom
and Dad are mad every day.

    Every day at school you cause trouble, and kids say
"Is that your sister?" I wish I never met you. I can hardly
wait to be eighteen so I can leave and never see you
again.

    You make me sick. I'll never adopt or even be a dad
because I might get stuck with a kid like you. I hope
you get married fast so we don't have the same name
anymore.

I HATE YOU,
Ben

Ben's feelings are not unusual and must be validated by his parents if he is to succeed in moving beyond them. He, and other children in his situation, should not be expected to understand and accept their new sibling's negative behaviors. Their protestations that "It's not my problem" are close to accurate. Their parents made the decision to adopt the difficult sibling, and it is not fair for parents to expect their other children to coparent that child. Just as the adopted child has experienced loss, so have the other children in the family. They may have lost a peaceful home, happy parents, a safe environment, and a trusting atmosphere.

In such cases, some children find it helpful to keep a journal, write letters, or rant into a tape machine. A support group, where both biological and adopted children who are relatively problem free get together with others who share similar situations, can also be beneficial. They are relieved to discover that their intense feelings are not unique to them. They learn that a comfortable life with a disturbed child is hard to come by. They can feel less guilty about their anger and hatred and be encouraged to let go of it.

POSSIBILITIES

Not all birth children have such a hard time accepting their new siblings. Most families who adopt sibling groups are glad they did. They look back and can't imagine their children growing up apart. The new siblings, once integrated into the family, seem so connected to each other and to their birth siblings that it is impossible to believe they could grow up separated from each other.

> Don, age ten, always said he hated his nine-year-old sister, Ellen. He insisted he didn't want to live with her and his two other siblings, six and five, but they were placed together anyway. Shortly into the placement, Mom and the younger children left for a short trip. Ellen got the flu, and Dad was in charge. "It was remarkable," the dad said. "Don wouldn't leave Ellen's side for a moment. He made sure she was covered with a blanket, got her food, and hovered over her. He really loves her. I can't imagine them growing up without each other."

Many workers who do searches in agency records for adult adoptees report that most who were adopted as older children search not for their birth parents but for their siblings. As adults, they understand why they were removed from abusive parents but find it incomprehensible that they lost their beloved brother or sister. The public needs only to watch reunions on television shows to see the joy siblings show as they are reunited after thirty, forty, or even fifty years. Of course, if we begin to place more children together, they won't have to search for each other — they'll all grow up together in the same home.

Most birth children love their adopted siblings. Often an older adopted child becomes a brother or sister before becoming a son or daughter. Even if there are difficulties, the children learn to love and bond as they become one family. In many instances, birth children become very defensive of their new siblings. Although they may feel justified in complaining about problems, outside parties had better not criticize! Birth children often become the adopted child's support person after the parents pass away, especially if the adopted sibling has significant problems throughout his life.

Like all families, siblings—adopted and/or birth—have arguments and problems, but in the long run, they are there for each other. After all, without siblings, our children would have no aunts, uncles, or cousins. The links, love, and memories forged by siblings as children ease many a difficult path for them as adults.

TEN

GIVING YOUR CHILD A HISTORY

Regina's Bag of Tricks

We often hear parents, social workers, and therapists discuss helping a child get ready to talk about his past, but we seldom see much work being done to facilitate the process. We can't help but wonder precisely what one does to help a child get ready to process the fact that his birth mother died or that his birth father sexually molested him. We know of one foster mother who was told by the agency that placed her twelve-year-old foster daughter that the child was not ready to know that she is biracial!

The best time to talk about the past and to prepare for the future is now. Obviously, the day after a child learns that the state has obtained permanent custody and he won't see his birth mother again is not a good time to introduce him to an adoptive family. Common sense must prevail, but for the most part, directness is the best policy.

The procrastination that we often witness seems to be due more to the adult's discomfort with the issues than the child's ability to deal with them.

An adoption worker recently described a child to a couple and their social worker. "Of course," she said, "Raina won't be ready for adoption for six months." When questioned about what was being done to get the child "ready," she drew a blank. She just knew that someone somewhere needed six months.

Children are not loaves of bread waiting to rise. If a person intends to help them understand their past and move on to their future, something has to be done—and the best time to start is usually the present.

Ideally, the work should be done prior to adoption, but it's never too late to start. In fact, it is wise to redo the work over time as a child's developmental, emotional, and cognitive abilities evolve. A parent's response to the question, "Where do babies come from?" would differ greatly if asked by a two-year-old or a sixteen-year-old. The same is true when discussing adoption, the child's past, and his resulting emotions.

Another consideration is that many older children who are adopted have special learning needs. While such children are quick to be labeled developmentally handicapped in the classroom, we often forget that the same disabilities affect their emotional maturity. Simply discussing issues across a desk does not always work. These children may need varying tactile and experiential tools to help them comprehend the confusing parts. The information must often be repeated in different ways, at different levels, and at different times. Once is seldom enough.

All of us spend at least some time wondering who we are and why we are. For a child who has faced many moves and a chaotic life, these are difficult questions to answer. But as elusive as the answers may be, they are vital if the child is to mature into a functional adult. Whether it is a parent, social worker, teacher, friend, or therapist who is working with the child, the techniques that we will present can be used to help the child understand and integrate his past.

For the sake of simplicity, we will refer to these people as "helpers." While it is often most effective if the tasks we suggest are accomplished by a trained professional, that solution is not always practical. So whomever you are—whatever your relationship to the child—we wish you much success in helping the kid you care about.

Corrective information is essential to any helper since without it, he or she cannot help the child resolve the right things.

Review pages 92–97 in chapter 6 for suggestions on how to gather as much information as possible about your adopted child. Once armed with adequate information, the helper can then try various techniques to assist the child in dealing with his past.

THE TIMELINE

Take a sheet of graph paper and cut it horizontally. Tape it together to create a long strip of paper. Make sure there are enough squares so that one square represents one month of a child's life—from birth to age twenty-five or so. (Three hundred squares will do nicely.) This will help dispel the eighteen-and-you're-out mind-set that most foster children have.

Have the child select a color for each of his placements. If, for example, he was with his birth mother for four years and chooses blue to represent the birth home, he colors forty-eight squares blue. If he was removed and returned, he uses the same color each time he returned. Underneath the line, the child or the helper writes who lived there, why the child moved, and any other available information. Continue coloring and writing notes up through the present placement.

Even adults, when confronted with a colorful depiction of the child's moves, will sometimes make comments like, "I knew he moved twelve times, but now I can see what it means." Also, many adoptive families find new hope when they see how long a child's life was compared to his life with them. As one adoptive mom said, "A year with us seemed like forever, but when I see the other twelve, I realize how little time we've actually been working with him. He's come a long way."

Children are sometimes amazed by this visual depiction.

Barbara, age sixteen, was adopted when she was eight. She had lived in an extremely abusive birth home for four years, and her behavior as a teen was terrible. After making the timeline, she sat back and said, "I've lived here longer than anywhere. I don't need to act like them anymore," she said, pointing to the time she spent with her birth parents. "I need to act like them," she said, indicating the ninety-six squares that represented the time with her new family. A quick fix? Not quite, but it was a way for Barbara to start a new way of thinking.

Another benefit of the timeline is that it provides a way for children to begin to sort out their anger. In many cases, the anger they feel toward their neglectful or abusive birth parents is imposed on their adoptive parents. The helper can direct the child to place one hand on the birth home time and the other hand on the adoptive home time. A discussion about protective love and a reminder that the adoptive parents didn't even know the child when the abuse occurred can have significant results.

The timeline can be used as an ongoing ritual, taken out periodically so the child can color in more time with the adoptive family. It provides both a continuing opportunity to discuss the past and an affirmation of the permanency with the current family.

> Claire was adopted from a Russian orphanage when she was ten months old. At age seven, she still feared being returned. Developing a timeline with her helped her understand the concept of permanency and accept the reality that she was not leaving her adoptive family for any reason.

PHOTOGRAPHS

Photos are vital to all of us. If we knew we had only a few minutes to snatch possessions before a fire, most of us would include family snapshots—an irreplaceable reminder of our past.

Since adopted children seldom have pictures of themselves at an early age, they may have trouble conceptualizing themselves as infants or toddlers. As a result, they sometimes form faulty images of their past.

> Monica, a pretty ten-year-old when she was adopted, was convinced that she had been an ugly baby. She would patiently explain to the adults in her life that a mom would be mean only to an ugly baby, and since her birth mother abused and neglected her, it was proof that she was—and still is—an unfortunate-looking creature. This belief was attacking her self-esteem.
>
> Her helper managed to find a worker at the very first agency that handled her birth mother's case. The worker, unable to meet Monica because of the geographic distance, spent forty-five minutes on the telephone describing what a beautiful baby she was. She had seen her as a newborn in the hospital and had worked with her birth mother for a

year. The expression on Monica's face — as well as the resulting changes in her belief system — were well worth the price of a telephone call. The same worker was able to track down Monica's first foster parents, now retired, and find an early — and quite adorable — photo.

This visual image, combined with the auditory picture painted by the worker, helped Monica move away from her position of self-blame for her early neglect to justifiable anger at the birth mom who failed to care for her. For the first time in her life, she began to believe that the abuse was not her fault.

Most children in the system have no photographs, but some detective work can often uncover at least a few. Any helper who has witnessed the delight of a child who has been given a photo of himself at an earlier age, his birth mother, a sibling, a pet, a former house, or any significant person or event knows that the effort expended in tracking down that photo was worthwhile. For internationally adopted children, photos of foster parents or orphanage workers can be very helpful. If a child chooses not to accept a picture of someone from his past, his feelings should be respected. It can always be tucked away safely in case he wants it later.

When gathering photographs, the best advice is to start at the beginning. Some hospitals keep a newborn picture in the child's file. Schools sometimes have a photo of the child stapled to his folder. Birth relatives can sometimes be contacted through an agency and may be willing to exchange baby pictures for a current snapshot. Social services agencies may have photos of a child in their records. Sometimes these are merely shots of bruises or scars documented for the court. With the aid of a therapist, it may benefit the child to confront his injuries.

Modern technology has come to the rescue of a photo problem. If a hospital, school, agency, or family member doesn't want to share a picture because it's the only one, a high-quality color copy can be made. Several smaller photos can even be taped together on to a sheet of paper and a single copy generated. Or a camera can be used to take a picture of the original photo, often with excellent results. A local camera buff can help you, or you can set it up yourself with a little effort. (Use good lighting, minimize the glare, and get as close as possible.)

Many helpers fear, often justifiably, giving a child the only copy of a treasured photo. Such a picture can be torn to shreds in a rage, destroyed by another child to get even, or lost in the shuffle of a move. A color copy kept by a responsible person will ensure that the only photograph of a birth mom is not lost.

Conversely, the child can be given the copy, and the original stashed away for safekeeping. More often than not, the child—instead of destroying the photo—kisses it, fondles it, or sleeps with it under his pillow.

There is no reason why a child should not have, at the very least, current photos of his life. If he is getting ready to be adopted, the process must include recent photos of himself, his foster home and family, school, and friends. Turning a camera over to a child to capture what he deems to be important can be very revealing. (If a child is not responsible enough to handle a good camera, he can be given a disposable one, available at most discount and drug stores.)

> Matthew, age thirteen, photographed the refrigerator in his foster home—both open and closed. He even took close-ups of the ketchup bottle to let his new parents know that "I eat just about everything with ketchup." Food was obviously a primary issue to this growing teen.

Adoptive parents, too, can use photos to help welcome a new child. A family album—including snapshots of the family members, their home, church, school, pets, and activities—can be presented to the child by way of introduction. It can even be designed with the new child's interests in mind—focusing on the family cars and basketball backboard for a teenage boy, the swing set and fish tank for a young child, and the neighborhood park and junior high for a school-age child.

THE LIFE BOOK

This is perhaps the most important, least implemented, and seldom understood tool available to help a child. The life book is a process, not a finished product—an autobiography that incorporates the discovery and discussion of a child's life experiences. It can be created on videotape, audiotape, or the most common form — paper. The easiest system is a three-ring binder with plastic sleeves to protect the pages. This allows for flexibility, enabling the child to make chronological additions as new information becomes available. Colored paper, markers, crayons, stickers, wrapping paper, and the child's artwork can all be used to decorate the book.

Like all autobiographies, a child's life book should start at the beginning. The title page should include a current photo of the child and whatever title he chooses. "Ty's Life Story," "The Stupendous Ty," "All About Ty," and "The Life and Times of Ty" are examples of titles he might select.

Page two could feature a copy of the original birth certificate or, if it is unavailable, any birth information the helper might have. A chart available at any library or on the Internet can provide the relevant day of the week. This is a good place to put a baby picture of the child too, but in its absence, a photo of the hospital where the child was born can suffice.

Don't make the mistake of cutting out a photo of another baby from a magazine and telling the child it's him. Small children would probably believe you at first but would ultimately become confused. An illustration of a baby from a coloring book or a line drawing works much better, as it is obviously not this child. The birth information can be entered by the child, or younger ones can listen while the helper recites the facts and writes them down.

After entering the birth information, the time is right to discuss with him what you know about his mother and father. As the helper, it is your responsibility to provide all the facts you can. Help the child compute the time that has gone by, since children freeze people at the time of separation. If a mother was sixteen when the child was born and twenty when he was taken away from her, help him figure out how old she is now that he is eight. Compare this information to other people that the child knows.

For example, if you have a sixteen-year-old neighbor, ask the child what kind of mom he thinks she would be. Talk about the kind of parenting skills his birth mom had and encourage him to recall positive memories of her. Ask questions like "Was she funny?" "What sorts of things did you like to do with her?" "Could she sing?" This allows him to hold on to good thoughts about her, since Department of Social Services records usually contain only negative information.

The positive memories must be balanced by a discussion of problems in the birth home. While most children will, in time, talk about these issues, many people think it's cruel to bring up anything negative. But allowing a child to believe that everything was wonderful when he lived there only contributes to feelings of being "kidnapped" by his adoptive parents.

If his life book addresses only the good aspects of the birth environment—and the child clearly remembers hunger, anger, and confusion—no purpose is served for him.

Curtis, age thirteen, spent two years in residential treatment from the ages of eight to ten. His therapist there spent most of the time trying to dispel the boy's fantasies about his past. His fantasies were about police chases, drug busts, and serving as the lookout during drug buys. He described his birth mother as the drug queen of the rural county where he lived.

After Curtis was adopted and his life book begun, his helper uncovered old newspaper articles that confirmed everything the child had said about his early life. At Curtis's request, information about his birth mother's drug involvement was added to his book. His new therapist felt it was harsh to include this information, but Curtis believed it was an important element of understanding his past. After all, if there were no problems in his birth home, he never would have been adopted.

A child's life book needs to include birth siblings, as well: their names, birth dates, and where they are living. Photographs of brothers and sisters are a plus. Additional features might be lists or pictures of likes and dislikes, sports activities, and hobbies—and, of course, important memories such as moves, foster families, and court actions. Encourage the child to draw pictures of people and things he remembers. Since many hurt children come from transracial, multiracial, and interracial backgrounds, check out art and teacher supply stores for crayons in multiple skin, hair, and eye tones. Do not lose sight of the fact that not everyone in his life may be the same race as he is.

The best life books are the ones that are made with the child's participation. If he refuses to comply or is too young to get involved, the book can be prepared for him. In reality, the only bad life book is the one that's never made. If a child comes to you with an existing life book, it should be reviewed often, talked about, and readily available for updates. It should not be shared indiscriminately—for example, at show-and-tell—but should be respected as an important part of the child's world. A comprehensive guide to the creation of a life book can be obtained for a minimal fee from the Three Rivers Adoption Council. (See the "Resources" section at the end of this book.)

CARDS, LETTERS, AND NOTES

Written correspondence is a great tool for communicating with children. Since national card makers do not generally offer adoption cards beyond congratulations and announcements geared to infants, helpers need to use a bit of imagination. A best-wishes-in-your-new-home card could be sent by a former foster parent to a child in a new adoptive home. A congratulations-on-your-achievement card could be an appropriate message for a child in residential treatment who made it out of a locked cottage into an open one. Postcards and thinking-of-you greeting cards could be sent to a child between visits to enrich the time spent apart.

Let's face it—everyone likes to get mail, and most of the children we're talking about get none at all. Many card companies today have a special line designed for parents to send to their children—complimenting them on a clean room, a good report card, or just being a fun kid—that are wonderfully appropriate for hurt children. Written communication provides kids with keepsakes, perhaps for the first time in their lives, creating for them a past to hold on to as they move into their future.

THE WATER EXERCISE

To perform this exercise that enables a child to integrate the past with the present, you'll need a large pitcher, several glasses in varying sizes, and water. This exercise has been used successfully with children from age five to seventeen and requires knowledge of the child's history.

The conversation between the helper and the child goes something like this:

HELPER: This water pitcher represents you at birth, Jon. What's inside?

CHILD: (Peering inside) Nothing.

HELPER: That's right. We are all born needing food, clothing, water, love, and lots more. Now, when you were born, you went home from the hospital with your birth mom, right?

CHILD: Right.

HELPER: And you lived with her for five years. That's a long time. (The helper chooses a large glass—the size of the glass represents the quantity of time, not the quality of time—and fills it with water.) Your mom gave you food, water, and changed your diapers—she gave you all she could. (She dumps the glass into the pitcher.) But are all of your needs met? Are you full? (She indicates the partially filled pitcher.)

CHILD: No.

HELPER: You're not full because she couldn't keep you safe (or feed you enough or whatever is appropriate). So you went to the Smiths and stayed there for two months. (The helper selects a smaller glass and fills it with water.) You left because you scribbled with a magic marker on their brand-new siding. They gave you all they could. (She indicates the full glass and dumps it into the pitcher.) Now, which part is the Smiths and which part is your birth mom?

CHILD: (Inevitably, the child looks into the pitcher and registers amazement.)

HELPER: You can't tell because it's all mixed up inside of you. (She continues to fill glasses and add water to represent each subsequent placement—talking about the length of time the child spent in each home and discussing the positive and negative aspects of each move. It is important that she does not fill the pitcher completely. Finally, she puts the pitcher under the faucet.) Your adoptive parents don't want you to forget any of these people. Your new parents love you, and they know that all these different people made you who you are. They want to add to this and fill you up with love so you have enough to fill you and more for everyone you care about. (She then lets the pitcher overflow.)

This exercise has been effective in many situations. Prior to adoption, it can help a child understand why adoption is a good solution for him. Afterward, it can relieve anxieties that falsely link acceptance of the adoptive family with rejection of every other family the child has known.

FAMILY TREES

Family trees of both the birth family and the adoptive family can help a child sort people out and gain perspective on his past and present. Each individual's name, date of birth, and relationship to the child should be included. Remember, all young children have difficulty understanding that Grandpa is Dad's dad. To the child separated from his birth family and entering a new one, the confusion is greater still. To assist him in his comprehension of who's who, make relevant notations under each family member's name on the tree. For example: Bruce Jones—your uncle, your birth mom's brother; Tom Smith—your grandfather, your adopted mom's dad.

THE SIBLING GAME

Ideally suited to help separated siblings bond before being placed together in an adoptive home, this game works equally well to help any children begin to fit into a new home.

We'll use the example of a group of four children. The first child rolls a die. A 1 requires him to answer a question about the oldest sibling, a 2 relates to the second-oldest child, and on down the line. A 5 requires an answer to a general question, and a 6 is a free point. The first person to reach twenty points wins the game.

Examples of sibling questions are:

- What color eyes does _____ have?
- What grade is _____ in?
- How old is _____?
- Name something that you and _____ both like to do.
- Tell me something I don't know about _____.

Examples of general questions are:

- What's the difference between foster care and adoption?
- What's your birth mom's name?
- What's your social worker's name?
- What's the best dinner your birth mom ever made?

We have played this game successfully several times with the same group of siblings. The first time we played, the oldest child, age ten, commented, "I knew I got two years older since we left Mom, but I never knew my brothers and sisters did too." The sibling game helped the children reconnect to one another and review their history.[1]

The game can also be played after adoption with new siblings to facilitate bonding. Questions about the new child and existing family members can help everyone grasp just how much knowledge, history, and experience there is waiting to be shared among them.

JUST TALKING

Some helpers make the mistake of thinking, *He never talks about the past . . . his birth mom . . . his sister . . . so they must not matter to him.* This belief is seldom true since children think about these people nearly all the time. They simply have no way to verbalize, organize, or test the truth of their memories and feelings. As a result, their thoughts slip into negative actions, depression, or unresolved feelings. Once a helper opens up topics of the past, a child's fears, beliefs, and sadness have a chance to be released.

DEALING WITH THE HOLIDAYS

Holidays can often generate feelings of tension, loneliness, grief, and sadness for a hurt child and his new family. Many adoptive families experience the holiday horrors of November and December instead of the holiday cheer. It is interesting to note that children's records reveal that moves from one home to another frequently occurred during these stress-filled periods.

The holidays are especially difficult for those who have experienced a major loss. They tend to sink into bouts of depression, reflection, and mourning as they grieve for "what could have been." So, too, do hurt children often experience extreme sadness during a season that's meant to be festive. They may miss birth parents, foster parents, siblings, or other meaningful people. The gifts they receive — no matter how grand — cannot make up for their loss. It is for this very reason that a longed-for toy bestowed during the holidays is often smashed to pieces by the new year.

A foster mom asked her eleven-year-old foster daughter to list the things she wanted for Christmas. The child dutifully wrote:

1. I want my mom to stop doing drugs.
2. I want to go home.
3. I want to live with my brother.
4. A doll.

"Already," the mother lamented, "I can't give her what she wants most."

The best way to ease a child's pain during the holidays is to acknowledge his past. Families can use Advent wreaths, Hanukkah candles, or Kwanza candles to light every night for the people their child misses. They can also share feelings about their own relatives who have passed on or moved away — reinforcing for their child that his emotions are perfectly justified.

One family we know provided a small Christmas tree just for their adopted daughter. Every day, she made a paper ornament that bore the name of someone she missed. The jumble of names — birth parents, foster parents, therapists, social workers, friends from her residential treatment center — comprised the story of her life and losses.

Food is another important component of holiday traditions, and the absence of a particular treat can make a child's holiday seem strange.

Over the course of five years, Jane lived in four foster homes, two residential treatment centers, and a group home. Finally settled into an adoptive home at the age of fifteen, she made this sad revelation to her new family.

"When I lived at home, my grandma always came for Christmas. It was the safest time for me because no one ever abused me when she was there. On Christmas morning, she always made orange muffins—when I woke up and smelled them, I knew Christmas was here. Everywhere I've ever lived I hoped someone would ask me what I'd like to eat on Christmas. I have the recipe, but no one has ever asked."

By simply talking with a child about his past holidays, a helper can gather specific information and try to incorporate the child's fond memories into the adoptive family's traditions.

FACING THE DEATH OF A LOVED ONE

A visit to a cemetery can play an important role in helping a child come to grips with certain realities. Although there are few true orphans among the children in the system, many of them have experienced the death of a parent, grandparent, or other loved one. Locating a copy of the person's obituary and taking the child to visit the grave can facilitate the grieving process. If an actual grave site is unknown, a local genealogy society may be able to help locate it.

CELEBRATING THE PAST

Some families adopt several children, and in the day-to-day activity of work, school, and home, they can lose sight of their children's past. We know of one family who adopted three unrelated sons, one by one, as young teens. One Sunday a year, they host a foster party in a local park. All of their sons' past foster families—including parents and their children—bring a potluck dish and spend the day together. It becomes a sort of crazy family reunion since no one is actually related, but everyone has a wonderful time and each adopted child gets to celebrate parts of his past that are meaningful to him.

COMMEMORATING PLACEMENT DAY

Other families celebrate "gotcha day"—the day their child was placed with them or the day the adoption was legalized. This ensures that at least once a year, the life-altering event of adoption is celebrated. A single mom who adopted six children takes them all to a special restaurant to commemorate each child's placement. In each case, the restaurant of choice is the first place she took that child during visitation.

MOVIE NIGHT

Movies can be a great way for a child to process ideas and feelings, especially if he is a poor or pre-reader. *Pinocchio* is a great family movie that addresses the issues of adoption, lack of conscience, and lying. (Poor Geppetto probably could have used a good parent support network.) Other movies popular with the adoption set are *Yours, Mine and Ours*; *Angels in the Outfield*; *Free Willie*; *Tarzan*; *Problem Child*; and *Martian Child*—but you and your child had better be in a good place when you watch the latter, or he may get some new ideas.

A follow-up discussion of the movie can lead to questions like, "So, Brad, if the story of Pinocchio were true, how long would your nose be?" This is inevitably followed by giggles and gentle conversation—a pleasant alternative to arguments and defenses. Sometimes watching and interacting with other people's stories is a great way to spark a child's memories and get him talking about past feelings, losses, and joys.

The methods we have outlined may not help the most seriously disturbed children. Sometimes, however, they may be the catalyst that facilitates the exposure and integration of a child's past in a life-altering way. Certainly, it's worth a try to help a child move on by using a few simple, inexpensive interventions. After all, you need every trick you can get your hands on.

ELEVEN

TREATMENT FOR THE HURT CHILD

Making It Effective

For therapy to be effective, it must be directly related to the issues that the family and the child are experiencing. Specific problems warrant specific solutions, and boilerplate methods serve no purpose. In most cases, finding the right therapist to point out the right path is the first step toward family harmony.

We continue to hear complaints from adoptive parents that many mental health professionals blame them for their child's current problems. It is an unfortunate fact that many of those who attempt to provide treatment to adoptive parents with disturbed children know very little about issues related to adoption. They may not have an adequate understanding of complex trauma and its impact on development. This is particularly alarming when we realize that they not only fail to provide effective therapy but also solidify the child's existing pathology and complicate subsequent therapeutic efforts. It is not unusual for us to work with families who have seen four to six other mental health professionals without results.

Part of the reason for this ineffectiveness is the fact that while graduate training enables therapists to deal with the neurotic personality, it does not adequately prepare them to deal with individuals who have not yet made it to a developmental level that is complex enough to be capable of being neurotic. Children with developmental delays—social, psychological, cognitive, emotional, and neurological—who have been in traditional therapy tend to be extremely skilled at figuring out the therapist's goals and style. They effectively assume the role of victim, and the therapist responds with sympathy. Rarely does a clinician challenge a "victim" child, which is precisely what needs to be done when the child is externalizing his problems or projecting blame. When the therapist buys into the pseudovictim role, his sympathetic response serves to reduce the child's capacity to make the kinds of changes that will improve his level of adjustment.

Because many children who have experienced neglect, abuse, and abandonment have not yet developed an internalized set of values by which they judge themselves and others, they are not able to receive and experience empathy, nor can they develop insight. They project blame onto others and onto objects. They blame their adoptive parents for causing their anger, and they blame toys for breaking. They blame things that could not possibly be responsible for anything.

Most often, children or adolescents who engage in projecting blame are those who have not yet developed a conscience. These same children are adept at engaging others in a superficial manner; thus, therapists, teachers, and outsiders to the family feel that these children are easy to be around and that they are truly misunderstood by those who should know them best—their parents. These kinds of children are most likely those with a disorganized attachment style.

BELIEVING THE PARENTS

Many children feign "poor me," and many professionals are quick to endorse their helplessness and lack of social competence. This victim stance is rarely accurate, and while the children and adolescents are initially satisfied with their success at hooking yet another adult, they ultimately hold him in contempt for "being so stupid." Many therapists have fallen into this category and will be of little help to the child and his family if they continue to blame the parents or the family system for the child's difficulties. Character-disturbed children and adolescents are highly skilled in engaging the therapist, when it should be the other way around.

It is an interesting dichotomy that the same therapists who are easily taken in by disturbed children find it difficult to work with the parents. Since their efforts are focused on helping the parents understand and tolerate the child, the implied—and sometimes direct—message is that the problem is one of parenting. When parents are influenced to feel that their own issues are to blame, they may assume the I-need-to-change role. Even when they objectively know that they were perfectly functional prior to becoming adoptive parents, they may be led to identify themselves as the ones who should change. When their thinking no longer matches their experiences, they can feel crazy.

Many parents with whom we have worked describe years of nonproductive therapy. At the suggestion of therapists whose empathy focused solely on the child, they kept charts of chores, doled out rewards and stickers, and imposed monetary fines. They compromised their values, altered their expectations, and skewed their rules. They were therapeutically robbed of their parenting roles, resulting in an unexpected shift of power from them to their troubled child. Once this occurred, there was little reason for their child to change.

It is our strong belief that any therapy with adoptive children whose development has been compromised must actively include the parents. To do otherwise may cause further fragmentation in the parent-child relationship.

After many failed attempts at therapy, adoptive parents frequently become defensive, guarded, and overly controlling in their relationships with therapists. Once this happens, the parents are likely to look as if they are, indeed, the ones who need help. We often ask parents, "Did you feel and act this crazy before you adopted Bobby?" When we approach them from a humorously empathic point of view, we generally get a response like, "Finally, we've found someone who understands!"

Providing therapeutic support to adoptive parents serves two important purposes. First, it helps to counteract years of minimization and disbelief by mental health professionals, teachers, social workers, and extended family members. Second, when parents feel supported, they are able to receive, process, and utilize the information they receive from the therapist. They will listen to an ally differently from someone who is blaming them and are then open to making any necessary changes.

We are always clear with our clients about one issue: Adoptive parents of previously abused children are *not* responsible for the problems these children have, but they *are* responsible for doing what they can to help alleviate them. While we don't blame adoptive parents, we do expect them to assume a role that is strong, committed, resilient, and persevering.

ADDRESSING COMPROMISED DEVELOPMENT

Developmental change occurs within the context of intense interpersonal relationships. The relationships forged in the birth family — although locked in faulty thinking and ultimately causing developmental arrest — were intense. As a result, a strong connection developed between the abused child and the abusing parent. It is important to remember this dynamic and to understand that our positive relationships must be equally intense if they are to counteract and compete with the abusive relationships that initiated and solidified the child's pathology.

Therapy with hurt children must include high energy and intense focus, close physical proximity, frequent touch, confrontation, movement, much nurturing and love, eye contact, and fast-moving verbal exchanges. These elements should be present in the normal bonding cycle described in chapter 3. One goal of therapy, then, is to approximate what occurs in the healthy attachment cycle, thus reworking the process that was so traumatically interrupted early in the child's life. Therapy that is detached, nondirective, and passive is seldom received by the child as it is intended by the therapist. It is most often viewed as cold, uncaring, uninvolved, boring, and useless.

It is, however, extremely tolerable because it does not make demands on the child. A nondirective therapist who does not push his client can always tell the parents, "We had a good session today. See you next week." Of course they had a good session — there were no expectations to be dashed! It felt okay to the child since there was no confrontation; it seemed productive to the therapist, who may have gained new insights about the child. But the parents, frequently left out of the therapeutic process, leave the session wondering what was so good about it, especially when they see no change in their child's behavior. The it-may-get worse-before-it-gets-better rationale should not endure for years.

If a child is to be freed to move beyond the developmental stage at which he has been stuck, his faulty thinking patterns must be challenged and confronted. Cognitive restructuring is a critical component of treatment. If the child's distorted thinking patterns are not altered, treatment cannot be considered successful. Since thinking causes and directs behavior, the thinking and acting (cognitive and behavioral) processes require intervention and remediation.

While addressing cognitive and behavioral issues, appropriate therapy must also be experiential. Psychodrama, role-play, creative movement, and artistic expression may be utilized to further access a child's primitive feelings. Nonverbal processes frequently reveal meaningful issues and areas for new exploration.

Scientists who study brain development are uncovering exciting physiological information that should encourage therapists and parents who want to help developmentally challenged children. Ongoing research into physical and psychological trauma and its relationship to brain development provides powerful evidence that early trauma significantly interferes with normal development in a growing child's brain. Because compromised development is rooted in physiological as well as psychological causes, effective treatments must utilize a variety of strategies.

The explosion of information and knowledge in neuroscience and Developmental Trauma Disorder has led to many new treatment alternatives since the first two editions of *Adopting the Hurt Child* were published. In the following segment, we will discuss many of these now available treatment options.

THERAPEUTIC INTERVENTIONS

In this book's first and second editions, the focus in this section was on what was then called holding therapy—a term that seems to limit the scope of our current treatment process. The term was not used to mean physical restraint, nor was it meant to be synonymous with rage reduction.

At the time of our initial writing, we had already come to believe that children with Developmental Trauma Disorder had layers of issues and usually had more than one diagnosis. Typically, we are seeing children who meet criteria for PTSD as well Reactive Attachment Disorder. As we began to see more involved biopsychosocial issues, treatment strategies began to change. No longer was catharsis assumed to be *the* solution for children experiencing high levels of dysregulation on a rather consistent basis.

Holding a child is a nurturing act, and we continue to use it in treatment. We encourage parents to use nurturing holding as a component of the overall parenting process. Gentle physical interaction is what healthy parents do from the moment a child is born or adopted. The controversy behind such behavior perplexes us because if a parent did not have close proximity with a child, we would think there was some sort of neglect or even psychological detachment on the parent's part.

The holding we do is with the child's permission and cooperation; those from age nine to late adolescence must agree to the process. If they do not, we do not proceed.

When we ask a child or teen why he thinks we want him to lie on his parent's or therapist's lap, the usual answers are reasonable, such as, "So I can look at you." One older adolescent with a history of sexual abuse replied, "Because I didn't get holded when I was little, and I need it now." If the children understand what is going on and why, the adults around them should have little trouble engaging in holding as well.

Therapeutic holding mobilizes development because the close physical proximity involved in holding a child results in an interpersonal closeness that cannot be duplicated in any other therapeutic format. Holding also produces physiological benefits that are reflected in a child's attitude.

Dr. Temple Grandin's work with autism reveals how deep physical pressure produces a calming of the neurological system.[1] Helping a child develop the capacity to reach a calm state is critically important. When he can learn to regulate himself, his out-of-control periods will become less intense, less frequent, and ultimately nonexistent.

Terry, age thirteen, seemed to be in a state of hyperarousal when he arrived for his therapy appointment. After a period of holding, the therapist decided to help Terry relax. She encouraged the child to close his eyes and gently move his head back and forth. Almost immediately, his entire body eased up and his mood changed dramatically as calmness set in. Terry's awareness of this change was keen, and he readily verbalized — with much surprise — what he had experienced. This was a calmness that was unfamiliar to him.

In many instances, children who have grown accustomed to high levels of stimulation and dysregulation are initially uncomfortable in a relaxed state. As a result, they may engage in some sort of behavior to speed up their environment. When this happens, they must be helped to get back on track. Activities involving movement — gross motor actions, followed by slower moves — usually prove helpful.

Many children have discovered how to get in a calm state on their own. Their behaviors may seem odd if their parents don't understand the purpose of their actions.

Tommy, four years old, was always trying to crawl into very tight spaces. He slept with lots of blankets on top of him and on occasion would wedge himself between the mattress and box springs of his bed. He seemed comforted by the pressure, the tightness, and the apparent tranquility it brought him.

Tommy's behavior seemed less odd to his parents once they understood that he was attempting to calm himself. The sensory integration dysfunction literature certainly explains such behavior, as does Dr. Grandin's work with both animals and people.

The examples of Terry and Tommy clarify how important holding in therapy is. It provides the kind of comfort — both physiological and psychological — that many children crave, even though it often appears that they are constantly trying to avoid touch. They actually may be attempting to avoid the light stimulating touch that may occur in casual social or family settings.

Holding does not result in a quick fix but rather in a jump start. The child and therapist can access feelings that would not be readily apparent through talk therapy alone. Dr. Daniel Hughes' book *Facilitating Developmental Attachment* offers many insights for both parents and professionals. He frequently states, "Emotional attunement between parents and child is crucial for therapeutic success."[2]

Such attunement can be expedited through holding since it would be nearly impossible for the child not to experience the feelings of the person who is holding him. In treatment, it is critical for the child/adolescent to feel what the parent/therapist feels because it may be the child's first experience of synchronicity with another. This experience offers the child an opportunity to connect with and attach to the parent.

Most of the professionals who advocate holding are in agreement about the following elements:

- Emotional contact between the child and the person holding him is heightened.
- Holding may produce emotional responses that are unlikely to occur in any other kind of therapeutic intervention.
- Corrective emotional experiences may occur during, and as a result of, holding.
- Holding enhances the child's capacity to attach.
- Holding increases the child's attachment to the parents.
- Holding provides physical closeness and emotional security, which are reassuring to the child whose feelings often frighten him.
- Therapists who do holding are more aware of the child's nonverbal experiences — the physical tensing, relaxing, and breathing — than they would be if they sat across from him with no physical contact.

When attempting to jump-start arrested development, holding is powerful. It is precisely what happens to a "normal" child in his first year of life, providing him with a foundation of nurturing, trust, safety, and security. These four elements merge to set the stage for later development. They help ensure that cause-and-effect thinking will develop, which leads to identification with the parent, which leads to the formation of a conscience. If a child is developmentally stuck, growth must be activated before genuine behavioral change can be expected. Since development is sequential, it must be activated at the point where the child became fixated, regardless of his chronological age.

When children are able to develop a sense of being safe in a relationship, they can then tolerate a wider range of affective experiences, allowing feelings such as sadness, hurt, and fear to surface within a secure context. They have less need to control their environment, and they no longer have to create chaos as a deflective maneuver.

Bud had experienced a difficult childhood. His mother, Sylvia, was intellectually limited and claimed to have had only one date with his father. She knew his name, but she denied knowing anything more. She had numerous children by numerous men, and none of the fathers was involved with his respective child.

Sylvia had become fatigued with what she perceived as her mothering role. By objective standards, she had performed few, if any, of the roles one would associate with a mother. Her five children had struggled simply to live. She cared little *about* them and less *for* them. She sought and found her comfort in the many men with whom she associated. They, in turn, regarded her as nothing more than an object, useful to meet their physical needs.

After much social service intervention, Sylvia decided that she no longer wanted to be a parent. One by one, she gave her children to the child welfare system. One Halloween, she decided to have a party. She also decided that at the end of the party, she would have a social worker come to remove Bud. As planned, the family gathered for the Halloween festivities, and also as planned, the worker arrived to remove Bud after the refreshments were enjoyed. Bud never understood why he was leaving. Looking back, he assumed that the party was a going-away celebration. But he was the one who left — quickly, and without explanation.

He was finally adopted, four years later. Rage-filled and confused, he presented several dilemmas to his new parents — acting as if they were responsible for his prior traumas. Specifically, he directed his rage at his adoptive mom. He tried to hurt her emotionally in every conceivable way. When emotional damage did not suffice, he resorted to physical threats that culminated in an attempt to kill her with a weapon. The family had had extensive professional help throughout the placement, but nothing helped.

Finally, they participated in an intensive treatment program that utilized holding and focused on repairing damaged attachment and reducing Bud's anger. During treatment, Bud experienced much of his rage and was able to direct it at the therapist. He became more open and was more accessible during his sessions. His range of feelings increased, and his level of giving and receiving affection was dramatically enhanced. His capacity to attach developed, and his interactions with his parents became more meaningful.

Depression coexisted with Bud's attachment difficulties, and this became an ongoing issue that emerged episodically. During these times, he became dysregulated and destroyed property—usually his bedroom and belongings. But as his connection to his parents and his therapist grew, his relationships continued to develop, even through his worst times.

Ongoing therapy centered on Bud's losses, grief, depression, and rejection. Anger issues were more easily resolved, but progress was neither steady nor consistent. Periodic regressions marked his overall progress. Bud's treatment outcome was positive, but not without difficulties.

As people continue to grow, they become more developmentally complex. This complexity adds dimensions to the personality, increasing the number of issues that need to be addressed. Bud's capacity to receive and give love has increased significantly. His level of rage remains reduced, and his level of self-examination is heightened. Much work still must be accomplished, but his developmental process has been activated and we predict positive long-term adjustment.

As stated earlier, most experts on therapeutic holding agree that corrective emotional experiences can be facilitated during the holding process. While no therapy can change what has happened to a child in his past, his perceptions about his experiences can be altered if he is helped to reframe his circumstances and responses and thus gain mastery over his greatest fears and losses.

For example, people often ask—usually with great reservation—about holding a child or adolescent who has been sexually abused. What better opportunity for a corrective learning experience? Here we have the elements that were present during the prior abuse except one—the sexual activity. We have the child. We have touch. And we have adults who are coordinating the situation. What, then, can be learned by the child who has been sexualized early in his life? He learns that touch can be okay. It can be safe. It can be nonsexual. He learns that control by adults who can be trusted does not have to result in a negative experience. He learns that his parents and his therapist will stay with him during his most painful work. When asked how it feels to be held, a child may say, "This is how I was abused." Such a comment provides an excellent opportunity to address his painful feelings.

You may have a specific child in mind and are wondering how it would be possible to get him to agree to participate in holding. Prior to adding holding as a component of our work, we, too, would have made this query. The answer is surprisingly simple.

Most of the children with whom we work respect directness, clarity, and honesty—even though they don't do a good job with any of these qualities themselves. We merely tell them that we have found holding to be very helpful for many kids who have problems similar to theirs. Since most of these children have been in traditional talk or play therapy for years with a variety of therapists, they often view holding as a new challenge. They think it might turn out to be more fun than playing cards for another two years. In addition, the fact that they don't know us—remember that they often prefer to be with strangers—sets the stage for them to give it a try.

Very few clients refuse to participate in being held by their parents. If they are hesitant, we talk until we get agreement. Absolute refusal usually indicates a poor prognosis for change, and without agreement from the child, we never attempt a holding.

While initially being held, most older adolescents (ages sixteen to eighteen) look perplexed. When asked about their thoughts and feelings, they often respond with something like, "You know, this is really weird. I thought I'd hate it, but it feels kinda good. This is bizarre—being held at my age."

We most often follow this comment with a simple, yet powerful, question: "Did you get this when you were supposed to?" Never has any child—even the most difficult and resistant—responded with an affirmative answer.

During holding, the therapist must be especially aware of the dynamics of transference and counter-transference, almost universally recognized as integral components in the development of the psychotherapeutic relationship. Transference, simply put, occurs when the feelings that the client has for others are attributed to the therapist. For example, if the client is angry with a controlling parent, he might transfer that anger to the therapist and endow the therapist with the qualities that he associates with his parent. His continuing interaction with the therapist may also be colored by these feelings of anger. Ultimately, transference aids the therapeutic relationship because it allows the client's issues and feelings to be resolved effectively.

Counter-transference, on the other hand, refers to how the therapist emotionally responds to the client. The therapist's feelings toward the client are connected to the therapist's own issues and may interfere with the process if they are not acknowledged and managed well.

Issues of transference and counter-transference are more apparent during holding than in traditional therapy. The transference process emerges quickly and is the dynamic that brings about change in the child. He is able to work through his most intense, disabling feelings with the therapist—spurred on by the physical closeness and contact that speed up the formation of the transferential relationship.

Counter-transference issues also emerge quickly and more intensely during holding. The therapist's feelings may become part of the therapeutic process since holding requires a genuine sharing of self with the child that differs greatly from the more traditional relationship of professional distance. Because love, nurturing, and physical contact all come into play, the therapist must be aware of his own feelings regarding such issues.

The themes of loss, separation, abandonment, love, and caring are always present. The painful past that is part of each abused or neglected child is always difficult to address, but it is essential to focus on all the details and factors associated with that abuse. While it is not uncommon for angry feelings toward the abuser to surface within the therapist, they must be handled appropriately. Even though the child may be angry with his birth mom for not protecting him from abuse, the therapist's anger at her may serve only to trigger the child's defense of someone he loves. When in such a defensive mode, he cannot disengage from the fantasized relationship he maintains with her.

While all therapists must be clearly aware of the counter-transferential process, they should be particularly cognizant of the fact that holding may generate greater confrontation with their own emotional baggage than other kinds of treatment.

Mental health professionals who are interested in doing holding should get specialized training prior to beginning the work and should have on-going supervision and consultation once they start. Others may choose to adapt some intervention strategies that approximate holding situations.

We have found that simply decreasing the amount of physical space between the therapist and the child increases the amount of emotional contact the child experiences and also expedites the overall therapeutic process. Simply put, the closer the therapist is to the child, the greater the chance for an effective, active therapeutic process. Sitting knee-to-knee, face-to-face, seems to ensure the delivery of the message. Eye contact, too, is more easily established when the spatial boundaries between people are narrow. Most hurt children are hypervigilant, and physical closeness guarantees their attention and helps activate the growth process.

Another adaptation of holding is to have the child lie on a couch or on the floor with the therapist sitting at his head. Essential eye contact is more easily maintained in this position than from across the room or from behind a desk, and emotional contact is more likely to be established. The therapist, by the very nature of his location above the child, is more central and better able to direct the therapeutic processes and interactions.

Regardless of the type of intervention used, it is critical to differentiate treatment for hurt children. They are not good candidates for the kinds of therapy that prove beneficial to those who are not developmentally delayed. A family systems person may want to apply his specific methodology to everyone with whom he works. A professional interested in working with suppressed memories may have the inclination to assume that the problems presented by the child are symptomatic of actual events unknown to him. Therapists interested in attachment theory may assume that all of the children who come to them need attachment work.

It is crucial for all mental health professionals to prevent their theoretical interests and philosophies from guiding their work in an undifferentiated manner. They should not follow the same pattern with all of their patients any more than a physician should perform the same medical procedure just because that's where his expertise lies. Each assessment should be an assessment of the individual. Treatment, then, must be based on that which is differentially determined in the assessment.

Eye Movement Desensitization and Reprocessing (EMDR)

The contribution Dr. Francine Shapiro has made with the development of Eye Movement Desensitization and Reprocessing (EMDR) brings yet another dimension to treatment for the hurt child. EMDR helps people revisit their trauma via their memories, reprocess and desensitize these memories, and resolve their feelings about them.

"One of the basic premises of EMDR," Dr. Shapiro says, "is that most psychopathologies are based on early life experiences. The goal of EMDR treatment is to rapidly metabolize the dysfunctional residue from the past and transform it into something useful. Essentially, with EMDR, the dysfunctional information undergoes a spontaneous change in form and meaning—incorporating insights and affects that are enhancing rather than self-denigrating to the client."[3]

While it is not completely understood why or how EMDR works, we have found it to be helpful with children and adolescents in attachment therapy because it quickly accesses anxiety rooted in their past. A hurt child's genuine feelings about past traumatic experiences are often deeply buried, yet these hidden memories and feelings frequently dictate how they interact with others in the present. EMDR allows the affective component of the child's past trauma to emerge in a safe setting, where it is then desensitized and resolved through the rapid eye movement process.

A trained therapist begins EMDR by explaining the process to the client. For children, the explanation needs to be simple and direct; adolescents are able to understand something more complex. When we do EMDR with a child with attachment difficulties, we often begin by telling him that there is something that can help take away the yucky feelings from old, bad memories. Would he like to know more about it or try it? Almost all children agree to learn more.

We ask the child to describe an old memory that still feels bad to him. We try to get all the details—particularly sensory information (color of clothing worn, smells, sounds, tastes, tactile sensations). We ask him what part of the memory is most vivid. What is the worst part? What is he feeling? Where in his body does he feel it? Then we elicit horizontal eye movements by instructing him to follow the movement of our fingers back and forth in front of his eyes. Other stimulation, such as alternating tones through headphones or tapping on the hands, can also be used.

After several sets of these eye movements, the child is asked what feelings, thoughts, and images came up for him. This process is repeated until the child reports feeling less discomfort about the original memory he described. The whole EMDR process is client-driven and directed, and the therapist should refrain from interpreting the client's memories for him.

EMDR has also helped some of our clients develop and/or access a personal historical narrative. During EMDR sessions, we have seen children fill gaps in their memories, helping heal the wounds they experienced. They did not necessarily access new memories but rather had a context into which they could organize their memories.

Adam, an adolescent adoptee from Korea, continued to focus during an EMDR session on a little boy with curly hair sitting in a big room by himself. After several sets of eye movements, he moved into other images. Yet at the end of the session, he remained perplexed about the curly hair. He saw this little boy as himself, but he had no explanation for the hair, since his is straight.

We talked to his adoptive parents about this, and they informed him that his birth grandmother had given him a permanent prior to his going to the orphanage. This small piece of information, while not earth-shattering, provided Adam with one more detail in a still incomplete picture of his past.

Knowing these morsels about one's life is very important to some adoptees—such details provide a link, a connection, and an attachment to the past. This is important because strong, positive past connections can help strengthen present and future attachments.

For children and adolescents, the typical EMDR protocol used with adults may not be appropriate. Most EMDR proponents feel that the most important component of the procedure is bilateral brain stimulation, which can be achieved in several ways. Sometimes throwing a ball back and forth—switching hands for each catch and toss—will do the trick. We also use a small pulsating device called a TheraTapper, which consists of a control box connected to two small pulsers held by the child. The pulsers vibrate in an alternating fashion, and the child can determine both the speed and the intensity of the vibrations. The stimulation is comparable to the vibration of a pager or cell phone, and since many kids today are interested in technology, they usually find these little devices very intriguing.

Sensory Integration Dysfunction Treatment

The early trauma experienced by children who have attachment difficulties affects every aspect of their existence. One area commonly affected is the sensory system—the part of the brain that organizes and processes sensory input and uses the input to respond appropriately to a particular situation.

Tatiana, three years old, always seemed restless and uncomfortable when her mother dressed her. She would begin to pull at her clothes, become agitated, and engage in tantrum behavior. Her anger escalated until she would rip at her clothes. One day after she successfully undressed herself, she attempted violently to remove the tags from her garments. Her mother finally understood just what was bothering her daughter. These tags were the obvious cause of Tatiana's distress and exaggerated response. Most children are not even aware of the tags in their clothes, and even if they are, their sensory system processes the touch message in a way that does not even result in heightened arousal, much less full-blown tantrums. After discussing Tatiana's behavior with the family's therapist, a referral was made for an evaluation of the child's difficulties.

Marty went to his therapy session directly from school, where his parents picked him up after recess. The drive to his appointment took more than an hour, and they reported that the trip was unremarkable. As Marty entered the office, the therapist noticed a rattling noise coming from his shoes. When asked about the noise, Marty responded, "Oh, there must be some stones in my shoes," and he promptly emptied a huge amount of gravel onto the floor. Together, Marty and the therapist counted thirty medium to large pieces of stone. Marty said he hadn't noticed anything in his shoes. Most of us can barely tolerate even one small piece of anything in our shoes, much less thirty rocks! Marty, unlike Tatiana, was totally under-responsive to something that would cause extreme annoyance to almost everyone whose sensory system is functional and well-integrated.

When a child has what seem to be unusual responses to sensory input—such as sound, touch, movement, food/mouth activity, and temperature—he might be helped by an occupational therapist certified in sensory integration (SI) therapy. The therapy's goal is to help align the child's senses—to bring his sensory awareness to a more normal state and to help him respond to sensory input in an appropriate manner.

For example, an SI therapist working with a child who has sensory difficulties may provide deep pressure to a child with tactile problems, or she may brush the child's arms and legs before engaging him in other activities. Movement is an important activity in a person's life, so if a child has issues around movement, the therapist will develop activities that help the child get accustomed to the kinds of movements he avoids or fears.

Many children adopted internationally from orphanages have difficulties with food, texture, chewing, and swallowing. Often they were fed a kind of gruel from a bottle with a large opening in the nipple. They never needed to learn to chew or suck properly. For a child with these problems, an occupational therapist would develop specific activities for the parents to do which would desensitize and accustom the child to new textures in his mouth.

Parents can locate therapists who are trained in sensory integration therapy by calling hospitals or private clinics that offer occupational therapy. Parents should ask specifically for a professional who is SI certified.

Neurofeedback

In recent years, more attention has been given to neuroscience and what it teaches us about the brain and its relationship to what were formerly thought to be exclusively psychological or psychosocial conditions. Now most people would agree that we must focus on biopsychosocial elements of all diagnoses. It was not all that long ago that the mental health world saw schizophrenia as a psychological disorder. It was believed that the so-called schizophrenigenic mother presented conflicting and confusing messages to her child that resulted in the development of this devastating brain disorder. Today, nearly all professionals, almost without exception, recognize that schizophrenia is clearly a brain disorder.

Sebern Fisher, MA, a leading expert on neurofeedback and its utilization in the treatment of Reactive Attachment Disorder, shares that Reactive Attachment Disorder is a "disorder of stark overarousal, and it is a disorder of the right hemisphere (of the brain). Once we begin to recognize Reactive Attachment Disorder as a disorder in brain development in all realms, structure, chemistry, and timing, we can also begin to see the possibilities for treatment through training of the brain."[4] Fisher aptly indicates that Reactive Attachment Disorder predicts conduct disorder in adolescence as well as antisocial personality disorder in adulthood. In addition to the two conditions just mentioned, Reactive Attachment Disorder may also lead to the development of oppositional defiant disorder, narcissistic personality disorder, and borderline personality disorder.

Fisher goes on to state that "neurofeedback is a technique of operant conditioning which directly changes brain function, in particular the timing of specific regulatory networks in the brain. It most dramatically affects arousal regulation. In doing so, this 'brain training' can normalize the propensity to high arousal seen as the hallmark of Reactive Attachment Disorder."

This is a noninvasive strategy for helping children with regulatory disorders develop the necessary internal skills to achieve and maintain regulation. Most parents of children who have attachment spectrum disorders will welcome any change that results in fewer episodes of dysregulation, such as tantrums and violent behavior. This is, after all, an important goal of therapy.

Maria was adopted as an infant. Her birth mother had used alcohol throughout the pregnancy. Maria had a wide array of challenges, but the one that caused the most disruption was her frequent episodes of dysregulation. Sometimes the trigger of these episodes was clear, but on other occasions, Maria's parents had no idea what the precipitating event was. Often, the only hope of ending the "meltdown" was bedtime because once Maria started to become dysregulated, it seemed that the behavior became locked-in for the remainder of the day.

By Maria's fourth birthday, her parents had already consulted with a psychiatrist, who prescribed a psychostimulant for ADHD, a mood stabilizer, and an antipsychotic medication. While there was some improvement as a result of the medication, the frequent periods of dysregulation continued. Maria then began neurofeedback. Soon her parents noticed that she was calmer and less reactive to day-to-day stressors.

Over a few months, the tantrums that had disrupted the entire family became an unusual occurrence. When Maria did become dysregulated, the episodes were brief and less intense. As she gained confidence, she was able to remain regulated throughout the day. Ultimately, her stimulant medication was reduced, and she discontinued taking both the mood stabilizer and the antipsychotic.

Family Attachment Narrative Therapy

The attachment relationship provides the primary context in which a child develops an understanding of self, others, and the world. Trauma in early life, especially when it involves the attachment relationship, can profoundly affect a child's internal beliefs. Children who experience early life abuse and neglect tend to construct incoherent, chaotic life narratives with faulty conclusions about personal value and their role and responsibility in relation to the maltreatment. Such internal beliefs can result in problems in multiple areas, including behavior, stress regulation, and peer relationships.

Family Attachment Narrative Therapy is designed to shift the destructive beliefs formed by children who suffered early life maltreatment.[5] The methodology uses narratives, or therapeutic stories, told by parents to help children construct new meanings from previous life experiences. Effective narratives integrate factual and emotional information, helping the child to reprocess his experiences and reach new conclusions about them. Narratives are divided into four types: claiming, trauma, developmental, and successful child.[6]

Family Attachment Narrative Therapy builds on strengths in the parent-child relationship, relying on parental sensitivity and attunement to the child's internal emotions, thoughts, and motivations. Therapists recognize the key role of the parent in the child's healing, and they support parental expertise. Working in partnership with parents, therapists facilitate parental use of narratives. As the parents better understand the child's internal working model and how it has been affected by the trauma, their empathy increases and their innate need to provide protection and healing is activated. This results in sensitive, attuned narratives that explicitly challenge the child's faulty internal beliefs and provide a healing experience.[7]

Dylan was not feeling that he was a part of the family, so his parents sought professional help to increase the security of his attachment. They began with a claiming narrative.

"If you had been our baby from the beginning, Dad and I would have spent months getting the nursery ready for you. I think we would have decorated it with jet planes because we would have known you'd love them. When you were first born, we would have counted your fingers and toes and kissed the end of your nose. You were the most beautiful baby. We would have been there every time you made a noise to check if you were hungry, wet, or just wanted to be held."[8]

Activities Involving Movement

Occupational therapists often use movement when helping children with Sensory Integration Dysfunction, which was discussed earlier. More and more people are beginning to understand how movement can be helpful for children and adolescents who have experienced complex trauma. At a recent conference on attachment disorders at Harvard, there was discussion regarding just how important gross motor activities may be in correcting regulatory problems—behaviors that parents would describe as meltdowns, hissy fits, and tantrums. After high arousal, the children and adolescents are helped to regain a sense of calmness. In the ebb and flow of life, the individual's capacity to maintain or regain regulation—that is, to get back in control of oneself—is of paramount importance.

Many activities—such as sports, drama, dance, creative movement, martial arts, and yoga—can be helpful to hurt children. We frequently talk with parents who are so frustrated with their child's difficult behaviors that they want to use these activities as a reward for improved or good behavior. We strongly suggest that involvement in any activity that is organized, instructive, and constructive be a part of day-to-day living and not subject to restriction or revocation for unrelated behavior.

Use of Music

As mentioned earlier, sensory experiences are sometimes profound, and it is for this reason that we attempt to activate and/or access a child's sensory world. It seems safe to say that people are often transported to a different level of affective-emotional experience as the result of hearing music. Sometimes the music will be from one's past. Other times new music creates a different sensory experience and launches us into what will become a part of our "new history."

Parents have been singing to their children for generations, and most often this music provides a level of comfort for the child. In all probability, it also offers a dyadic attunement experience for the parent and the child, which leads to the development of the improved regulatory processes—one of the goals of attachment-focused therapy.

The therapists at ABC of Ohio introduced music as a regular component of our treatment program. The use of music as an adjunctive part of therapy has taken root, and we are now routinely lubricating emotions with a variety of calming tunes.

Animal-Assisted Therapy

Service dogs are being utilized in greater numbers than ever before. In addition to guide dogs for the blind, canines are now being used for the hearing impaired and the physically handicapped. In some prison programs, inmates train rescued dogs to be service dogs. Many people find it easier to relate with empathy to a dog rather than to a person.

Many organizations use animal-assisted therapy as a component of their attachment-focused programs. Adolescents in residential treatment centers learn to train dogs to help other people, sharing with the animals a common history of trauma, loss, and abandonment. As the adolescents explore their trauma experiences, they gain insights while they learn about the stories of the dogs they are training.

Many of the children and adolescents with whom we work participate in therapeutic horseback-riding programs. They get both the benefits of the physical movement and the emotional fulfillment that results from caring for the horses, and they learn something about reciprocity as well as cause-and-effect thinking.

The relationship between people being cruel to animals and committing violence toward other people is well documented. Helping children develop empathy with animals may go a long way toward preventing future aggressive behavior toward people and animals.

Theraplay

Theraplay—not to be confused with play therapy—promotes attachment among family members by using play. The Theraplay philosophy varies from play therapy in that it is more directive and uses the parents and/or therapists as the primary objects of play. It offers an interactive way to increase and strengthen attachment through structure, nurture, challenge, and engagement.

The therapist uses many techniques to direct the participants' activities to improve eye contact, positive interactions, and attachment between the child and parent. He or she works on building an engaging relationship with the family unit in an effort to change the child's perceptions of both self and parents and to enhance the quality of attachment among all family members. For more information, contact the Theraplay Institute listed in the "Resources" section.

A toddler group consisted of three children adopted from foster care and three children adopted from other countries—all under five years of age. The mothers learned Theraplay strategies to help promote stronger connections to their children. One of their favorite activities was to close their eyes and attempt to find and identify their child through touch. For the adults, the exercise seemed silly at first, but the children seemed surprised that their moms could find them with closed eyes. They appeared delighted and giggly—an emotional state the mothers rarely saw.

Any activity involving food was a true hit, but the one that seemed particularly productive was when the mothers fed the children yogurt with a baby spoon—a process that they had not had the opportunity to do before. The mothers expressed satisfaction at having met other mothers whose children were presenting challenges at home, and the children seemed to enjoy the time they spent with other children. The group activities promoted improved attachment and interactions between the mothers and their children, and it provided ideas of how to use play at home.

Medication

A common question that frequently arises during therapy is whether or not medications should be used. Some parents summarily reject information about medication with the common arguments, "I don't want my child to use drugs; I'm not much of a medicine person; I don't even like to give my child aspirin." However, the fact remains that there are mental disorders that are clearly biological and respond well to appropriate medication. It would be as foolish to ignore the role of prescription drugs for some children and adolescents as it would be to ignore the use of insulin for diabetics.

Parents need to rely on the health-care professionals with whom they are working for guidance and expertise. In addition, the behavior of a child on medication should be monitored carefully. We have seen dramatic improvements in those on medication. We have witnessed those who experience little or no change. We have even seen children who exhibit worse behavior after taking medication. Parents should never attempt to alter dosages without first consulting the prescribing physician. Such alterations are unhelpful—at the very least—and can be outright harmful.

Medication probably serves its most beneficial purpose when used in combination with supportive services and appropriate therapy. There is no medication alone that can restructure the personality and further its development. Human development occurs through intimate connections with others, and it is this human vehicle that ultimately leads to an individual's capacity to give and receive love and to become a participating, contributing member of society.

Providing Truthful Information

As we explained in chapter 7, family of origin issues move into the adoptive home in an adopted child's heart. They cannot be ignored if treatment for the hurt child is to be effective.

For therapy to work, the child's previous families — birth, foster, and/or adoptive — must be acknowledged. These families have all contributed to the person the child has become, yet too often there is an effort to delete them. While some adoptive parents and therapists attempt to diminish the importance of earlier families, the child may struggle harder to retain them emotionally. It is difficult for the new parents to understand how the child — now perceived as theirs — can have allegiance to those who have hurt him. But difficult as it may be, good therapy makes use of information about these families.

In our work with children, we like to spend as much time as necessary digesting birth family information. We are constantly addressing truth in an effort to either validate the child's memories and/or experiences or to correct misperceptions or incorrect information that may have been shared with the child.

As children move through the foster care system, their perceptions become their realities, and we find that what they often hold to be fact may be untrue. Children who have lived in orphanages most often have little or no birth family information. In many cases, they have been given false information in an effort to provide them with some sort of history. Many have been given names and birth dates by orphanage staff.

While we always feel that the truth is of primary importance, each family must determine whether or not any search activities are feasible, in the child's best interest, and consonant with the child's current level of adjustment and functioning. Families can deliver truthful information in a neutral manner. The most important ingredient is the truth itself, and the child will process what you tell him within the context of his current situation. He may need to repeatedly revisit the truth, the story, his former life. He may even "forget" what you told him, so don't hesitate to remind him again and again.

People often assume that the search process cannot start until the child reaches the age of eighteen. In reality, this age has little significance and merely serves to set up the child for distorted perceptions of what occurs at the point of legal adulthood. Many adolescents are no better prepared to face the world at eighteen than at a younger age. We recommend that parents and therapists refrain from making promises such as, "At eighteen, you can live on your own, look for your birth parents, and connect with your brothers and sisters." The search for birth relatives can be undertaken at any age. It should, however, have relevance for the child, not just the adoptive parents.

> Robert had been taken from his birth mother at the age of seven. He had been severely neglected by her, sexually abused by her boyfriend, and appeared to have the physical characteristics of Fetal Alcohol Spectrum Disorder. He was eventually adopted by a family with many difficulties — so many difficulties that Robert could no longer remain in their home, despite the fact that he had been with them for eight years. He was placed in foster care and underwent therapy, and finally the adoption was legally dissolved.
>
> Robert longed to be in touch with his birth mother. We felt that even though she had been a very poor parent, his intense desire to see her needed to be addressed. After a brief and easy search, she was located. She had been sober for five years, was successfully raising another child, and had made major changes in her life. Robert began to visit her, and both mother and son entered therapy together. Ultimately, Robert's birth mother legally adopted him.

Although this case is not typical, it illustrates that birth parents and family dynamics can change over time and may be able to play a meaningful part in a hurt child's healing process. All avenues of support should be explored — even when they appear to be extreme, as in Robert's case.

Because all past attachments help promote future attachments, they should be acknowledged, supported, and nurtured. Unfortunately, some people still embrace the belief that if a child remains too connected to his foster parents, he will fail to bond to his adoptive family. The absurdity of this notion is best illustrated when we compare it to adult relationships that develop via a common acquaintance. Imagine if a friend arranged a blind date for you, and then you and your date had to end your association with the matchmaker in order to allow your relationship to develop. On the contrary, familiar acquaintances can be a bridge to new relationships and should be considered a valuable resource. The decision about whether or not to maintain connections with former families, however, should be left to the child.

The child's response to a meeting with his previous families is the most important factor in determining whether or not the meetings should continue. Are there negative behavioral changes each time a contact is made? If so, these changes should be evaluated. What do they mean — to the child, to the new parent, to the birth relatives, to the previous foster family? Answers must be found before any decisions are made to continue, suspend, or terminate these contacts. We have not seen any one thing destroy or save a placement. Having a great reunion with birth parents will not repair a dysfunctional adoption — conversely, a negative experience will not doom an adoption that is developing smoothly.

Interest in having contact with the birth family has its own developmental course for the adopted child. At any point in time, he may have more or less interest in the process of locating birth relatives, which may be confusing to his adoptive parents. "We spent all of this time trying to find your birth mother, and now you don't want to see her!" they cry. They should remember that it is their child's response that should guide them. Perhaps the child wanted only to know if his mother is still alive, where his father lives, or whether or not there are any new siblings. Over time, his attitude may change, and these vacillating needs and desires must be respected by parents and therapist alike. As long as the child is not endangered by contact, he should be allowed to take the lead.

THE PARENTS' ROLE IN THERAPY

While we have consistently stated that we as therapists support parents, we want to make it clear that this support is not carte blanche. Of course it is the parents' right and responsibility to call the shots in their families, but it is our responsibility to help them make appropriate changes in their interactions with their child that coincide with our therapeutic work with the child.

We are constantly amazed at the reports we hear about therapists who treat children without informing the parents of what happens in therapy. The parents of our young clients are always involved — either by their presence in the treatment room or in the observation room. While we have high regard for the confidential nature of some therapy, we firmly believe that the parents of character-disturbed children must be aware of what we are doing.

We are honest with the child, and our openness has always proved effective. The children with whom we've worked respond well to a contract that states, "Your parents are important people in your life. Because we believe they are the best people to help you, we want them to know everything that goes on in our work. There are no secrets here, and there will be no secrets about what goes on at home."

This would not be the prescribed treatment contract with a high-functioning adolescent who is working through typical adolescent issues, such as identity or dependence-versus-independence conflicts. Just as the treatment itself must be differentially developed, so must the treatment contract.

Most parents whose children have developmental delays and attach-ment issues—both of which are manifested through significant behavioral problems—become much too serious about everything. They become the child's opposite: He assumes that nothing is serious, which leads the parents to assume that everything is serious. They allow themselves no levity. They take nothing in stride. Instead, even small issues become major issues in their eyes. Their problems and miseries lead to the loss of support of family and friends, and they drift in a sea of isolation.

Like all of us, the adoptive parents have unresolved psychological issues. Since hurt children seem to have button-locating radar, their parents' issues are generally targeted for exposure, aggravation, and agitation. If there's a button that can be pushed, these children will find it. And once they zero in on it, they push mercilessly.

Every day spent with a disturbed child heightens parents' awareness of their own issues. Most often, their unresolved struggles are reduced to power-and-control battles with their child. And once the parents are engaged in a battle initiated by the child, they have a difficult time pulling out.

Treatment efforts must therefore be focused on at least two dimensions. First, the parents' issues need to be explored and resolved. Simultaneously, they must be given the practical strategies and tools for correcting the emo-tional imbalance in their homes. As a result, the therapist often assumes a multidimensional role with the parents, serving as mentor, advisor, psycho-educator, supporter, confronter, and guide.

We have worked with many parents who report that the child's issues seem to be reactivating his responses to the trauma he experienced in childhood. A rather common occurrence is that of childhood sexual abuse. Many, if not most, of the children and adolescents with whom we work have had early sexual trauma. Some of the parents, also, experienced similar kinds of abuse. The parents have reported that they thought that they had dealt with their own trauma, but when their child began demonstrating sexualized behaviors, their old feelings surfaced with much intensity. Not only do they describe feeling surprised, but they also feel overwhelmed by what they thought had long ago been put to rest.

We most often work with parents as part of a comprehensive team — comprised of the social worker, adoption placement worker, and referring therapist. This treatment team must work closely together if the hurt child is to grow and make the changes that may be necessary for him to stay in his adoptive home.

The team process includes a complete assessment involving a structured, written autobiography by each parent; a marital assessment for couples or an individual one for single parents; and a family assessment, done in conjunction with the child's assessment.

When the assessment indicates a serious problem, we help the parents become emotionally disentangled from the child's web of conflict, confusion, and trauma. As they begin to lighten up, they make two joyous discoveries: They get more pleasure and satisfaction out of parenting, and their child is more drawn to them.

The latter is precisely what we want to happen. When the child is drawn to the parents, the balance of power begins to change. The child begins to wonder, *What's up? Why are they so happy? What's going to happen?* The breakthrough question is soon to follow — sometimes verbally, sometimes behaviorally — "Can I join you in this happiness?"

Once parents recognize the dimensions of the power struggles created by their child, they become empowered. They can stop reacting to his every move. They can cut the puppet strings and in doing so free themselves as well as their child.

As startling as it may seem, the child does not enjoy the role of puppeteer. Fundamentally, he does not want to manipulate, lie, and play games — it's difficult work, and it's hardly fun. When it's no longer an option, he is relieved. He is free. He can pursue a new life. His parents are then firmly in charge and in a position to do what parents are supposed to do: provide, protect, love, nurture, and control.

As the child's power is neutralized by his parents, they can help him redirect his energies in a more productive way. Instead of monitoring him, they can exercise their strengths at parenting him. Instead of alienating their other children, they can respond to them. Ongoing therapy can help them recognize new developmental strides and understand new and old behaviors in a clearer context. The meaning of a particular behavior at an early developmental stage differs greatly from that same behavior after growth has been reactivated. For example, when a disturbed nine-year-old seeks autonomy, it has a much different significance than the same activity exhibited by a now-healthy fifteen-year-old.

It is imperative for parents to take breaks from therapy, school problems, court problems, and any other unpleasant issues that are part of the package of raising a difficult child. When they take good care of themselves, they continue to grow and develop. They become stronger. More comfortable. And they can laugh at things that used to send them rushing to the therapist. They gain an awareness that there are more good times than bad at home, and that awareness is a source of pure joy.

There is no denying the excitement we feel each time we see parents change from reactive to proactive. It is precisely at this point that we know significant progress is in the making. The child has begun to grow, and the parents are just far enough ahead of him to encourage and celebrate his ongoing journey.

TWELVE

WHEN ADOPTION FAILS

Parents and Kids in Crisis

No one likes to face it, but not every international or domestic adoption is a success. Sadly, tragically, some children simply cannot make the adjustment to an adoptive family—any adoptive family. There are also parents who cannot make the adjustment to a child with special needs—any child. Sometimes the adoption fails quietly, with the child simply hanging out until he is old enough to leave. Sometimes it fails after repeated struggles. And sometimes it fails when the parents decide the safety and well-being of the other members of the family are being seriously jeopardized.

Quiet failures seem to occur when the child is unable to form healthy attachments, but it is clear that his best interests are served by remaining in the home. He may annoy and irritate, but his behavior never escalates to outright disruption. He lives in the house but never becomes part of the family. Like a boarder, he simply stays until it is time to go, and then he moves on. In many instances, such kids just disappear, possibly returning to their birth families. If they call, it is only for money or some other kind of help. Occasionally, something clicks with these children in their mid to late twenties. They suddenly appear again, wanting to become part of the family.

Bill was adopted at age ten after being removed from his parents' home because of serious, repeated, multiple-perpetrator sexual abuse. He and his younger brother and sisters had "starred" in child pornography videos.

By the time he became a teenager, Bill's anger was expressed as complete disregard for every rule his parents laid down. He broke rules about school, curfew, alcohol, sex, and drugs. At eighteen, he hit the road, drifting a few states to the west. Suddenly, at twenty-three, Bill sent his parents a Christmas card with a picture of his bride and their baby. Months later, he phoned and shyly asked if he could bring his family home for a visit. While the relations remain tentative and the bond fragile, his parents are amazed at what a good father and husband Bill is trying to be.

Other children are not so kind. They leave a trail of torn families and broken spirits in their wake.

Ron, eleven, began his journey through the system when he was removed from his birth home at six months because reports by a doctor indicated that he was not receiving necessary medical care. He was returned after six months in foster care. His mother, raised in foster homes and institutions, was ill-equipped to handle the pressures of parenting. Life in the home was chaotic, abusive, and violent. But because Ron's father had a good job, the home appeared clean and well cared for to the casual observer.

When Ron was four, his twin sisters were born into the chaos. They, too, began the bumpy development of neglected kids. During the next seven years, Ron and his sisters were separated from and reunited with his parents six times. The parents always seemed to do just enough—quit drinking, cleaned the house, bought a few groceries, stopped their violent fighting—to convince authorities to return the children one more time. But each time, they quickly returned to their old habits, and the children were finally freed for adoption. Separated from his sisters in foster care, Ron seldom saw them as he moved twenty-three times before being adopted at age eleven. He lived in his birth home, foster homes, preadoptive homes, group homes, and a residential treatment center. At one point, an attempt was made to reunify Ron with his twin sisters in a foster home. When Ron terrorized the girls with threats, physical violence, and attempted sex, the experiment ended.

Because of his history, Ron was placed in an experienced adoptive home with four older children. At first, everything seemed fine. Although Ron used a lot of abusive language, he seemed particularly close to his adoptive mother. He went out of his way to be polite and engaging to her. It looked as though this "last chance" was going to work.

Then Ron's behavior changed. He refused to listen to his mother or do anything she asked. While remaining loving and cooperative to his new dad, Ron went to extremes to upset his mom. He ran away, urinated in her closet, refused to eat the food she prepared, and became increasingly violent toward her and the other children in the family. Because his father saw none of this for a while, he remained loyal to Ron for a time. He simply could not believe this charming boy was purposely directing anger at his wife. Ron's new mother became frightened. She began keeping her distance from him and dreaded returning home after work. Depression deepened as she saw her family being systematically destroyed by this new child. Ron began asking his father to divorce his mother so that they could be a family without her.

The parents tried traditional therapy, respite care, linking with the past (including visits with his sisters), and every parenting technique imaginable. The harder they tried, the worse Ron's behavior became. His adoptive mother began to realize that the only hope of preserving her family was for the boy to leave. Because Ron was still actively charming his adoptive father, Dad was less willing to accept that drastic solution. As time passed, however, he became more aware of, and concerned about, the abuse that his wife and other children were experiencing at Ron's hands. When the family's dog died under mysterious circumstances and Ron began to threaten his mother's life, the father gave up.

As the family wrestled with feelings of failure, anger, and despair toward Ron, he became more honest. He told his parents and therapist that he didn't want a new family. His birth mother had pledged eternal love and he was holding on to that, despite the fact that he had not lived with her for years. He was waiting for his mom, and no one else would ever be able to take her place. He admitted that he liked his adoptive family, but he already had a mom and did not want another. If his father would leave her and his other children, that would be all right. Otherwise, he would never show her respect, never love her, and never join the family.

The family, to preserve itself, had to say good-bye to Ron. His rage and violence sent him on his way through a series of placements that will likely continue until he is eighteen. His adoptive family, beaten and battered, began the painful process of healing.

Children like Ron have a definite agenda and the stalwart perseverance to stick to it, no matter what attempts their adoptive parents make. In Ron's case, it seems the one thing he held on to throughout multiple moves was his desire to reunite with his mother. To accept a new mother would have clashed against that single-minded goal.

Many times, the hurt child has strong fantasy-laden ties to his birth family. The parent becomes the archetypal ideal mother or father who is the only one who can truly love him. Part of the fantasy is to believe that if he goes through enough social workers, enough foster homes, enough failed adoptions, "they" will finally give up and let him go home. He may paint, often with the unintentional help of professionals, a rosy picture of his former life. By avoiding the disclosure of painful truths, adults hope to protect him from the harsh reality of his past. But this only serves to confuse him.

While reviewing a history supposedly written by both a child and his social worker, we read that he didn't live with his birth parents because of "money problems." The child, who had the history in his possession for years, had no idea what this meant. When we discussed budgets he said, "Oh, you mean Dad took all the money from us, spent it on booze and drugs, then beat us and we had no food." That is hardly the picture "money problems" conjures up for most people. Facing reality, no matter how grim, helps a child heal and allows him to join successfully with a new family. And it gives him a rational explanation for having been moved from his birth home.

CHILDREN IN FEAR OF REJECTION

Hurt children are often so frightened by intimacy that they will go to any lengths to avoid it. They are afraid to love because people in their past, those who should have loved and protected them, hurt and abused them. Their deep assumption is that their adoptive parents, like everyone in their past, will hurt them and leave them. When that happens, it will be much easier to be left by people they hate.

Underlying that simple thought pattern is the belief that they are not lovable, that no one will love them anyway. In the past, the words "I love you" were often followed by abuse, neglect, abandonment, or sexual advances. They have come to believe that there is something so wrong with them, something so ugly inside, that no one could ever love them.

They will bend any rule, take any stand, and challenge any authority to be in control of every situation. Evoking anger, frustration, and distance is their primary goal. Their actions may include:

- Making mealtimes a point of discord by rejecting any semblance of acceptable behavior. Some children go so far as to vomit at every meal to avoid receiving any nurturing from their parents. More common behaviors include food hoarding, out-of-control eating, binges, and animalistic table manners.
- Creating conflict at every bedtime. They may refuse baths, trash their bedroom, refuse to sleep, and roam the house at night, creating havoc and terror.
- Disrupting school activities by challenging, ignoring, or aggravating all authority. Bus drivers, teachers, hall monitors, principals, and everyone else may grow to dislike or fear these children.

Such a child has learned one lesson well: If he creates enough trouble, his new parents will finally crack under the strain and send him on his way. He "wins" in two ways: He experiences a smaller amount of pain than he would have if he allowed himself to attach and then had to leave, and he is able once again to play the role of victim by being rejected. He will gain sympathy because of the rejection and will prove his theory that he is truly unlovable.

When a child has decided to provoke rejection, he is remarkably resourceful in his methods. Every button the parent has will be pounced upon and thrashed. The child will often disgust his parents by refusing to wash or comb his hair, brush his teeth, or take a bath. His room may become a lair, filled with the offensive odors of urine, rotting food, and body odor. Every day we hear of children and adolescents who urinate and defecate all over their homes and their bodies. Boys are biologically equipped to be more creative when they urinate. We have heard stories of boys urinating into family mouthwash, down heating ducts, on walls, on carpet, and all over furniture.

> Tiffany, age twelve, was adopted as a toddler. Her new family had no information about her early years and no realization of the impact those years would have on her life. Tiffany loved to urinate in inappropriate places. She would often take food to bed to hoard, urinate on it, and then eat it.
>
> When her menses began, she refused to wear sanitary napkins, preferring to soil herself and any furniture she could. If forced to wear a napkin, she removed it and left it soiled in public rooms or in her parents' bed. Although nothing was known of her history, her bizarre behavior suggests that Tiffany suffered extreme abuse and/or neglect.

Because we hear of these patterns so often, we believe there may be more to them than just an unpleasantly convenient way to nauseate parents. Such behaviors may be the child's unconscious attempt to recreate the familiar odors of his birth home. Anyone who has made visits to the homes of families who have lost their children because of neglect can attest to the distinct smell that combines urine, feces, and cleaning solutions. Just as we all have certain smells that trigger sensory memories and even emotions, so might nauseating smells serve the hurt child. In his way, he is clinging to his birth parents at a deep level.

Children determined to create rejection are often fixated on violence. Through threats, preoccupation with gore, and vicious actions, they scare family, friends, teachers, neighbors, and other children. As their behavior intensifies, they may be asked to leave scouting groups, churches, sports teams, and so on. Sometimes the violence is so extreme that parents have to terminate the adoption in order to protect the lives of others:

- On the way to therapy, the family stopped at a drive-through for soft drinks. The mom noticed that when she tried to take a sip, her straw was clogged. Her daughter had put pills into her drink in an attempt to poison her.
- He was bigger than his brother by sixty pounds. In the swimming pool, he stood on his brother's back, forcing him under water. It took his parents and two lifeguards to get him off. "I wanted him dead" was his explanation.
- "My brother had breathing problems," said another child. "I liked to put heavy objects on his chest and watch him turn blue. It was fun."
- Twins thought they were cutting the brake line on the car their mom would drive to a meeting. Luckily, they were bad mechanics and cut only the emergency brake line. "We want her dead," they explained.
- "I knew something was wrong," said one foster mother who had smelled kerosene in her lemonade. "Luckily, he's not too bright — he kept waiting around. I finally told him I knew something was in it and I wasn't going to drink it."

This seems to be the stuff of bad television movies, but they are true — if rare — stories of how violence in a child's past and the intense anger it fosters can breed violence in their present lives.

ADOPTIVE PARENTS ON TRIAL

To the unschooled, these children can seem like the victims of the adoptive family. An outsider may see the child as being rigidly controlled by his parents and treated differently from other family members. When he gains sympathy from these people because his clothes are worn out (because he trashed all his good ones), he scores a moral victory. When strangers disapprove of his parents' controlling behavior, he has scored another. He has succeeded in making a loving, caring, kind, nurturing family seem quite the opposite, which is exactly what he wanted. He takes the sympathy and alliance of outsiders as further proof that this is not a good family. His parents, struggling to protect others from his extreme behavior, face a double bind. They cannot let up on him for fear of what he might do, and they receive no support from others. It is truly a no-win situation.

A colleague of ours was once called into a family crisis. She shared that the adoptive mom had said some "horrible things" about the child. The mom told her daughter, "You never wanted to be adopted. You have done everything you can to get out of this family since the day you got here, and you have made me hate you." The therapist was amazed when we commented that the only horror was that it was probably all true. Even therapists trained in dealing with troubled children can fall into the trap of believing the child incapable of creating this much pain and anger in her mom. Instead of supporting parents in their honesty, they blame them for telling the truth.

When a hurt child's behavior escalates to the point of violence and he hurts members of the family, other children, teachers, or pets, many parents are forced to concede defeat. But other families persevere, parenting against all odds until their child reaches maturity and can move on as an "adult." These hardy families often go to extremes to prevent the loss of the child. The pain, rejection, distress, and abuse the child inflicts on them are hard for the outsider to understand. These are couples who haven't been out together in years because no one will babysit. They have locks on bedroom doors for safety. They lock up the pantry and even padlock the refrigerator. They have no friends, no helping relatives, no support systems left. Still they struggle on. They have exhausted every form of therapy and tried every conceivable parenting technique, and nothing works. Some have even tried exorcism in their attempt to reach the loving child they think must surely exist beneath the layers of rage.

They increase control to the point that outsiders view them as a little crazy, if not downright abusive. Their child has no freedom, never leaves the yard, has no friends. What people do not understand is that the parents think they are acting in the best interests of all by protecting both the child and those he might harm. As the child's behavior escalates, the parents' control may approach the absurd.

"What we consider normal," explains one parent, "other parents think is insane. We lock our soft drinks in the car trunk. We have alarms on windows and doors and chains on our refrigerator." Professionals, seeing these parents for the first time, marvel at how such crazy people were ever approved to adopt a child. Odds are, these parents were not so extreme until they adopted a child whose own dysregulation was so great that it generated a reciprocal response in them.

In addition to the stress of attempting to control their child's behavior, these parents feel enormous guilt and shame. They intended to adopt a hurt child and nurture him into a whole person. Instead, they are less parents than jailers, less nurturing than controlling, less accepting than rejecting, less loving than hating. They may have fantasies of hurting, or even killing, their child. What kind of monsters, they wonder, could feel such anger toward a child? Relatives, coworkers, friends, and some professionals often add to these feelings. Into this mix, toss a child who can be completely charming and engaging to all outsiders, and it is a small wonder that these parents feel insane. The same child who put his fist through a wall and pulled a knife on his mother is a charming, helpful, compliant child in respite care.

Parents who plod on in the face of such defeat are sad. They are sad that they cannot reach their child, no matter what they try. They are sad that their hopes and dreams of parenthood have been so brutally crushed. If they have other children, they feel guilt and sorrow over what the adoption has done to them, especially if the adopted child has hurt one of the children. Instead of sharing a Walt Disney adventure, they have hurled the family into a Stephen King novel.

Often, the hurt child creates conflict between his parents to improve his odds in the battle. To one parent—usually the father—he is kind, respect-ful, and agreeable. To the other parent, he is uncooperative, mean, and cruel. Soon his parents are arguing about him. His father accuses his mother of being too strict, of expecting too much, of failing to give him a break. His mother counters by accusing his dad of not supporting her, of believing the child instead of her, of being a pushover. Often, dads arrive home to a crisis night after night. Mom can take no more and demands help in angry and bitter ways. Dad, newly arrived on the scene, feels none of the anger and sees only the result—an angry mom. He does not see the child's behavior that pushed her to this point. Nor does he see the smug look of satisfaction on the face of the child who has orchestrated the scene.

This tendency to alienate, punish, and hurt mothers more than fathers is one we see often. Because mothers give birth and are often the ones left to take care of a child, a hurt child often perceives them as the ultimate betrayers. They are the ones a child feels should have protected them, cared for them, fought for them, and loved them. Because the child is angry at his birth mother for failing to do her job, he directs that anger at her substitute—his adoptive mom. She pays for taking the birth mother's place, for being the woman who could actually parent him. Her caring seems only to intensify his anger at his birth mom. After all, if he is as lovable as this woman thinks he is, why didn't his birth mother take better care of him?

In addition, the child may view a mother as the weaker parent. It is always easier to attack the weakest in the pack. The child may be repeating a multigenerational pattern. In most abusive homes, women are consistently demeaned and attacked, so the child may be acting out behaviors he learned on a very basic level. Even if he was removed from the abusive home before he could talk, he internalized the attitudes directed at women by the "winning" side. He wants, after all, to be a winner too.

Marital conflicts add stress to an already overwhelming situation. The parents can't agree on a solution, and one may feel pressed to choose between the spouse and the child. If a divorce occurs and one parent keeps the child, the child has won the ultimate victory. He gets what he wants—someone all to himself. But he loses far more than he gains. If the parents decide to give up the child, one parent may still blame the other and be unable to forgive.

WHEN IT'S TIME TO SAY GOOD-BYE

A child cannot continuously abuse others and remain in a family. Just as an abusive spouse needs to leave the home or an abusive parent needs to relinquish the child, so it may be necessary for an abusive child to be removed from the family to keep the others in the home safe. Sometimes it is possible to remain legally involved in a child's life, even though he lives elsewhere. Other times families elect to terminate parental rights.

Dissolution, the term given to ending adoptions, is a painful, permanent step that is sometimes necessary. It should not be the first step, but it can be the only alternative left when all other options have been exhausted.

Sometimes all that's left is to say good-bye.

Many times the adoptive family's pain continues. Parents are left with shattered dreams, mangled marriages, and angry children. While the family members may learn to forgive, none will forget the trauma they have been through. Adoptive parents must grieve the loss as deeply as any parent who loses a child. And they must struggle with their guilt, self-inflicted blame, and deep sense of failure. Some international adoptions dissolve when the families, with the help of agencies, go through the legal process of finding new adoptive parents for the children they feel they can no longer care for.

There are too few resources for families who are left hurting and angry. After an adoption fails, parents are often ignored by the agency that placed their child. Workers, unwilling or unable to face the parents' sadness and their own guilt, avoid the family and do nothing to help them heal. The parents are unfairly cast into the role of the offender after they have exhausted themselves and all resources in desperate attempts to keep and help their child. Alone, they grieve.

It is important to remember, however, that not all failed adoptions end this sadly. Remember Ron's parents, who had to terminate their parental rights after Ron's repeated abuse? A year after Ron left, his adoptive parents decided to take the skills they had honed with Ron and try again. They adopted a group of young brothers and sisters from the same agency. About their decision, they say, "If nothing else, Ron taught us a lot. We went into the next placement with our eyes wide open. We learned many parenting skills from Ron, and we are all fine now. We still hear from him once in a while . . . I guess our relationship is the closest he will ever have to family."

A child sometimes disrupts one family, only to move on and be adopted successfully by another. Sometimes this is because the child received help to better prepare him; sometimes it is because he feels more "at home" in the second adoptive home. When his behaviors are better known, a better-equipped family sometimes can be found to help him. Just because one adoption experience fails, a child is not necessarily doomed to repeated failure, nor is the next family to adopt him consigned to chaos and defeat.

THIRTEEN

WHEN ADOPTION WORKS

Healing the Hurt Child

For every adoptive failure, there are many, many more successes. Parents who adopt a hurt child who is eventually able to attach and become part of the family seldom regret the experience. They often learn more about themselves than they bargained for and may work harder than they wished, but they invariably share a deep pride and profound joy at playing such an important role in a child's life.

As one dad who adopted a sibling group of four noted, "I don't want to be remembered for working in a factory for thirty years. I want to be remembered for doing a good job with these kids. They make my life worthwhile."

A mother, looking back at five years of therapy, police intervention, school problems, and family turmoil, said, "Would I adopt her (at thirteen) again? You bet. I learned so much about myself and the world. She's in a place she never would be without us. She's so much better. I never suspected it would take so long or be so hard, but it's the best thing I ever did."

These parents are among the thousands who have experienced the unique miracle of entering a hurt child's life and helping him change for the better. As therapists, we often feel battered by the overwhelming obstacles in the road for these children, but we look back with awe at the miracles we have seen.

THE CHILD WHO HEALS

When a child takes the step to really become part of a new family, it is a true miracle. He is choosing to join on an emotional level with the very thing that has hurt him the most. He accepts the joys, sorrows, connections, and complexities that are part of a family—an acceptance both foreign and frightening. As he makes this leap of faith, he begins to reciprocate affection genuinely. He begins to care about family members and lets go of the need to control every situation. He becomes just a kid.

Many times, this shift is signaled by a child's movement, or regression, back to an earlier developmental stage. Now that he has let go of control, he can allow himself to fill in some of the gaps in his developmental process. He may become suddenly shy and act much younger than his years. As the angry, tough, older-than-his-years facade begins to crack, a real child begins to emerge. At this point, he may ask for and need emotional parenting in a new way. This positive forward/backward step must be taken in the safety and privacy of family time.

A ten-year-old may seem more like a toddler as he plays peekaboo or engages in finger-and-toe games. An adolescent may begin snuggling up on a parent's lap to watch television. A twelve-year-old boy plays baby, crawling on the floor while babbling. A sixteen-year-old boy cuddles in his father's lap, sobbing, after discussing his early life. The child is asking for and allowing himself to be parented in a way he's never known. To be allowed this privilege is a gift that a parent should keep private in order to protect the child's dignity.

Rachel was a hyperactive eight-year-old whose temper tantrums were legendary. Not content to lie on the ground, she flung her body around the room. One positive in her life was that she loved and nurtured her dolls. When she moved into her adoptive home, her new mom rocked and bottle-fed her every night. Rachel played baby, not speaking. Her mom held the bottle, rocked, maintained constant eye contact, and told Rachel how pretty she was, how she was going to be okay now, and how she was a good girl. After three months in her new home,

Rachel stopped her tantrums. "I don't need to," she explained. "I have a new mom now. I know because she fed me and told me she loved me."

Children who have been rejected so often sometimes need a strong dose of reassurance before they will allow the bond to form.

Jay was in a therapy session with his adoptive mother, father, and therapist. After hearing the dismal story of their week together, the therapist stated, "The only solution I can see is to give him back."

"Give him back?" cried Jay's mother, standing up and facing the therapist like a mother bear protecting her cub. "I will not give him up! He's mine!"

From that point forward, there was a new bond between mother and child. "I truly claimed him," said the mother, "and he knew it. He knew he was my child."

Being treated well, like a baby should be, can help a child fill in the gaps in his development.

John, age four, stayed home when his brothers and sisters went to school. His adoptive mom held him close for hours. She tickled, kissed, and bottle-fed him. His eyes never left hers. At the end of six weeks, John had stopped hitting, swearing, and spitting. "It's hard to believe," his mother said, "but he's a different kid."

Most often, the child makes these shifts gradually, so parents realize how far he's come only in retrospect. Old, negative behaviors that a child used to distance people fall away as he begins to emulate and internalize family members' values. He begins to invite people into his life instead of striving to keep them away.

When this shift occurs, the child is no longer on the defensive and will replace negative behaviors with new approaches. He may stop stealing, lying, and hoarding food because those behaviors no longer serve his purpose, which has now become a healthy desire to join with people. Spending time with him will actually be fun. He will begin to make friends, not enemies, and will learn to enjoy family events instead of sabotaging them. School, though perhaps not a top priority, will cease to be an arena for conflict. His sense of humor becomes real, and the charm of the past loses its glib texture. Most important, his parents can begin to trust him.

Once this transition begins, the child may become more open about himself, his feelings, and his past. He may begin to share secrets with parents about his birth family or his life in foster homes. No longer a victim, he begins to accept the reality of his birth family and learns to enjoy, and appreciate, the present. He starts to believe he may have a better future in store than his vision of early death, prison, or street life. There is hope.

Although the shift is both definite and permanent, not every day will be sunny. Normal developmental issues that face all parents will arise, but confrontations will not have the intensity of the past, nor will they necessarily be linked to the past. Most problems become typical kid issues. A child may still argue about cleaning his room, but he is not likely to demolish it.

The child, who has sometimes lived in the family for years, finally becomes a member who wants to be accepted as such.

Vincent was starting kindergarten for the second time when he entered his adoptive family. As a baby, he had been tied up and left for days in his crib. He had also been placed with the same foster family three different times.

The family who adopted Vincent had adopted before and were experienced. They were told that he was hyperactive, had problems with stealing and lying, and never felt pain. At first they saw none of this, as Vincent stole their hearts with his intelligence, affection, and musical talent. But the problems began and quickly escalated. He stole a valuable heirloom bracelet from a neighbor. Three times he was brought home by the police — for stealing, setting a fire, and running away. He lied so much that it was impossible to ever believe him. The school constantly called with complaints about his behavior. Once he fell from a bike and, though gashed deeply on his leg, said he felt no pain.

Fortunately, the family's social worker was familiar with both

Attention Deficit Hyperactivity Disorder (ADHD) and Reactive Attachment Disorder. Vincent was diagnosed and placed on medication for his ADHD. His behavior at school and in the community almost immediately improved. Next, his parents found a therapist familiar with attachment problems. Through holding, she helped Vincent deal with his feelings. Finally, the family implemented many parenting techniques presented in *Parenting the Hurt Child*, one of our other books. Armed with new tools and a child who was trying to change, they were able to make progress. It took a long time for everyone to come together, but within a few years, Vincent was on the honor roll. His stealing declined to a few incidents a year, and the family began to function with joy and love for one another.

ADJUSTING TO POSITIVE CHANGE

Even the most positive change requires adjustment. Parents and other family members have established habits in the way they treat the hurt child. Some families must confront the fact that they have lost the family scapegoat. Without realizing it, they expect certain behaviors from the child, who has trained them well. Now that the behaviors are present less often, the family must adjust, and it may be difficult. Parents who have learned from their child that good behavior was usually just a cover must now learn to trust his honest, good actions.

As the family's attention eases off the child, they may discover other areas that have been sadly neglected for some time. Businesses, marriages, and relationships with other children and with people outside the family may have fallen into disrepair. Many parents realize they have done nothing for themselves for months. Now that the resources are once again available, they will often flounder as they learn new roles and new ways to spend time, money, and energy.

During this time, a parent can cause more problems than the child. Because misconduct is reduced, parents may jump on every infraction with unnecessary harshness. The child is in a no-win situation. If he behaves well and tells the truth, no one believes in him. If he behaves poorly, he is in trouble. This is a time when parents must risk letting go of old, angry feelings and trust their child. It is not easy, and progress may be halting, but it is up to the parents to allow it to happen. They don't need to enthusiastically praise every positive action, but they can note and support their child's efforts.

> Charles had been a handful. He stole, lied, and did nothing his parents asked. After attachment therapy he began to change, but his parents didn't let up. He was too much of a problem, and they wanted him removed. When confronted, they admitted that he no longer stole or lied. He was good in school. His transgressions were rather minor and age appropriate. The problem was that the family was now off-kilter. What had been the all-consuming problem — Charles — was no longer the focus. Problems with their marriage and their other children began to surface. It was such a habit to blame Charles that no one stopped to realize these "new" problems were not his fault. As the family's focus shifted away from him onto other problems, it frightened everyone. They were charting new territory without a scapegoat.
>
> Charles was terribly confused. He had changed, and he was being good, but no one was happy. His parents didn't want him as he was, so maybe his role of bad kid was better. Through continued therapy, the entire family came to view things differently, and Charles was welcomed as a contributing member of the family.

Take time to enjoy the child. This is when healthy bonds are forming, and it is the perfect opportunity to connect happily with one another. In fact, the good times together will do more to strengthen and smooth the path than any parenting technique.

GROWTH AND REGRESSION

Remember, the hurt child's progress will not always be consistent, and some regression is to be expected. That's because human growth is never constant. People move forward and acquire new skills and then appear to slip back and lose them again. Remember, though, that the regressions do not go back further than the peak of the last growth spurt.

This diagram illustrates the idea:

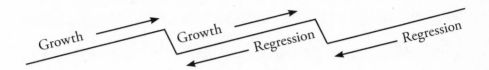

Even in regression, the pattern of growth continues to advance. The child still retains all the new skills and new capacity he gained and is not going back to his old ways.

Anyone who has been on a diet can relate to this conception of progress. After weeks of learning new, healthy habits, stress can prompt a potato chip binge. Even as the chips are going in, the brain is reminding us that this is not the proper way to deal with the situation. In this case, guilt is less effective than support. It's the same with parenting. Instead of shaming the child for relapses, a little understanding and positive nudging back on track can work wonders to help him continue moving in the right direction.

One of the reasons a child regresses is that the old behavior is a connection to his birth family. There is a deep-seated fear that if he loses the behavior, he will lose that connection. In order to help him let go of the past behavior, parents need to be gentle. As they make the present a more loving, caring, attractive place to be, he will have an easier time moving out of the past.

Attachment is not a static thing. As the child continues to participate and become part of the family, the attachment deepens. One way to strengthen the bond is to reflect on earlier times without bringing back the negative emotions. By talking about the past they shared and laughing about the tough times they went through as a family, the child can be eased forward. It is important for him to know that his parents do not hold his past behavior against him.

One of the most important realities for adoptive parents to accept is that the hurt child may never meet "normal" expectations that parents tend to place on children. He may never do particularly well in school and may never attend college. He may live at home far longer than other children — because he had so little time to grow up. And he will be the product of all of the people who have touched his life, both positively and negatively. Accepting the child for who he is, rather than condemning him for who he is not, is the surest way to strengthen his attachment as he moves forward to adulthood.

> Noel was adopted at sixteen. She and her adoptive parents were able to form a solid attachment, but still, Noel became pregnant at eighteen. She moved in with her boyfriend shortly thereafter, leaving her parents with broken dreams of having her in the house for several years while she attended college. While they must deal with their own disappointment, they are secure in the knowledge that they have given Noel a place to call home. She knows that they are there for her and that she can return home if things don't work out with her boyfriend. She also knows who to call with parenting questions and where to go to get help studying for her high school equivalency tests. While it is not a picture-perfect outcome, Noel's parents were able to give her many benefits she would not have experienced in the foster care system.

Parents of hurt children need to focus on being happy with what they have given, rather than sad about imperfect results. The might-have-beens must be grieved but with the knowledge that their child now has a forever family. He has a home where he can leave his yearbook, bring his children, and spend holidays. He has a history and fond memories. And he has a family who loves him and serves him — a model of behavior he has internalized that will aid in his own parenting one day.

Many times, parents who adopt a hurt child find themselves doing it again. "It's like cross-stitching," a single adoptive mom of six said. "It's kind of addicting, and you never know how it's going to come out until it's done."

For all the tears and trials of parenting a hurt child, the payoffs can far exceed the heartache. As a society, we owe these parents a debt for all that they have invested and endured. While their children may not be perfect (none are), they have been given the tools to become competent, responsible, loving adults who will be contributing members of society. That is a tremendous gift to the child . . . and to all of us.

FOURTEEN

SUCCESS STORIES

Four Families Who Made It Work

In our many years of working with adoptive families, we have witnessed countless success stories that reinforce our belief that there is hope for hurt children. We would like to share some of these case histories with you to give you a glimpse of how patience, perseverance, and appropriate interventions can open up a troubled child's heart . . . to show you that even devastating pain really can be transcended.

Mike, the adolescent you met in chapter 1, was adopted again at age seventeen and has become quite a success. Once he settled, permanently and finally, into his adoptive home, his life continued to change for the better. As he grew to realize that the unsettling nature of multiple placements was truly behind him, his personality blossomed. He began to develop a wide range of interests and knowledge. Now exposed to a life with a solid base, he, too, has become a more solid individual.

Mike's commitment to wrestling earned him a high school state championship title and a junior college national championship. In addition, he was a two-time NCAA qualifier and has since competed both nationally and internationally with success. He graduated from a four-year university and has a career in coaching at the university level.

Mike is able to depend on his adoptive family as a point of reference in all of his activities and involvements. Even though his early years were filled with interruptions, he continues to grow and develop just as other young men his age. In fact, his growth in many areas far exceeds that of his peers. His level of independence is balanced with a normal level of dependence on his family, allowing him to move on to adulthood.

All indications suggest that Mike's once tentative life now has connection, direction, definition, and focus. He embraces a future that would have been impossible to achieve prior to being adopted.

Jeannie entered the system at the age of eight, a victim of both sexual and physical abuse imposed by her birth father and four brothers since she was five. The placement process separated her from her birth sisters, who were adopted by an out-of-state family who refused to allow her any contact with her siblings.

While in foster care, Jeannie was moved five times because of her behaviors. Stealing, lying, and running away became her way of life. She eventually landed in a juvenile justice facility where she was incarcerated for theft. When it came time for her release, she was a confused and angry thirteen-year-old—with no preparation for the outside world and nowhere to go.

An inexperienced single woman agreed to take Jeannie in. Supported by the placing agency, her therapist, and her family and friends, she rose to the challenge of parenting this difficult child. Jeannie, on the other hand, tried everything she could to drive her new mother away. When she ran away, her mother picked her up at the police station. When she stole from a local store, her mother made her repay the owner. When she screamed, "You're not my mom!" she readily agreed but demanded respect in spite of the fact.

After several years, Jeannie began to trust that her new mother was different from the other families she had experienced. Here, she felt, she could grow up safely. She finally abandoned her defenses and attached to her mother. Slowly, significant changes began to take place in her life.

One of her biggest problems was a fear of closeness and physical affection — the result of her early sexual abuse — and Jeannie's adoptive mom began working on this during their early days together. She started by giving her daughter gentle back rubs and brushing her hair while they watched television. With the help of an attachment therapist, she began to do holdings with Jeannie. Jeannie ultimately learned that touch could be safe, and she began to look forward to her special close times with her mom.

Her initial discomfort with any show of affection gave way to an acceptance of emotional displays. She empathized with the feelings of others and cried when she felt sad. Over time, her fear of intimacy reversed itself and she was capable of having close friends and dating like any other teen.

Jeannie gained a family and a future. She recently graduated from college and now has a job in the medical field. She is engaged to be married and is planning a big wedding. While those who claimed to know her best predicted that she would be a high school dropout and pregnant by fifteen, Jeannie loved proving them wrong. And not only has Jeannie's life changed, but so have the lives of the children who are yet to be born to her.

Today, instead of leaning on the system, Jeannie contributes to it. With a family to depend on, she is interrupting the intergenerational cycle of abuse.

Half-siblings Quentin and Yvonne were neglected because of their birth mother's medical problems. From the ages of seven and one respectively, they cared for her for six years until she died from cancer. During this time, they lived on nothing but sandwiches and doughnuts.

When Yvonne was three, she was sexually abused by her uncle. Although her mother took her to the hospital and reported the abuse to authorities, she was too ill to follow up with appropriate counseling. Her disease tapped her energies and her resources, leaving nothing to spare for her daughter.

After she passed away, the children—then ages thirteen and seven—lived on their own for about two months. Having slipped through the safety net that is provided for children, the two survived by foraging in trash bins behind fast-food restaurants. They came to the attention of authorities when they were evicted from their apartment for delinquent rent. Their landlord confiscated their property and pets, and the children were left with nothing but each other. Neighbors finally reported them as homeless. Their fathers and families were unknown and/or unavailable, so in the eyes of the system, they were orphans.

Separated in foster care, they longed for each other as the last remnants of a torn family. Finally, one family took on the challenge of adopting them both when Quentin was sixteen and Yvonne was ten. Despite Quentin's age, negative behaviors, and emotional problems and despite Yvonne's past sexual abuse and the family felt that these children deserved a chance at a life together.

They let the children develop at their own pace and were willing not to push for intimacy. By giving them the space they needed, they allowed them to grow and heal. Quentin's and Yvonne's stealing habits—fine-tuned over years of stealing to survive—eventually stopped when they learned that they could depend on their parents to provide for them.

Although Quentin was sometimes an aggressive adolescent, he was always gentle with his sister. He was eager to continue the parenting role he had established with her, so the family allowed him to do so. They felt that the history the siblings endured—enhanced by a powerful love and bond between them—was a special gift that they should be free to share.

If adoption had not been a viable option for Quentin, he would have been emancipated at the age of eighteen. Odds are great that he would have joined the ranks of the homeless. And since he required medication to combat his emotional problems, there was great likelihood that he would have drifted into the adult mental health system.

Instead, his adoptive family helped him get on the right medication to control his depression. And by permitting him to have the parenting relationship that he wanted with his sister, he soon lost the need to care for her, allowing his parents to take over. He completed high school, attended junior college, and discovered an interest in computers. He is now self-sufficient, lives on his own in an apartment, and is a great big brother to Yvonne.

Yvonne was finally able to face her grief over the death of her birth mother. Once she felt safe in her adoptive home and once her basic emotional needs were met, he was free to express her real feelings. Family therapy with her brother and her parents enabled her to deal with her early sexual abuse and the loss of her mother. Today, Yvonne is a successful high school student. She is active in drama and is looking forward to a career as a teacher.

She and her brother — thanks to the parenting of a wonderful adoptive family — have moved beyond tragedy to triumph. Their grief over their mother's death will always be with them, but the help they have received allows them to keep her in their hearts while letting in their new parents, as well. They have been able to deal with the past and have a positive outlook for the future.

Paul, an only child, lived with his birth mother until he was eleven. Throughout his young life, a string of "dads" came and went. All of these men had characteristics in common, and all of them vented their aberrant behaviors on him. They were all physically abusive in a random way. Each time Paul thought peace had finally come, a new terror assailed him.

He was thrown into walls, whipped with electrical cords, tied up with duct tape, and even locked in a closet for days at a time. One night he was awakened by the cold, sharp sensation of a knife against his warm skin. His latest dad, drunk, threatened to cut his throat. Paul suffered these atrocities at the hands of men he barely knew, and he had no idea why he was being brutalized.

In fact, none of this "punishment" had anything to do with Paul's behavior. But, of course, Paul didn't understand that. He learned to lie constantly when questioned at school about his bruises and his home life. He tried his best to cover up and keep his mother's current man happy.

Paul's mother kept him on a strict diet. Usually he went without breakfast and had a peanut butter or cheese sandwich for lunch and dinner. Mom and the dads always dined on far better fare, and once Paul tiptoed downstairs to sneak some leftover meatloaf from his parents' dinner. He was caught and beaten, but he felt it was worth it. For once, he wasn't hungry.

Paul once tried to burn down the house, hoping that he and his mother would move on without the latest dad. His plan failed. Often he ran away, but his mother always brought him back.

Mom had been raised in a series of foster homes and had no parenting or coping skills to help herself or her son. One day, when Paul was eleven, she simply left him in aisle B3 of a large grocery store.

When the Department of Social Services entered Paul's life, the agency first sent him to an emergency foster home. He stayed there briefly, while arrangements were made for long-term foster placement. The new family was very controlling, and Paul did poorly. They were a highly structured and organized unit — the opposite of everything he was used to. He was unable to cope and began to take his frustrations out on the younger children in the home. He hit, pushed, and kicked them in order to express his anger and to control those he viewed as weaker.

Paul felt that to survive he must be in control of someone . . . anyone. His experiences had taught him that when adults are out of control — as they most often were in his life — he had to take control to stay alive. His concept of survival was directly linked to being in charge, even if he wasn't very good at it.

The foster family eventually requested that Paul be removed, and he was placed in a far less structured home in the country. This family gave him more control over his own life, and he enjoyed the freedom of leisure activities, such as going to the pool and playing ball. He began to act more responsibly, he learned limits, and he demonstrated age-appropriate behaviors.

Through this family, he became involved in group therapy. Although he viewed it as useless, he managed to pick up some social skills from the other boys in the group. His therapist — described as intrusive by some, but considered an okay guy by Paul — managed to break through Paul's defenses and get in touch with the frightened little boy that he really was.

With his therapist, Paul did not work on understanding the abuse that he'd endured — after all, there was no logical reason for it in the first place. Instead, they focused on grieving and accepting it. In his words, Paul dumped "tons of anger" until he had only a "pocketful" left. He was able to accept the fact that even though he loved his birth mother, she was not a good parent. He understood that she would never change, and therefore he could never go back to her.

Paul was placed in a permanent home, and plans were made for adoption when he was fourteen. He was capable of being honest with his new parents and learned to negotiate rules with them that were mutually agreeable. He still maintained an aura of aloofness, however, and would often set up his own failures. For example, he would join a sports team, fail to show up for practice, and get thrown off the team. He would do his homework, "forget" to turn it in, and get a failing grade.

His last big grandstand occurred the day before his adoption hearing. Panicked at the concept of what was about to happen, Paul convinced himself that this new family would ultimately reject him as his birth mother had. He was terrified at the prospect of emotional intimacy with these people and fearful of the finality of legalization. *What if they start abusing me after the adoption?* he thought. *How will I ever get out of it?*

He flew into a rage and threatened to kill his adoptive parents. A crisis call was placed to his social worker, and his therapist was immediately notified. Feeling safe in a holding with his therapist, Paul vented his rage at being abandoned, abused, and unloved. He expressed his fear that his new family couldn't possibly want him if his own birth mom didn't. Given a safe environment in which to express his anger toward his mother and his fear of future rejection, Paul began to calm down.

In spite of the upheaval, the family went to court the next day to finalize the adoption. His parents said they were ready to make the commitment, and Paul could do as he pleased. They nervously gave their testimony to the judge, and then Paul — much to their relief — agreed to the adoption.

This move marked only a tentative step toward emotionally joining the family. Paul didn't commit completely until two years later, when another special-needs child was taken in by the family. The new girl's rage, anger, and manipulation drove Paul right into his family's arms. He was indignant at the way she treated "his" family, even though he had done precisely the same thing. He defended them at every opportunity, fuming at the new child for mistreating "the best parents in the world."

Slowly, over time, Paul became the son his parents longed for. He cheerfully attended tutoring and changed his grades from Ds to Bs. He joined a sports team and stayed with it. He made gifts for his parents — a demonstration of both his skill and his love. Today, Paul is well on his way to becoming a mature, responsible adult.

It is stories like these that inspire adoptive parents to keep on trying. Most children who would otherwise grow up lost and unattached to anyone can make it in families who know how to parent them. As they are enriched by the love and security of the family, they also learn to be better parents to their own children. At last, the intergenerational cycle of abuse and neglect can be put to rest.

Even when a child has a less dramatic turnaround than those whose stories we have illustrated here, his parents can still take pride in knowing that he is better off because they became a part of his life. And generations to come will reap the rewards of the good parenting skills the adoptive parents have passed on to their child.

It is time, we believe, to direct every resource possible toward helping the hurt children of our society and their adoptive families. We need to make every effort to create environments where these children can flourish and grow into the best adults they can be. If we don't, we all suffer.

FIFTEEN

REFLECTIONS FROM THE TRENCHES

What It's Like to Hurt and Heal

The adoption triad—the birth family, the adopted child, and the adoptive parents—comprises every adoptive situation. Whether or not all parties are actively involved, they all exist in memory, in loss, or in the present. They have a lot to say about their experiences, and we've asked some of them to share their thoughts and feelings with us.

You will find a wide range of emotion in the following reflections. We thank all of those who agreed to participate and hope that their insights and comments will help you gain a clearer understanding of the personal dynamics involved in the adoption process.

■ ■ ■

"When Theresa and Robert were removed from me, I was a drug and alcohol addict. I cared more about myself and my wild life than my kids. I didn't deserve to have my kids. My boyfriends were my life's interest. They had to be pleased and taken care of. The kids got in the way; they were a bother. Even though I felt I loved them, I didn't want to do what kids need their moms to do.

"Now I am sober and more organized. I have had another child who

I take care of, and I plan to get Robert back since he got tossed out of his adoptive home. Theresa is doing good with her adoptive parents."

— *Martha, birth mother who lost custody of her two children*

■ ■ ■

"The adoptive parent classes are over. The anxiety and excitement of the first meeting with our new son are in the past. Past, too, is the month we spent going back and forth on weekend visits — a five-hour trip each way. We'd spend the five-hour drive there planning what we were going to do and the five hours coming home talking over every detail of the visit. During the week, we'd hurry to cram all the things we'd normally do on weekends into those few free hours after work. We'd rush to get that last coat of paint on his room, buy that last piece of furniture . . . then the weekend arrived, the dog went back to the kennel, and we hit the road again.

"Finally, the day arrives when we sign the placement document that says we're almost parents. Yes, we have the day-to-day responsibility. Yes, we have 'our' child at home with us, and we can start to become a family. But the county is still there, still in control. We really don't think that will be a problem. Our son holds our hands, calls us Mom and Dad, and begins to cling to us.

"On the first trip to church, everyone rushes to meet the new family member. They're not really sure how to act, and we see in them the awkwardness we felt just a few weeks earlier when we met our new child for the first time.

"At home, things are wonderful. Our son behaves perfectly. We figure that everything we were told beforehand was about those other kids out there. Those parents who came and talked to our class are to be pitied for all the rough times they had. Why, our child isn't exhibiting any of that behavior! Oh, there have been a few moments when our child whines or forgets to turn off the hall light, even though we've told him a hundred times. That's normal childhood behavior, isn't it? And lots of kids have problems wetting the bed. Ours comes in and wakes us to tell us and doesn't hide his soiled laundry. And we really don't understand why anyone was so adamant that we take restraint training.

"Then something changes. I'm not sure whether he changed or I just woke up from the dream. He still isn't willing to do what we ask him. If we scold him or say no to him, he says we're treating him just like *they* did (the treatment home, the old foster parents, or maybe even his birth parents). Then the threats start: 'If you don't let me do XYZ, I'll run away.' 'You can't spank me, or I'll tell everyone you're abusing me just like my *real* mom.' 'You can't make me do that; you're not my real parents.' 'You don't love me; you're just doing this for the money.'

"Then the first tantrum happens. We look at this wonderful child whom we've comforted during those early nightmares—the child we've read to every night until his face takes on that angelic glow of sleep. And in his place is a monster—threatening us, ripping up his school papers, literally bouncing off the walls—and our minds go into overload trying to remember how to restrain him. And that horrible thought creeps into my mind: 'Why did I do this?'

"And soon, the storm is over. We've gotten him settled down, my heart has returned to its normal beating pattern, and I think, 'Okay, so that's over and now we can go on.' He's tested us and now knows better than to try that again. After all, we've shown him that we have things under control and he doesn't have to worry about our beating him or locking him in a closet or any of the horrid things they told us his birth parents did. We've proven to him that we are the perfect parents, and we know he's so grateful for the whole learning experience. For weeks, things go along so well. We've reached a new level in the relationship and the chaos is all over.

"Then I get the phone call at work. 'Come get your son. He's being suspended for biting his teacher.' None of my friends' children have ever been suspended. I put in the frantic calls to our adoption worker and our son's psychologist. 'You have to expect setbacks when you're making progress,' they tell me. 'This is a good sign. Be happy; your child has bonded to you.' My question is, 'Do I really want to make this much progress?'"

—*Beverlee, adoptive mother whose son was eleven at placement*

■ ■ ■

The following three comments are from birth siblings who had not lived together for six years. After that time, they were reunited in an adoptive home.

"When we all moved in together, it was really weird. It was like moving in with strangers. I loved my brothers, but I didn't know them anymore. We had been apart for six years, almost one-third of my life. It took a lot of time to get to know each other again."

—*Holly, age nineteen, adopted at sixteen*

"Mom and I were talking about my cousins. They fight with each other all the time. She said all brothers and sisters fight like that. She said she noticed that we didn't, and she wondered why. I told her that being taken away from each other for six years stays in your memory. You appreciate your brother and sister more."

—*Shawn, age sixteen, adopted at thirteen*

"It was good."

—*Stephen, age ten, adopted at seven*

■ ■ ■

The children's adoptive parents have this to say:

"Our hardest times are when something comes up that makes us realize how much our kids have missed. Things we took for granted as children that helped us become the people we are today are missing. Simple things like waking up every morning knowing that Mom and Dad will be there."

—*Ben, adoptive father*

"I'll be telling them stories about my childhood, and I'll look in their eyes and know they haven't a clue what I'm talking about. That's when that overwhelming feeling of sadness hits me with such a force I can't move. I grieve for the childhood my kids never had."

—*Sharon, adoptive mother*

■ ■ ■

"You can't take someone out of his family and put 'em in another one and expect 'em to act like nothing changed—no matter what age they are."

— *David, age sixteen, adopted at four from El Salvador*

■ ■ ■

"The thing that stands out in my mind most about my treatment is how before my treatment I never grew or needed a coat because with all the hate and anger I never felt anything. But after my treatment, because of finally learning to accept love and nourishment, I grew to be a big sports star and I could feel more. I would like to thank the treatment for all I have."

— *Bryon, age sixteen, adopted at nine*

■ ■ ■

"I had a bad birth mom because I was in alcohol when I was born."

— *Marcus, age six, adopted at three*

■ ■ ■

"At the time of being put up for adoption, it feels like the worst thing in the world. But as you grow older, you learn how strong you have become from that experience. The worst thing to do is give up. There are parents out there for every child—ones who will love you more than you could imagine. It was awhile before I could give my father the love he was giving me. The only love I thought I could get was from my birth family. But I was wrong. If I had waited for the promises they made to me, I would have missed out on the best thing in my life—my *real* family. I know it hurts to not be with your birth family. But being with the ones who love and care about you can heal that."

— *James, age twenty-three, adopted at fourteen*

■ ■ ■

"Sandy and I were married twenty-two years before we made the decision to adopt. As the years went by, we became more and more depressed as we realized we were going to spend the rest of our lives with no children or grandchildren. Sandy comes from a large, close-knit family where get-togethers for holidays and birthdays are very important. Even though we enjoyed getting together with all the nieces and nephews, the trip home was always rather quiet. Finally, one day in October 1991, after not talking about it for seventeen years, we made the decision to adopt. Here it is four years later, and we have three sons—Ken, seventeen; Ed, fifteen; and Josh, eleven. These three boys have been the biggest challenges of our lives and also the most rewarding experience anyone could ever imagine."

—*Bill, adoptive father*

■   ■   ■

"While waiting to become an adoptive parent, I created in my mind a dream of what my child would be like and what this phase of my life would encompass. When our child was finally placed with us and we discovered that he was unattached, I began a grieving process for the loss of my dream. The process included denying that this could be happening to my child and to me. Then anger and outrage took over when parenting this unattached child became time-consuming and emotionally draining. When acceptance finally came, I had lost a good portion of who I am. These phases appeared, disappeared, overlapped, and intertwined. The piece with the most emotional impact, however, was the overwhelming sadness over the death of my dream—the kind of sadness that you can feel only when it involves loving your child."

—*Kathy, adoptive mother*

■   ■   ■

"We were just tickled when our children were placed with us. They reminded me of sunshine and flowers. Everyone was so happy to be together as a family . . . they all fit right in. It was fun, exciting . . . all the children's noises—in and out the door, asking for cookies, asking for me. When little children are around, you get to do little children things. I loved it."

—*Larsenia, mother of six adopted children—two sibling groups of three—and two birth children*

■   ■   ■

"It was hard waiting for an adoptive family. I was scared because I might get parents I didn't like. I wanted it to happen soon—I had no patience. I told some kids, and they thought it was weird. I imagined what the people would be like, and it turned out good. Waiting kids shouldn't be thinking bad things. It usually turns out good.

"I was afraid to leave my foster parents and my friends. I thought I might never find new ones."

—*Bobbie, age fifteen, adopted at ten*

■ ■ ■

"Colleen was nearly fifteen when she was placed with us for adoption in the fall of 1991. Since then, she has had a remarkable history of moves in and out of our household. From the day she came to us, she has always found at least one other family in the area, wormed her way into their good graces and into their home for frequent visits and overnights, called the adults Mom and Dad, and, on occasion, begged them to adopt her, letting us know that 'They understand me.'

"There have been at least ten of these families over our three-plus years with our daughter. It seems she keeps moving because she knows no other way of coping with the real world and because this is how she controls her world. It's her only familiar way of life and her protection against being moved.

"I am certain her problem is the result of having been moved in and out of group homes, foster homes, relatives' homes, and children's homes from birth until the age of fourteen. A court psychologist recently estimated that she was moved at least twenty-seven times in her brief life span.

"The bad news is, next to the system that retained and trained her for so many years, she is still her own worst enemy. The good news is, now that she's eighteen, we can keep on being the one thing in her life that doesn't change. We can be her loving parents. But we don't have to reopen our door and take part in her self-destructive drama of manipulation and endless moves."

—*Mary, adoptive mother*

■ ■ ■

"My own experience tells me there are many keys to a successful adoption—none of which are as easily done as they are said. For me, it was a matter of showing me, giving me some tangible proof that the caring and security were real, that these weren't mere words of love and devotion but that all these things were real and could and would be there for me.

"My adoptive father of twelve years showed me these things. I tested, I pushed, I rejected. Through it all—rejection, drugs, alcohol, prison, and failure—he was there, showing me with much more than words. Thus, I felt the need to give all these things back to him—the devotion, the love, the security, all the things he has given to me. I had to give these things back to him because he so unselfishly gave of himself to me. To be there, to stand strong and never give up. To give and to take on both sides of the issues. Parent and child both. This, I feel, makes for a successful adoption."

—*Patrick, now an adult, adopted as a teen*

■　■　■

"Before I gave birth to my daughter, I made two life-changing decisions. The first decision was to relinquish her for adoption so that she could be raised by a loving family who would provide for all her needs while she grew up. My second decision was that no matter what, I would once again be reunited with her and let her know that I have always loved her. When we met, the hole in my heart was finally sealed forever. The precious child whom I had given birth to eighteen years ago was returning to my life. We were separated by love and now have been reunited by that same love."

—*Denise, birth mother*

■　■　■

"Adoption has given me a whole new life. A life that I never had before. A life that most kids with natural parents would die to have. Before I was adopted, I felt sorry for myself because I didn't live with my natural parents. Now that I am adopted, I feel that I am the luckiest person in the world. I'm lucky because when things were going bad, I was adopted by the best possible parent that a kid could ever want. I wouldn't trade my life for anything in the world."

—*Brian, adopted as an adolescent, now a college graduate*

A CALL TO ACTION

As we finished this book and reviewed its contents, we continued to have thought after thought about what we said, what we didn't say, and what we might have said. Our consciences worked overtime as we looked back at what we had written and wondered how our various audiences would think and feel about our attitudes, philosophies, and methodologies. We then reminded ourselves that *Adopting the Hurt Child* is but one book, and it is not meant to be all things to all people.

Certainly, our intention was not to provide an answer for every clinical, social, and political issue concerning adoption. Instead, our goal was to focus on core issues that we feel have the greatest impact on the ultimate success or failure of the adoption process. Our perspective is but one angle—a view that may be incorporated into another to help expand an understanding of effective adoption practices.

We believe that the symptoms we have described throughout this book are the result of fractured child development. It is clear that we, as a society, must work to ensure that each child has the chance for uninterrupted development. Of course, when the child can do this within his own family of birth, it is best. But because this is not always possible, we need to smooth the path to permanent adoption if these children are to have a chance. Policies that prevent or delay children from being adopted once the idea of reunification is eliminated must be reviewed with an eye toward helping these children more effectively. Case histories—and they are numerous—that tell of seven years and twelve placements in foster care should no longer be the rule.

Those who share our view can help address the concerns we have illuminated in *Adopting the Hurt Child*. Some of you may work to correct problems that exist within the system. Others may facilitate change on a child-by-child or a family-by-family basis. Both kinds of efforts are critical and will help affect adoption in positive ways.

Any call to action that results from this book will provide the much needed momentum to facilitate change. It is our hope that *Adopting the Hurt Child* will shine light on the important issues we have delineated and inspire individuals to:

- Allow children to remain in their birth homes when safety can be ensured
- Remove children only when it is necessary for their safety, both physical and emotional
- Limit repeated, failed reunification efforts when all evidence points to continued damage to the child
- Limit the number of moves (placements) a child has prior to adoption placement
- Examine a foster care system that has strayed far from its intentions of providing one temporary home for a child
- Do everything necessary to facilitate a hurt child's capacity to develop strong, secure attachments to others
- Preserve all positive prior attachments, such as birth family and foster family
- Empower and inform adoptive families — both parents and children — so they can knowledgably examine adoption within its entire scope, including events that led to the child's removal from the birth home and how the child's history can be preserved and used to strengthen his present and his future
- Recognize that although adopting a hurt child has its difficulties, understanding these difficulties is the first step toward achieving great success — for the adopted children, for the adoptive parents, and for all those whose lives are touched along the way

To the thousands of children who wait for adoption . . . to the thousands already living in adoptive homes . . . to the thousands who are yet to be born, we wish you love, health, happiness, and a safe place to live. May you each find the care, joy, tenderness, and peace that you deserve, and may your todays and tomorrows be filled with love.

*People only unmask themselves in the privacy of love or friendship.
One has to treat them with care and tenderness. Each is unique
and we may never see another like him. We must protect him from
injury if we are to share his life.*

ANAÏS NIN

NOTES

PREFACE

1. www.acp.hhs.gov/programs/cb/stats — research/afcars/tar/report14.htm.
2. Numbers vary based on geographic location and the age of the child, so we have used a mean from the Child Welfare League of America's National Data Analysis System. In addition, since residential treatment varies by the child's specific needs, age, degree of supervision, and treatment, the numbers presented reflect a mid-range cost.

CHAPTER 2

1. *Diagnostic and Statistical Manual of Mental Disorders* (IV-TR American Psychiatric Association, 2000), 127-130.
2. Adapted from Foster W. Cline, MD, *Understanding and Treating the Severely Disturbed Child* (Evergreen, CO: Evergreen Consultants in Human Behavior, 1979), 87–109.
3. The National Child Traumatic Stress Network, "Complex Trauma in Children and Adolescents," Cook Alexandra, PhD, Margaret Blaustein, PhD, Joseph Spinazzola, PhD, eds., www.nctsnet.org/nccts/assetido ?id=478.
4. M. S. Ainsworth, M. C. Blehar, and E. Waters, *Patterns of Attachment: A Psychological Study of the Strange Situation* (Oxford, England: Laurence Erlbaum, 1978).

CHAPTER 3

1. Foster W. Cline, MD, *Understanding and Treating the Severely Disturbed Child* (Evergreen, CO: Evergreen Consultants in Human Behavior, 1979), 28.

CHAPTER 5

1. M. Elizabeth Vonk, "Cultural Competence for Transracial Adoptive Parents," *Social Work* 46, no. 3 (July 2001) 246–256.
2. Versions of this exercise are widely used in adoption training programs. We were unable to identify the originator of it and therefore cannot give proper credit.

CHAPTER 7

1. Department of State, "Immigrant Visas Issued to Orphans Coming to the U.S.," http://travel.state.gov/family/adoption/stats/stats_451.html.
2. Anna Marie Merril and Betty Laning, "Who Are the Children? A Perspective on International Adoption," *Adoptalk*, Summer 1997, 4–5.
3. Maureen Leister, MA, MPS, and Maye Van Arsdel, MS, "Adoptive Family Ties" (presentation at Building and Growing: A Conference on Adoption and Child Development, Auckland, New Zealand, June 1997).
4. Susan Soon-Keum Cox, *Outside Testimony Hearings before House Foreign Appropriations Subcommittee*, 102nd Cong. 1st sess. 1991.

CHAPTER 9

1. Gloria Hochman, Ellen Feathers-Acuna, and Anna Huston, "The Sibling Bond: Its Importance in Foster Care and Adoptive Placement" (National Adoption Information Clearinghouse, 1992), 2.
2. Some information in this chapter originally appeared in a resource guide for adoptive parents: Regina Kupecky, "Siblings Are Family, Too" (Pittsburgh, PA: Three Rivers Adoption Council, June 1993).

CHAPTER 10

1. Regina Kupecky, "Siblings Are Family, Too" (Pittsburgh, PA: Three Rivers Adoption Council, June 1993).

CHAPTER 11

1. Temple Grandin, "Calming Effects of Deep Touch Pressure in Patients with Autistic Disorder, College Students, and Animals," *Journal of Child and Adolescent Psychopharmocology* 2, no. 1 (1992).

2. Daniel A. Hughes, *Facilitating Developmental Attachment* (Northvale, NJ: Jason Aronson, Inc., 1997), 77.

3. Francine Shapiro, *Eye Movement Desensitization and Reprocessing—Basic Principles, Protocols, and Procedures* (New York: The Guilford Press, 1995), viii.

4. Sebern Fisher, MA, "Neurofeedback: A Treatment for Reactive Attachment Disorder," http://www.eegspectrum.com/Articles /Articles/InHouseArticles/RAD/.

5. J. C. May, "Family Attachment Narrative Therapy: Healing the Experience of Early Childhood Maltreatment," *Journal of Marital and Family Therapy* 31 (2006): 221–237.

6. M. Nichols, , D. Lacher, , and J. C. May, , *Parenting with Stories: Creating a Foundation of Attachment for Parenting Your Child* (Deephaven, MN: Family Attachment and Counseling Center, 2002).

7. D. B. Lacher, T. Nichols, and J. C. May, *Connecting with Kids Through Stories: Using Narratives to Facilitate Attachment in Adopted Children* (London: Jessica Kingsley, 2005).

8. Story contributed by D. B. Lacher for this book.

RESOURCES

There are many support groups, organizations, and much information available on adoption and attachment. We have not investigated all of these organizations, so inclusion on this list does not reflect our recommendation. Lack of inclusion reflects our lack of awareness and is not an intent to exclude. We offer the information to you for your own exploration.

Adopt a Special Kid (AASK), 8201 Edgewater Drive, Suite 103, Oakland, CA 94621; toll-free: (888) 680-7349; fax: (510) 553-1747, www .adoptaspecialkid.org.

Adoptees' Liberty Movement Association (ALMA), PO Box 85; Denville, NJ 07834; www.almasociety.org.

Adoption Assistance Hotline, (800) 470-6665. *Information on adoption assistance. Advocates for older-child adoptions. Sponsored by National Adoption Assistance Training, Resource, and Information Network (NAATRIN) through North American Council on Adoptable Children (NACAC).*

Adoption E-mail Lists Directory, www.comeunity.com/adoption/listservs .html. *Preadoption and postadoption annotated directory of adoption counseling. E-mail lists for adoptive families. Information on attachment therapy.*

Adoption Health Clinics, Many clinics have been set up nationwide to help parents with health issues relating to adoption. For a clinic near you, visit the following websites: www.med.umn.edu/peds/iac/otherprofessionals/ home.html; www.aap.org/sections/adoption/default.cfm.

Adoption Learning Partners, phone: (800) 566-3995; www
.adoptionlearningpartners.org. *Interactive online courses.*

Adoption Network, 4614 Prospect Avenue, Suite 550, Cleveland, OH
44103; phone: (216) 325-1000; fax: (216) 881-7510; www.adoptionnetwork
.org. *Triad member support group that assists with the search for biological
families.*

***Adoption Today* Magazine,** 541 East Garden Drive, Unit N, Windsor, CO
80550; phone: (970) 686-7412; toll-free: (888) 924-6736; fax: (970) 686-
7412; www.adoptinfo.net.

***Adoptive Families* Magazine,** 39 West 37th Street, 15th Floor, New
York, NY 10018; phone: (646) 366-0830; fax: (646) 366-0842; www
.adoptivefamilies.com.

ADOPTNET Support for Adoptive Families, www.adoptnet.org. *Support
for adoptive families.*

Adopt Us Kids, Adoption Exchange Association, 8015 Corporate Dr., Suite
C, Baltimore, MD 21236; toll-free: (888) 200-4005; www.adoptuskids.org.
Listing of waiting U.S. children.

American Academy of Adoption Attorneys, PO Box 33053, Washington,
D.C. 20033; phone: (202) 832-2222; www.adoptionattorneys.org. *Attorneys
who specialize in adoptions and adoption-related laws.*

American Adoption Congress, 1000 Connecticut Avenue, NW,
Suite 9, Washington, D.C. 20036; phone: (202) 483-3399; www
.americanadoptioncongress.org. *Assistance with all facets of adoption.*

American Psychiatric Association, 1000 Wilson Boulevard, Suite 1825,
Arlington, VA 22209-3901; phone: (703) 907-7300; www.psych.org.

American Public Welfare Association, www.apwa.org. *Referrals to agencies
for subsidies, funding, classification, etc.*

Annie E. Casey Foundation, 701 St. Paul Street, Baltimore, MD 21202;
phone: (410) 547-6600; fax: (410) 547-3610; www.aecf.org. *Fosters public
policies, reforms, and support for vulnerable families and children.*

ARCH National Respite Network, 800 Eastowne Drive, Suite 105, Chapel Hill, NC 27514; phone: (919) 490-5577; fax: (919) 490-4905; chtop .org/ARCH.html. *Training and technical assistance to respite providers.*

ATTACh, PO Box 533, Lake Villa, IL 60046; toll-free: (866) 453-8224; fax: (847) 356-1584; www.attach.org. *International coalition of professionals and parents working together to promote identification, intervention, and treatment for those with attachment difficulties.*

Attachment and Bonding Center of Ohio, 12608 State Road, Suite 1, North Royalton, OH 44133; phone: (440) 230-1960; fax: (440) 230-1965; www.abcofohio.net. *Preadoption and postadoption counseling. Intensive attachment therapy. The authors can be contacted at this location.*

Beech Brook-Spaulding, 3737 Lander Road, Pepper Pike, OH 44124; phone: (216) 831-2255; toll-free: (877) 546-1225; fax: (216) 831-0436; www.beechbrook.org. *Residential and outpatient treatment for children. Adoption services for special-needs children.*

Child Help USA National Child Abuse Line, toll-free: (800) 422-4453; www.childhelp.org.

Child Welfare Information Gateway, Children's Bureau/ACYF, 1250 Maryland Avenue, SW, 8th Floor, Washington, D.C. 20024; phone: (703) 385-7565; toll-free: (800) 394-3366; www.childwelfare.gov/index.cfm.

Child Welfare Institute, 111 E. Wacker Dr., Suite 325, Chicago, IL 60601, phone: (312) 949-5640; fax: (312) 922-6736; www.gocwi.org.

Child Welfare League of America, 2345 Crystal Drive, Suite 250, Arlington, VA 22202; phone: (703) 412-2400; fax: (703) 412-2401; www .cwla.org. *Child welfare laws and referrals.*

Children Awaiting Parents, 595 Blossom Road, Suite 306, Rochester, NY 14610; phone: (585) 232-5110; toll-free: (888) 835-8802; fax: (585) 232-2634; www.capbook.org. *Adoption agency. Provides lists of waiting children and parents.*

Children's Defense Fund, 25 East Street, NW, Washington, D.C. 20001; phone: (202) 628-8787; toll-free (800) 233-1200; www.childrensdefense

.org. *Legal work, advocacy, and education for children.*

Dave Thomas Foundation, 4150 Tuller Road, Suite 204, Dublin, OH 43017; toll-free: (800) 275-3832; fax: (614) 766-3871; www. davethomasfoundation.org. *Dedicated to increasing adoptions. Videos and posters available.*

Ethica: A Voice for Ethical Adoption, 8639-B 16th Street, Suite 156, Silver Spring, MD 20910, phone: (301) 637-7650; www.ethicanet.org.

Evan B. Donaldson Adoption Institute, 120 East 38th Street, New York, NY 10016; phone: (212) 925-4089; fax: (775) 796-6592; www .adoptioninstitute.org.

Evan B. Donaldson Adoption Institute: Voice for Adoption, PO Box 77496, Washington, D.C. 20013; phone: (703) 430-7600; www .adoptioninstitute.org/policy/polvfa.html. *Organization that lobbies for legislation regarding adoption.*

Families for Russian and Ukrainian Adoption, PO Box 2944, Merrifield, VA 22116; phone: (703) 560-6184; fax: (413) 480-8257; www.frua.org.

Family Builders Network, c/o Spaulding for Children, 16250 Northland Drive, Suite 100, Southfield, MI 48075; phone: (248) 443-7080; fax: (248) 443-7099; www.spaulding.org. *Network of specialized adoption programs and agencies.*

Family Resource Center on Disabilities, 20 East Jackson Boulevard, Room 300, Chicago, IL 60604; phone: (312) 939-3513; www.frcd.org. *Resource, advocacy, and funding for disabled parents with disabled children.*

Federation of Families for Children's Mental Health, 9605 Medical Center Drive, Suite 280, Rockville, MD 20850; phone: (240) 403-1901; fax: (240) 403-1909; www.ffcmh.org. *Advocacy services offered by chapters in every state.*

Holt International Children's Services, PO Box 2880, 1195 City View, Eugene, OR 97402; phone: (541) 687-2202; fax: (541) 683-6175; www .holtintl.org.

International Adoption Medicine Program, University of Minnesota, Attn: Dana Johnson, 717 Delaware Street, SE, 3rd Floor, Minneapolis, MN 55414; phone: (612) 624-1164; fax: (612) 625-2920; www.med.umn .edu/peds/iac.

Joint Council on International Children's Services, 117 South Saint Asaph Street, Alexandria, VA 22314; phone: (703) 535-8045; fax: (703) 535-8049; www.jcics.org.

National Adoption Center, 1500 Walnut Street, Suite 701, Philadelphia, PA 19102; toll-free: (800) 862-3678; www.adopt.org. *Referrals and information about special-needs adoption.*

National Child Welfare Resource Center for Adoption, 16250 Northland Drive, Suite 120, Southfield, MI 48075; phone: (248) 443-0306; fax: (248) 443-7099; www.nrcadoption.org. *Videos, books, curriculum, statistics, newsletter, and current and past resources.*

North American Council on Adoptable Children (NACAC), 970 Raymond Avenue, Suite 106, St. Paul, MN 55114; phone: (651) 644-3036; fax: (651) 644-9848; www.nacac.org. *Well-respected special-needs advocacy group whose annual conference is well attended by many parents and professionals. Excellent resource room. Yearly membership fee includes informative newsletter.*

Pact: An Adoption Alliance, 4179 Piedmont Avenue, Suite 101, Oakland, CA 94611; phone: (510) 243-9460; fax: (510) 243-9970; www.pactadopt .org. *Transracial adoption information.*

SEARCH Institute, The Banks Building, 615 First Avenue, NE, Suite 125, Minneapolis, MN 55413; phone: (612) 376-8955; toll-free: (800) 888-7828; www.search-institute.org. *Performed four-year study on infant adoption:* Growing Up Adopted: A Portrait of Adolescents and Their Families.

Tapestry Books, PO Box 651, Ringoes, NJ 08551; toll-free: (877) 266-5406; fax: (609) 737-5951; www.tapestrybooks.com. *Complete source of adoption books and tapes for children, parents, and professionals.*

Three Rivers Adoption Council, 307 Fourth Avenue, Suite 310, Pittsburgh, PA 15222; phone: (412) 471-8722; fax: (412) 471-4861; www.3riversadopt.org. *Inexpensive guidebooks (under $5.00) on a variety of special-needs adoption topics.*

U.S. Department of Health and Human Services, Children's Bureau, 370 L'Enfant Promenade, SW, Washington, D.C. 20201; www.acf.hhs.gov/programs/cb/index.htm. *Publications and research.*

Youth Law Center, 200 Pine Street, Suite 300, San Francisco, CA 94104; phone: (415) 553-3379; fax: (415) 956-9022; www.ylc.org. *National group helps families become familiar with laws and entitlements.*

RELATED READINGS

Adler, Alfred. *The Problem Child*. New York: Capricorn Books, 1963.

Ainsworth, Mary D., Mary Salter Blehar, Everett Waters, and Sally Wall. *Patterns of Attachment: A Psychological Study of the Strange Situation*. Hillsdale, NJ: Erlbaum Association, 1978.

Ames, Louis Bates, PhD, and Frances L. Ilg, MD. *Your Two Year Old: Terrible or Tender*. New York: Dell, 1976.

Askin, Jayne. *Search: A Handbook for Adoptees and Birth Parents*. Phoenix, AZ: Oryx, 1992.

Barnard, K. E., and T. B. Brazelton. *Touch: The Foundation of Experience*. Madison, CT: International University Press, 1990.

Barth, Richard P., and Marianne Berry. *Adoption and Disruption: Rates, Risks, Responses*. Hawthorne, NY: Aldine de Gruyter, 1988.

Belesky, Jay, and Teresa Nezworski. *Clinical Implications of Attachment*. Hillsdale, NJ: Lawrence Erlbaum Associates, 1987.

Blum, Deborah. *Love at Goon Park: Harry Harlow and the Science of Affection*. Cambridge, MA: Perseus, 2002.

Bowlby, John. *Attachment*. New York: Basic Books, 1969.

———. *Loss: Sadness and Depression*. New York: Basic Books, 1980.

———. *The Making and Breaking of Affectional Bonds*. London: Tavistock Publications, 1979.

————. *Separation: Anxiety and Anger*. New York: Basic Books, 1973.

Brazelton, T. B., MD. *Infants and Mothers: Individual Differences in Development*. New York: Delacorte Press, 1969.

————. *Touchpoints: Your Child's Emotional and Developmental Development*. Reading, MA: Addison-Wesley, 1992.

————. *What Every Baby Knows*. Reading, MA: Addison-Wesley, 1987.

Brodzinsky, David M., and Marshall D. Schecter, eds. *The Psychology of Adoption*. New York: Oxford University Press, 1990.

Clarke, Jean Illsely, and Connie Dawson. *Growing Up Again*. San Francisco: Harper & Row, 1989.

Cline, Foster W., MD. *Hope for High Risk and Rage Filled Children*. Evergreen, CO: Foster W. Cline, MD, 1992.

Cline, Foster W., MD, and Jim Fay. *Parenting Teens with Love and Logic*. Colorado Springs, CO: NavPress, 2006.

————. *Parenting with Love and Logic*. Colorado Springs, CO: NavPress, 2006.

Confer, Charles. *Letters to Foster Parents: More on Discipline*. King George, VA: American Foster Care Resources, Inc., 1990.

————. *Letters to Foster Parents: On Managing Angry Behavior*. King George, VA: American Foster Care Resources, Inc., 1989.

Crumbley, Joseph. *Transracial Adoption and Foster Care: Practice Issues for Professionals*. Washington, D.C.: CWLA Press, 1999.

Delaney, Richard, PhD. *Fostering Charges: Treating Attachment Disordered Foster Children*. Fort Collins, CO: Corbett, 1991.

Delaney, Richard, PhD, and Frank R. Kunstal. *Troubled Transplants*. Portland, ME: University of Southern Maine, 1993.

Dorow, Sara. *When You Were Born in China: A Memory Book for Children Adopted from China*. Saint Paul, MN: Yeong & Yeong Book Co., 1997.

Eldridge, Sherrie. *Twenty Life-Transforming Choices Adoptees Need to Make.* Colorado Springs, CO: Piñon Press, 2003.

———. *Twenty Things Adopted Kids Wish Their Adoptive Parents Knew.* New York: Dell, 1999.

Fahlberg, Vera, MD. *Attachment and Separation.* Chelsea, MI: Spaulding for Children, 1979.

———. *The Child in Placement.* Chelsea, MI: Spaulding for Children, 1981.

———. *A Child's Journey Through Placement.* Indianapolis, IN: Perspective Press, 1991.

———. *Helping Children When They Must Move.* Chelsea, MI: Spaulding for Children, 1979.

———, ed. *Residential Treatmen: A Tapestry of Many Therapies.* Indianapolis, IN: Perspective Press, 1990.

Fisher, Antwone Quenton. *Finding Fish.* New York: Morrow, 2001.

Foli, Karen J., and John R. Thompson. *Post Adoption Blues: Overcoming the Unforseen Challenges of Adoption.* Emmaus, PA: Rodale Books, 2004.

Geidman, J., and L. Brown. *Birthbond: Reunions Between Birth Parents and Adoptees: What Happens After.* Far Hills, NJ: New Horizons Press, 1995.

Gilman, Louis. *The Adoption Resource Book.* New York: HarperCollins, 1992.

Goldstein, Joseph, et al. *Beyond the Best Interests of the Child.* New York: Free Press, 1984.

Grandin, Temple. *Journal of Child and Adolescent Psychopharmocology* 2. Mary Ann Liebert, Inc., Publishers (November 1, 1992).

Gray, Deborah. *Attaching in Adoption: Practical Tools for Today's Parents.* Indianapolis, IN: Perspective Press, 2002.

———. *Nurturing Adoptions: Creating Resilience After Neglect and Trauma.* Indianapolis, IN: Perspective Press, 2007.

Gritter, James. *The Spirit of Open Adoption*. Washington. D.C.: CWLA Press, 1997.

Hochman, Gloria, Ellen Feathers-Acuna, and Anna Huston. "The Sibling Bond: Its Importance in Foster Care and Adoptive Placement." Rockville, MD: National Adoption Information Clearinghouse, n.d.

Hoksbergen, R. A. C. *Adopting a Child: A Guidebook for Adoptive Parents and Their Advisors*. The Netherlands: University Utrecht, 1994.

Homes, A. M. *The Mistress's Daughter*. New York: Viking, 2007.

Hopkins-Best, Mary. *Toddler Adoption: The Weaver's Craft*. Indianapolis, IN: Perspective Press, 1997.

Hughes, Daniel A. *Attachment-Focused Family Therapy*. New York: Norton, 2007.

———. *Building the Bonds of Attachment*. New York: Jason Aronson, 2006.

———. *Facilitating Developmental Attachment*. Northvale, NJ: Jason Aronson, 1997.

Jackson, Janet Alston. *A Cry for Light: A Journey into Love*. Self Awareness Trainings, 2005.

Jaffe, Eliezer David, ed. *Intercountry Adoptions, Laws and Perspectives of "Sending" Countries*. New York: Gefen Publishers, 1994.

Johnson, Spencer. *The One Minute Mother*. New York: Morrow, 1983.

Johnston, Patricia. *Adopting After Infertility*. Indianapolis, IN: Perspective Press, 1993.

Jordan, Barbara. *Preparing Foster Parents' Own Children for the Fostering Experience*. King George, VA: American Foster Care Resources, 1989.

Karen, Robert. *Becoming Attached: Unfolding the Mysteries of the Infant Mother Bond and Its Impact on Later Life*. New York: Warner, 1994.

Karr-Morse, Robin, and Meredith Wiley. *Ghosts from the Nursery*. New York: Atlantic Monthly Press, 1997.

Keck, Gregory C., and Regina M. Kupecky. *Parenting the Hurt Child.* Colorado Springs, CO: NavPress, 2009.

Keefer, Betsy, and Jayne E. Schooler. *Telling the Truth to Your Adopted or Foster Child: Making Sense of the Past.* Westport, CT: Bergin & Garvey Trade, 2000.

Klaus, Marshall H., MD, and John H. Kennell, MD. *Bonding: The Beginnings of Parent-Infant Attachment.* New York: Mosby Medical Library, 1983.

———. *Maternal Infant Bonding.* Saint Louis, MO: Mosby, 1976.

———. *Parent Infant Bonding.* Saint Louis, MO: Mosby, 1982.

Kranowitz, Carol Stock. *The Out-of-Sync Child: Recognizing and Coping with Sensory Integration Dysfunction.* New York: Perigree Books, 1998.

Krementz, Jill. *How It Feels to Be Adopted.* New York: Knopf, 1982.

Kupecky, Regina M. *Siblings Are Family, Too.* Pittsburgh, PA: Three Rivers Adoption Council, 1993.

Lamb, Michael, and Brian Sutton Smith, eds. *Sibling Relationships: Their Nature and Significance Across the Life Span.* Hillsdale, NJ: Lawrence Erlbaum Associates, 1982.

Magid, Ken, and Carole A. McKelvey. *"High Risk": Children Without a Conscience.* New York: Bantam, 1988.

Mansfield, Lynda G. *Don't Touch My Heart: Healing the Pain of an Unattached Child.* Glenwood Springs, CO: Families by Design, 2006.

Marindin, Hope, ed. *Handbook for Single Adoptive Parents.* Chevy Chase, MD: Committee of Single Adoptive Parents, 1992.

Maskew, Trish. *Our Own: Adopting and Parenting the Older Child.* Morton Grove, IL: Snowcap Press, 1999.

McNamara, Joan. *Adoption and the Sexually Abused Child.* Ossining, NY: Family Resources Adoption Program, 1990.

————. *Tangled Feelings: Sexual Abuse and Adoption*. Ossining, NY: Family Resources Adoption Program, 1988.

McReight, Brenda, PhD. *Parenting Your Adopted Older Child*. Oakland, CA: New Harbinger Press, 2002.

McRoy, Ruth G., Harold D. Grotevant, and Louis A. Zurcher. *Emotional Disturbance in Adopted Adolescents: Origins and Development*. Westport, CT: Praeger, 1988.

Meese, Ruth Lyn. *Children of Intercountry Adoptions in School: A Primer for Parents and Professionals*. Westport, CT: Bergin & Garvey, 2002.

Melina, Louis Ruskai. *Making Sense of Adoption: A Parent's Guide*. San Francisco: Harper & Row, 1989.

————. *Raising Adopted Children: A Manual for Adoptive Parents*. San Francisco: Harper & Row, 1986.

Miller, Margi, MA, and Nancy Ward, MA, LICSW. *With Eyes Wide Open: A Workbook for Parents Adopting International Children over Age One*. Children's Home Society of Minnesota, LN Press, 1996.

O'Hanlon, Tim, PhD. *Accessing Federal Adoption Subsidies After Legalization*. Washington, D.C.: Child Welfare League of America, 1995.

O'Malley, Beth. *Life Books: Creating a Treasure for the Adopted Child*. Winthrop, MA: Adoption-Works, 2000.

Pertman, Adam. *Adoption Nation: How the Adoption Revolution Is Transforming America*. New York: Basic Books, 2000.

Reitz, Miriam, and Ken Watson. *Adoption and the Family System: Strategies for Treatment*. New York: Guilford Press, 1991.

Rule-Hoffman, Richard. *The Attachment Potential Art Therapy Assessment*. Cleveland, OH: Inner Image Publications, 1992.

Samenow, Stanton E., PhD. *Before It's Too Late*. New York: Times Books, 1991.

Schooler, Jayne E. *Searching for a Past*. Colorado Springs, CO: Piñon Press, 1995.

———. *The Whole Life Adoption Book: Realistic Advice for Building a Healthy Adoptive Family*. Colorado Springs, CO: Piñon Press, 1993.

Severson, Randolph W. *Adoption Charms and Rituals for Healing*. Dallas, TX: House of Tomorrow Productions, 1991.

Shapiro, Francine. *Eye Movement Desensitization and Reprocessing—Basic Principles, Protocols, and Procedures*. New York: Guilford Press, 1995.

Siegal, Daniel J., MD. *The Developing Mind: How Relationships and the Brain Interact to Shape Who We Are*. New York: Guilford Press, 2001.

Siegal, Daniel J., MD, and Mary Hartzell. *Parenting from the Inside Out*. New York: Jeremy Tarcher, 2004.

Sorosky, A. D., et al. *The Adoption Triangle: Sealed or Opened Records: How They Affect Adoptees, Birth Parents, and Adoptive Parents*. San Antonio, TX: Corona Publications, 1989.

Stiffler, LaVonne. *Synchronicity and Reunion: The Genetic Connection of Adoptees and Birth Parents*. Hobe Sound, FL: FEA Publishing, 1992.

Toth, Jennifer. *What Happened to Johnnie Jordan?*. New York: Free Press, 2002.

Trott, Maryann C., Marci K. Laurel, and Susan L. Windeck. *SenseAbilities: Understanding Sensory Integration*. San Antonio, TX: Therapy Skill Builders, 1993.

Van der Kolk, Bessel A., Alexander C. McFarlane, and Lars Weisaeth, eds. *Traumatic Stress: The Effects of Overwhelming Experiences on Mind, Body, and Society*. New York: Guilford Press, 1996.

Van Gulden, Holly, and Lisa Bartels Rabb. *Real Parents, Real Children: Parenting the Adopted Child*. New York: Crossroads Publishing, 1993.

Verny, Thomas, MD. *Nurturing Your Unborn Child*. New York: Delecorte Press, 1991.

————. *Parenting Your Unborn Child*. Toronto: Doubleday-Canada, 1988.

———— *The Secret Life of the Unborn Child*. New York: Summit Books, 1981.

Verrier, Nancy Newton. *The Primal Wound*. Baltimore, MD: Gateway Press, 1993.

Ward, Margaret. "Sibling Ties in Foster Care and Adoption Planning," *Child Welfare* 63, no. 4 (July/August 1984).

Watkins, Mary, and Susan Fischer. *Talking with Young Children About Adoption*. New Haven, CT: Yale University Press, 1993.

Watson, Kenneth. *Substitute Care Providers: Helping Abused and Neglected Children*. Washington, D.C.: U.S. Department of Health and Human Services, 1994.

Whelan, David J. "Using Attachment Theory When Placing Siblings in Foster Care," *Child and Adolescent Social Work Journal* 20, no. 1 (February 2003).

Wood, Lansing, and Nancy Sheehan Ng. *Adoption and the Schools: Resources for Parents and Teachers*. Palo Alto, CA: Families Adopting In Response, 2001.

CURRICULA

James, Arleta. *Supporting Brothers and Sisters: Creating a Family by Birth, Foster Care, and Adoption.* 2006.

Keck, Gregory C., Regina M. Kupecky, and Arleta James. *Abroad and Back: Parenting and International Adoption.* 2003.

Kupecky, Regina M. *My Brother, My Sister: Sibling Relations in Adoption and Foster Care.* 2006.

For information on these curricula, contact the authors at the Attachment and Bonding Center of Ohio, listed in "Resources."

ABOUT THE AUTHORS

GREGORY C. KECK, PhD, founded the Attachment and Bonding Center of Ohio, which specializes in the treatment of children and adolescents who have experienced developmental interruptions. In addition, he and his staff treat individuals and families who are faced with a variety of problems in the areas of adoption, attachment, substance abuse, sexual abuse, and adolescent difficulties.

Dr. Keck is certified as a diplomate and fellow by the American Board of Medical Psychotherapy and is a diplomate in professional psychotherapy. He is a part-time graduate faculty member in the School of Social Work at the University of Akron and is involved in training for a diversity of agencies, hospitals, and organizations both nationally and internationally.

His memberships include the Cleveland Psychological Association, the Ohio Psychological Association, the American Psychological Association, and the National Association of Social Workers. From 1991 through 2000, he was a member of the board of directors of ATTACh, the Association for Treatment and Training in the Attachment of Children. He served as president for two years and was honored by the organization in 2001 with its annual award for outstanding contribution to the field.

Dr. Keck was given the Adoption Triad Advocate Award in 1993 by the Adoption Network of Cleveland, Ohio.

He is an adoptive parent and has appeared on numerous television and radio talk shows to discuss a broad spectrum of adoption issues.

■ ■ ■

REGINA M. KUPECKY, LSW, has worked in the adoption arena for more than thirty years as an adoption placement worker and therapist. Her services to children have been recognized by the Ohio Department of Human Services, which named her Adoption Worker of the Year in 1990.

She is currently a therapist with Dr. Keck at the Attachment and Bonding Center of Ohio, where she works with children who have attachment disorders. She trains nationally and internationally on adoption issues, sibling issues, and attachment.

Ms. Kupecky authored a resource guide, *Siblings Are Family, Too*, which is available through the Three Rivers Adoption Council in Pittsburgh, Pennsylvania. She has coauthored a curriculum with Dr Keck and Arleta James called *Abroad and Back: Parenting and International Adoption* and has written a curriculum on sibling issues entitled *My Brother, My Sister: Sibling Relations in Adoption and Foster Care*.

She coauthored a chapter in the book *Clinical and Practice Issues in Adoption — Revised and Updated: Bridging the Gap Between Adoptees Placed as Infants and as Older Children* and has also written several newsletter articles for organizations including Jewel Among Jewels, ATTACh, and NACAC.

Ms. Kupecky holds a Master of Arts in Teaching (MAT) from John Carroll University.

NavPress has the resources you need for your adoption!